THE
WORLD WAS
TOO FLAT

THE WORLD WAS TOO FLAT

DANNY RUSSELL

"Your story is our priority"

LitPrime Solutions
East Brunswick Office Evolution
1 Tower Center Boulevard, Ste 1510
East Brunswick, NJ 08816
www.litprime.com
Phone: 1-800-981-9893

Published by LitPrime Solutions: 02/10/2025

ISBN: 979-8-88703-438-6(sc)
ISBN: 979-8-88703-439-3(e)

Library of Congress Control Number: 2024920707

CONTENTS

BOOK 1

CHAPTER 1

It was mid May 1954, Jake Oldham and Elzie Tatum were riding down Tatum Hollow road heading home from school.

"Hey, Jake, pull over, I gotta pee", Elzie said.

Jake braked the 1950 flatbed half ton Chevy to a stop.

"Ok, cousin let er rip." Jake always called people he was fond of, cousin.

"On second thought, I need to pee myself." And with that, Jake got out on his side while Elzie had bailed his stocky frame out on the other side.

"Whew," Elzie said, "that coke we got at the store filled me up."

"Yeah, me too," Jake said, "I don't mind watering the county road."

The two boys rode to school every day together, as they lived neighbors. They got back in the truck and drove on home crossing Tatum's hollow which ran into Denton Creek.

"We got enough rain last week to let us finish plowing," Jake said, "but will we get enough to make a crop?"

"We hadn't made a crop the last two years because of the drought, maybe this is the year it will start raining again," Elzie said. "If we don't I'll bet your dad has to start selling stock."

"We've been luckier than most." Jake said. "Old Denton creek's got some springs that have kept us in enough water to keep the cows, but you're right, if we don't get some rain to fill our tanks, we're going to have to sell. Daddy says the price for cattle is rock bottom too."

The boys wheeled up in front of the Oldham home. Jake's parents had a two story frame home that his father had built when he married Jakes mom, Mary Phame. It sat just off Russell's loop and faced the road. Jake's grandparents lived on the farm about fifty yards from Jake's house. Jake's grandfather, Lige Oldham had farmed the place with his father, was the only one of his brothers and sisters to stay on the farm. Lige and his wife Berthie May had two sons P.D. and Clois. Clois was a ranch hand for the Donald Cross Bar T ranch. The Cross Bar T was a ten thousand acre cattle ranch that Clois had worked on since he was a teenager. He had not finished high school as he was considered slow by some standards.

The Tatum home was the next place over from the Oldham house. The Tatum's place actually belonged to Lee Pariot, Elzie's grandfather on his mother's side. After his wife had died, he had asked Elzie's parents, Lester and Ida Lou, to live with him and take care of him. He had suffered a light stroke and was no longer able to farm. Now Lester Tatum had been injured while serving in the Army, causing him to loose most of the use of his left arm and was crippled in the left leg. Jake's dad had leased Lee's land and Lester helped P.D. with the farm work.

Since 1951 there had been a severe drought, a lot of farmers and ranchers had sold a lot of stock because they had no water and very little grass. Somehow, because he had water, P.D. had held on to his thirty mama cows hoping the calf crop would get them through until the peanut harvest, if there was a harvest and P.D. planned his farm for a harvest. They would plow the bottoms, plant twenty acres to melons and the other fifty to peanuts and pray for rain.

"Hey Elzie, ain't that your Grandpa sitting on the porch with my Grandpa?" Jake asked.

"Yeah, that's him," Elzie said.

Lee and Lige were sitting on the front porch enjoying the moment as elders of their clan had earned the right to have leisure time.

Lee and Lige had grown up together in Montague County. Their daddies had been good friends as their grandpa's had been the early settlers settling this part of the county. They had withstood famine, beast, robbers and Comanche's to keep their places. Although Lee was five years older than Lige, they had gone to Franklin School together. Franklin was about a mile from their homes and they walked to school every day. It wasn't uncommon for Lee to walk up to the Oldham house to visit Lige and Berthie May.

"Lige, you got a plug of tobacco in your pocket?" "I'm fresh out," Lee asked.

"You know good and well I got a plug in my pocket. Berthie May never lets me run out. I only chew Spark Plug, will that do you?" Lige replied.

"Oh yeah I guess it will but I prefer White Tag Tensley myself," Lee replied.

"Well, old man, trot yourself down to Hunter's store and get you a couple of plugs and you wont be mooching mine," Lige said as he chuckled.

"By God, Lige, the next time I'm in Sunset, I'll get a whole box then I sure wont be asking you for non of that little sissy plug you pretend to chew."

Both men had a big laugh, as they sparred each other. They did it all the time but it was always in jest

"Hey look there, Lee, yonder comes two old boys full of piss and vinegar," Lige said.

"Wonder what they aim to do?" Lee said. The two men studied the boys. There was Elzie, a stocky boy with blondish hair and blue eyes around five foot six in height. Jake was about the same height, less stocky than Elzie, light blond hair and wide blue eyes. They boys were talking with Jake making gestures with his hands as Elzie listened with a mischievous grin on his face.

"They better aim to plow Denton Creek bottom," Lige said. "I told P.D. I'd have them boys on the tractors when they got home from school."

"Hell, Lige you and I could have plowed the field," Lee said.

"I know it, we could have, but you know since your spell, your

3

daughter wouldn't allow you on a tractor a'tall. Besides, those boys can handle it and working keeps them out of trouble"

Hey Grandpa! Both boys said almost in unison.

Jake looked with deep affection at his grandfather. Lige was thin short man of five foot two, graying hair that receded on each side of his temple, clad in overalls and his straw hat laying on the porch beside his chair, looking through wire rim spectacles. He wore his father's pocket watch and fine chain with a fob hanging in the middle. He sat leaned back in his chair with his arms resting on the arms of the chair. Lee was not any taller or heavier, a worn face and faded gray eyes. Liver spots spotted one side of his face. Both men almost always wore striped overalls, long sleeves and were never outside without a hat.

"What kind of problems are y'all solving?" Jake asked.

"We ain't solving nothing, just waiting on you two to get to the plowing and get your mind off girls,"Lee said with a laugh.

Jake asked, Grandpa, "Can I have a chew?"

"Well hell's bells" Lige said, "first this worthless bum takes half of my plug for a chaw, now you going after the rest of it?"

"Just a small cut," Jake said, as he took the plug and with his pocket knife cut off a small piece and put it in his mouth. You want any Elzie? Jake asked.

"Naw, I sure don't Jake it makes me sick, makes me puke like a buzzard," Elzie said.

Of course Jake already knew that. He had seen that in action one time when they were fishing. Jake had got some tobacco and they had shared a chew. All of a sudden Elzie had turned green and started puking his guts out. Jake laughed and laughed, but Elzie didn't laugh at all. All he could do was lay down and moan.

"Lige, what are you making so much noise about?" Berthie May came to the screen and ask. Berthie May was a good two inches taller than Lige and twice his size. She was solid as a rock and built like a big wooden barrel.

"|Now Gal," Lige said "this out here is man talk."

"My foot!" She snorted. "I heard you hollering about your plug tobacco. You know good and well you got three more plugs in here and that will last you a month, no more than you chew."

"Never you mind, now, Lige said, Lee you want supper?"

Berthie May turned back behind the screen headed back toward the kitchen, knowing that everything Lige had said was in jest. She knew that when she told him where to head in, he would head in.

"Oh probably not," Lee said. "I imagine Ida Lou will cook when she gets home from the plant. If Roxy was living, she could be cooking. Course Leck tries to cook but with one arm it ain't very easy for him. And I can't even boil water!"

"Well, stay and have supper anyhow. You ain't been over in a week, and we sure ain't through visiting." Lige said. "It don't take any more food for two than it does for three. It takes a whole table full for them two there though." Lige said, pointing at the boys. "Like feeding a whole thrashing crew!"

The boys headed for the shed to get the tractors. P.D. and Lester both had Model TO-20 Massey Ferguson's. They were top tractors for 1954. Most folks had Farmall's. In fact Lige owned a Cub model Farmall. It was ideal for a garden, which both families raised.

The gas tractors came to life easily and both were already hooked to the breaking plows. Jake went down to his dad's bottom and Elzie to his place. Only a fence separated the two bottoms. Since P.D. had leased Leck's place, he had installed a gate between the two fields.

The boys had started the day before and with luck they would finish by tomorrow. They had been plowing each evening for a couple of hours before supper.

About 6:30 just before the sun fell below the horizon in a cloudless sky, the boys parked the tractors back at the shed. Every day, Leck would check the oil, the transmission oil, and hydraulic oil, and would fuel up the tractors for the boys.

"You boys hungry?" Berthie May asked.

"Does the wild man live in the woods?" Jake replied.

"No use you getting smart now," she replied.

"Go wash your hands and I'll set your plates." Berthie may said.

Lige and Lee were already at the table, Berthie May had set Clois a plate as he usually came by and ate too. Clois was single and totally depended on his mother. He lived on the Donald ranch, which had a cook for the family and hands, but Clois liked to come over and tell his mama all he had done that day.

Jake and Elzie had just sit down when they heard Clois's Chevy truck drive up. It was a '52 model army green. Unlike Lige's black flatbed, Clois's truck had the standard stepside with the spare tire mounted right behind the driver on the side of the bed.

"Come on in Clois," Berthie May called. "Go wash and I've got your plate set." Clois nodded to everyone as he hung his hat on the hat rack, went into the bathroom to wash. The house hadn't always had an indoor bathroom. Lige wasn't sure he wanted it, but Berthie May had been insistent and had won out. The room had been built by splitting the store room which was just off the kitchen. The store room held an extra bed, and canning goods from the garden. Berthie had a wood cook stove in the kitchen but had recently purchased a propane cooking model. Occasionally she would revert back to the wood stove when it was cold weather. The house had originally been Lige's parents home, built in 1889. The original house was a log two room built by Lige's grandpa. However, Lige's parents, Henry and Caroline built the home from lumber cut in Gainesville. Henry's father and Indian fighter neighbor Bart Trailer had help build the house. Henry's father, Elias Elijah Oldham, had died shortly after they had moved in. Henry had died in 1945, but Caroline was still living but lived with a woman, a Mrs. Brown, who cared for old people close to Bowie. Caroline lived in another world and didn't know her family. It was hard for Lige to move his mother from the farm, but Berthie May didn't feel she could watch her mother in law all the time. She tended chickens, cooked for the family and seemed to be always busy.

"I don't know if P.D. and Mary are coming for supper," Berthie May said. She pulled her graying hair from her round face.

Both Mary and Ida Lou worked at the slack factory in Bowie. It provided a much needed income to the farms.

Now, Berthie May liked to cook and to be fussed over for her great meals. However in the Pariot and Tatum house, there was no second woman to help with the cooking and housework. Lee's wife had died in 1940 and it had been hard for the family, but they did the best they could. Sometimes Berthie May would send word to Leck for them to come and have supper especially if all the men were working together. When the gardens were in, Leck would help Berthie May and she would can things for the Tatum's. Leck and Ida Lou had five children. The oldest was Nolan, three girls, Laverne, Susan and Elwanda. Elzie was the youngest and still at home, the rest were grown and on their own.

In Jake's house, he was an only child. Although he was an only child he never felt he was alone, as he had grown up side by side with Elzie although Jake was a year older. The boys felt they were more like brothers than just friends.

Berthie May had fixed fried chicken, fried potatoes, a pan of cornbread, a bowl of gravy, and opened her last jar of green beans with new potatoes. I got two pitchers of tea she told them, so drink all the ice tea you want. Jake loved sweet ice tea. He could almost drink a full pitcher without blinking.

Each boy raked three pieces of chicken in their plates, green beans, fried potatoes topped with the gravy, and slab of cornbread.

"Glad I cooked two chickens," Berthie May said smiling.

The boys ate with a real gusto, as most teenage boys.

"Mama," Clois said, "Mr. Donald got two hundred cows, and I count em every day."

In Clois's world what he did was the most important thing there was and he always wanted to tell everyone about it sometimes dominating the conversation.

"That's good Clois," Berthie May said, "are you tired honey?"

"Yeah, mama, I'm tired, work hard" "But, I can't stay here, I have to go back to the ranch. They need me first thing in the morning," Clois said.

They were half through the meal when P.D and Mary came in.

"Ya'll want supper?" Berthie May asked.

Mary replied, "It would be nice tonight; Berthie, Ida Lou and I had a hard day."

"Well, run down there and tell Ida Lou and Leck to come up and eat too. Lee's already here so they might as well eat too, we got plenty. I'll make another pitcher of tea," Berthie May said.

"I'll fix the tea," Mary said.

"No, no, Berthie May said, you just sit down and fix yourself a plate.

"Jake you and Elzie go down and get Leck and Ida Lou; you can have chocolate pie when you get back," Berthie May said.

Both boys shot up from the table and headed for the door.

They didn't drive down to the Tatum place, they just ran down. It was a quarter mile from the Oldham house to the Tatum's.

Ida Lou was talking to Leck when the boys arrived.

"What you two up to?" Ida Lou said.

"Grandma wanted y'all to come to supper," Jake said. "Your dad's eating up there, so's mama and dad."

"Leck?" Ida Lou said.

"There ain't a better cook on Denton Creek than Berthie May Oldham," Leck said.

"Come on boys, I'll get my truck."

Ida Lou straighten her hair and came out on the porch when Leck drove up. Driving was difficult for Leck as he had to steer and shift the gears with one hand. Sometimes he would rest his left hand over the wheel to help guide while shifting the gears in his '49 Ford pickup. The boys loaded in the back with the tail gate down sitting on the edge while Ida Lou got inside.

It took only a minute for them to go from one house to the next. Lige and Berthie May's house was a very typical style of the 1890's. It was called a T house. Two front rooms, one a bedroom the other a living room, which in Lige's boyhood was another bedroom, and the third room was the kitchen. However in 1919 Lige had added rooms on both sides of the kitchen. The room on the south side was another bedroom and the room on the north side was where Berthie May stored her canning. It was in that room that the modern wonder, the bathroom had been added. The bathroom had two doors one from the canning room and one that opened to the outside, although in Jakes lifetime he had never seen the outside door opened. To the side of the kitchen was a screened in porch that opened to the kitchen and the bedroom on the south side. The porch contained a table that Lige's father had built for him when he and Berthie May had married in January of 1909. Lige and his father were always close. He had married but had lived with his parents because Henry needed him to help with the farming. It had been rough for Berthie May as Caroline had been difficult to get along with. She never liked Berthie May very much. She thought her too bossy, which she was.

"God Dog, Lige said, look here, there's Leck and Idy, come in and sit at the table. Berthie's got your plate set."

"Hello Lige,"Ida Lou said. "You and Papa getting along this evening?"

"We might Idy, if you'd buy the scoundrel some chewing tobacco!" Lige said.

"Lige you hush," Berthie May said. "Anybody can get out of tobacco. I can remember more than once when we couldn't buy it and you were out."

"And I walked the floor," Lige said.

P.D. was always a more serious minded person than his dad. He looked at the boys and said, "How much more plowing you got to do?"

"Oh, we'll be through by tomorrow," Jake said. "If we get through will it be all right if me and Elzie goes fishing?"

"Fishing," P.D. said, "you can't make a crop fishing."

"Now P.D." Berthie May said, "they can't work all the time. When they get through plowing, let them go fishing! Besides, I sure would like to cook up a mess of catfish."

"Boys," P.D. said, "when you get through breaking the land, you'll need to hook up the disc and disc it four times. Disc with the plowing, then cross ways, then diagonal, then back like the rows will be set. That way the land will be ready to start planting Monday. We'll plant the melons first, and then we'll plant the peanuts."

"We get that done, then can we go fishing?" Jake asked.

"Yeah, y'all can go fishing," P.D. replied.

"I got some chicken livers you boys can take for bait," Berthie May said.

After supper the table was cleared, Ida Lou and Mary helped Berthie May with the dishes.

Lige, Lee, Leck and P.D. set up to play dominos while Jake and Elzie sat on the front porch.

"Jake," Elzie, said, "you ever think about moving off this old farm. Is our whole lives going to be strapped to this damn old place?"

"Elzie, your not supposed to talk like that," Jake said.

"Why not?" Elzie said, "All the guys at school do and you never heard such cussing at the gas stations".

"Well, don't say that here," Jake said. "It sounds bad."

"I've heard your grandpa say God Dog a thousand times," Elzie said "and that's saying about the same thing."

"Forget it," Jake said. "No, I don't think about moving off this place. I love it here."

"But, Jake, you're going to finish school next year, then what?" Elzie asked.

"I'll probably get drafted, then I'll come back and settle into farming," Jake said.

"You going to get married?" Elzie asked.

"Oh, I don't know about that, I don't even have a girl friend," Jake said.

"I hear Debbie Crocket's eying you. Ya'll go to the same church." Elzie chimed.

"I never heard Deb's eyeing me. We're just friends. Yeah she goes to the same church, but so what? Angie Freeman goes to your church, is she eyeing you?" Jake asked.

"She got her eyes on all the boys at church. You know what?" Elzie said. "Last month we had a church picnic and I stole off with Angie. She's real sweet you know."

"What you mean she's real sweet?" Jake asked.

"Hell, Jake you stay in the woods all the time? Don't you know, she puts out," Elzie said.

"Puts out? Jake mused. Then it hit him and his eyes got real wide, you don't mean it!"

"I do mean it," Elzie said, "and I got some."

"You're lying, you couldn't done that at no church picnic," Jake said.

"I did too," Elzie said. "We slipped off into the Pastors study and locked the door. We made out on his couch."

Jake just stood there dumbfounded. Then, he grinned a big grin. "Wow," he said, "tell me all about it."

"Well good night" Ida Lou said."I'm sure glad tomorrow's Saturday and we don't have to go back to he factory."

"Me too," Mary said. "We have to have a break from time to time just to get away from that awful floor walker Bessie Hutson!" The women both laughed.

"Leck, you and Ida going to town tomorrow?" P.D.asked. "Me and Mary's taking a load of pigs to Fort Worth."

"Yeah, Leck said, we need a few groceries. We ought to buy Berthie May's since we eat here so much."

"Now you don't say that," Berthie May said as she hugged Ida Lou. "I am proud for you to come and sit at our table."

"At least buy that old man some tobacco." Lige said laughing.

With that they went out and home.

CHAPTER 2

Saturday morning the boys were up and early to finish the plowing. Just after breakfast the boys met at the barn, Leck had just finished fueling the tractors.

"Be careful boys," Leck said, "don't try to gut the earth just plow good and easy. You'll get done and get to go fishing. Poor old P.D., he never was one to relax much. He is always figuring ahead and trying to stay ahead of the game. Trouble is, boys, the game never ends."

In three hours they had finished the breaking. They had to unhook the breaking plows and hook up to the tandom disc. Elzie hooked Jakes up while Jake guided the tractor up to the disc. Then Jake hooked Elzie as he backed up to the other disc.

Each boy ran on their own properties disking the way P.D. wanted, first disking over the plowed rows knocking down the sandy turned soil getting the rough clods smoothed down. Then, they went cross the field the opposite from how they started. Cutting the ground diagonally was difficult because each row was a different length. The longest being in the middle, which was where they started disking, working toward the outside. Finally running the disc back in the original pattern they had started. By the time they finished, the fields were mellow and ready to plant.

That morning after Berthie May had fed her chickens and milked the two cows, she and Lige took the flatbed that Jake drove to school, for their Saturday ritual. They always went to Sunset and bought groceries and feed from Hunters store. Berthie would also sell her eggs and cream. She had three dresses to wear. She had two she used for every day, and the third on was going to town dress and church dress. The work dresses she had made from printed flour sacks. She sewed her underwear from white flour sacks and had two bonnets. The going to town and church bonnet was a dark blue.

Lige wore overalls all the time. He too had two pair, one for work and one for town and church. Since it was May and warm he had switched from his felt to a straw. He had two straw hats, and two winter felts, one for working and one for town and church. His town and church hat was the fedora type. Each Saturday he and Berthie May loaded in the flatbed, which had a floor shift, placing the carton of eggs between them and would head for town. They would make half a day out of it most times. Sometimes Lige wanted to go by the implement dealer in Bowie eye new tractors and get any parts he needed for repairs. If it was the second weekend of the month, then he and Berthie May would be gone all day. No matter what they had to do, they always went by Mrs. Brown's to see Lige's mother. She never knew they were there as she no longer recognized her children. They would mostly spend time with Mrs. Brown and see that all her needs were met.

The second weekend of the month was a special day in Montague County, called Second Monday. It had begun in the city of Bowie around 1890. Developed by the city fathers, it was originally set on the second Monday of each month for farmers to come to town and without needing city permits, allowed to set up in a designated place and sell whatever farm goods they brought. Many brought produce, eggs and cream, while others brought livestock. By the '50's, professional vendors had replaced a lot of the farmers, although farmers still used the event to sell things. They would carry a pig or an orphaned calf and any extra produce to sell at Second Monday. Second Monday had become Second Saturday and by Monday there were no vendors.

When Berthie and Lige went to Sunset, they would park by the store, get out of the truck and would walk to the back of the truck.

There they stood, looking like Laurel and Hardy, where Berthie May would go over her grocery list while Lige listened. Then he would pull out his father's watch from his bib and check the time, glance once more at his wife before walking across the street to the Sunset Guarantee National Bank where some twenty men would be standing on the corner to visit. That was Lige's favorite part of going to town. They would talk about their farming, the weather, price of cattle, who was doing what in national baseball while their wives bought the groceries in Hunter's store. The final purchase was feed from Hunter's feed store. The feed store was right next to the grocery store separated only by a wall. Usually Floyd Hunter took care of the feed but since his son Bud was a teen, he had let Bud load and sell the feed. Bud was a strapping boy over six feet with jet black wavy hair, muscled from heaving feed sacks, but was a gentle giant. Women always needed fifty pounds of hen scratch, or starter feed and the men usually bought a half ton of cubes. It was always the last item of the purchase.

Very few farmers bought dairy products or meat, because they had their own. In fact many brought eggs and dairy products to the store to sell or trade.

If Mary and P.D. didn't want to go to town, they let Berthie May get their groceries.

P.D. had heard on the radio's farm and ranch program that hog prices were up. So P.D. had placed his side boards on his '51 model Chevrolet and loaded up ten nice pigs. He and Mary would be gone all day hauling the pigs to the Fort Worth Stock Yard. Both P.D. and his parents would pack a lunch for their town trips and a jug of well water.

Once the disking was done, Elzie and Jake, skipping lunch, got their fishing gear together and headed for the creek which ran through the lower edge of both farms. Due to the recent rains the creek had come up a few feet, which would mean catfish in the pools.

Using chicken liver for bait, which Berthie May always saved, the boys were fishing on the bottom. Even though it had rained the creek was still clear.

"Grandpa said they used to swim in a hole down below our place,"

Jake said. "He said another fork hit this fork and it made a deep hole. He said him and his brothers, the Trayler's and his cousins used to spend the whole day swimming. He said the hole was so deep they hardly ever touched the bottom."

"Yeah," Elzie said, "my grandpa said one time they had a bet on with your grandpa's brother Chick, that he couldn't touch the bottom. So, Grandpa said he got up in a tree that had a limb overhanging the creek and dove off of it. He said he was under the water such a long time that that they started back in thinking he drowned, but just as they were going in Chick come choking to the top with a hand full of mud."

"We ain't never seen a pool in Denton Creek that deep," Jake said.

"No, but the fishing is probably just as good,"Elzie replied.

The boys caught ten nice catfish. They took them up to Berthie May's house cleaned and put the fish in a bowl of water in the ice box.

"Hey Elzie, let's go over to the Jim Harry lake and hunt squirrel," Jake said.

"Sure, but we'll have to walk cause I can't take Grandpa's pickup unless he says I can," Elzie replied. "And he went to town with mama and dad.

"Who cares, if we have to walk?" Jake said.

Each boy had a .22, which their grandpa's called a target gun. Each took a box of shorts with them. Shorts were less likely to ricochet.

"Want to take the dogs?" Elzie asked.

"I guess so, you know how much a squirrel hates a dog." Jake replied.

The boys had a dog each, Elzie's dog was named Rex, and Jake's, Hoover. The dogs were good for hunting. They could get a squirrel all excited and agitated while the boys were in position to plunk the squirrel right out of a tree.

Jim Harry lake was really an old slew that an old man named Jim Harry had built back in the early twenties. He built the lake with a team and Fresno creating a small dike like dam along Denton Creek. The slew filled up from the creek's overflow. The slew was about twenty acres in size. The old Jim Harry place was a six hundred acre farm that was now over grown with oak trees and a twenty acre lake. Old man Harry had died four years ago and his daughters had not yet sold the place. The daughters didn't use the place, nor had they leased it, most people fished the slew as they wanted.

Joining the Harry place was the Jasper farm, a four hundred acre farm owned by Jess and Bertha Jasper. Jess had come to Montague County with his parents and grandparents when Jess was seven years old in 1888. Jess and Bertha lived on the place and were probably Lige and Berthie May's best friends. They came to visit often and Lige and Berthie May went to see them as well. Actually the Jasper farm was directly across the road from the Oldham's place but the Jasper's farmhouse was on the north end of the land. Driving around the road it was probably two miles from the Oldham houses.

Jake often went with his grandparents to visit the Jasper's. Mrs. Jasper often made angel food cake, which was a real delight to Jake to get a big slice of it with fresh cow's milk. Mrs. Jasper always offered Jake cake when they came to visit. She and Berthie May would visit for hours and talk about old times. One particular habit Mrs. Jasper had was when she talked about her husband. She never called him by his first name but called him Mr. Jasper. It was an odd thing to Jake because his own Grandma called his Grandpa Lige. On the other hand his Grandpa rarely called his Grandma by her name but usually called her Gal. It always seemed to irritate Berthie May too, but she didn't quarrel with Lige over it.

Crossing the county road which was known as Russell's Loup, the boys crawled over the barb wire fence and entered the Jim Harry. The place was thick with oak timber except in the bottom where the slew lay. The bottom land was covered in Cottonwood, Bois d Arc, and Hackberry and native pecans. It was an ideal place to hunt turkey and deer as well as squirrel.

They soon spotted a squirrel high up in a cottonwood fussing at the dogs.

"You think you can hit that squirrel Elzie?" Jake asked. "I'll walk over to the other side of the tree so the squirrel will expose himself to you thinking he is hiding from me."

"I think I can hit the bugger," Elzie said.

"Just remember, if you miss, then I get the next shot." Jake warned.

The strategy usually worked every time. The squirrel would be sitting on a branch making a fuss at the dogs. However if he saw the shooter, the squirrel would move to the other side of the tree out of sight. But, if another person walked under the tree, the squirrel would move himself out of sight of the person under the tree, but exposing himself to the shooter. The dogs sometimes were good at making the squirrel expose himself. That is, good squirrel dogs knew to do that. They would circle a tree until one told the dog to stop.

Just so happened, that this squirrel was smarter than they were. He scampered up the tree and then jumped to a joining cottonwood and on to a pecan, then disappeared.

"Smart squirrel," Jake said.

"Too smart," Elzie replied.

Instead of shooting squirrel the boys ended up roaming around the edge of the lake shooting any water snakes and moccasins.

"Hey Jake," Elzie, said. "You thought anymore about what you're going to do after you finish school?"

"Have you?" Jake replied.

"Yeah, I've thought about getting a job if I don't get drafted," Elzie said.

"What kind of job?" Jake asked.

"Well Comie Jackson offered me a job working at his station there in Sunset."

"Doing what?" Jake asked.

"Oh, filling up the trucks that stop for diesel, greasing em, fixin flats."

"You gonna live at home and do that?" Jake asked.

"Well for awhile, but I might want to get married sometime," Elzie said.

"Yeah, you going to marry Angie since you pretended to be married in the pastor's study." Jake chided.

"No, not Angie, I don't know who I'm going to marry. I'll just meet her someday and we'll get married," Elzie said.

"Sounds like you've got yourself a real good plan, there cousin," Jake said.

"You making fun of me, Jake?" Elzie said.

"No, no cousin, but I don't think I'd go at that way."

"Tell me then Jake ole boy, just how you would you go about it."

"I hadn't thought it through yet Elzie, Jake said. But I probably would work at ole Comie's station say a year or so, and save all my money then I'd try to buy the station, so I could be the boss. Then I'd hire me some grease monkey to do all the dirty work, so I could be spick and span to court and marry. I'd probably marry ole Angie too, cause you already know she puts out. Wouldn't be no guess work about some other female."

"You horses ass," Elzie said.

Then Jake busted out in laughter as many times he and Elzie discussed their lives and what was to become of them, often Jake had a way of leading a person on trapping them in some hopeless situation before he sprung the trap and have a big laugh.

As the boys walked home, they noticed a pickup pulling into the Oldham drive way.

"Who's that wonder?" Jake said.

"I dunno, I can't make out whose pickup that is.." Elzie said.

When the boys arrived, they discovered the driver was another one of their best friends. It was Glen Ray Shelton. Glen Ray was the middle son of Elmer and Francis Shelton. Glen's oldest brother was Cooper and youngest brother was Morgan. Cooper was two years older than Jake, and Morgan was ten years younger. Elmer and his brother Lloyd owned several gas stations in Sunset, Bowie, Nocona and Alvord. They also lived on a farm and ran cattle. Sometimes for school money, Cooper and Glen Ray would raise watermelons. However, since Cooper had graduated from high school, he had been in Denton going to college. He was the only kid in his class to go to college.

"Glen Ray!" Jake shouted, "What you doing?"

"Looking for ya'll," he said as he pulled his six foot lean frame out of a brand new Chevrolet pickup.

"Hey, who's pickup is this?" Elzie asked.

"My dad's," he said. "Just got it the other day, he let me drive it over to show ya'll."

"Can we ride in it Glen Ray?" Jake asked.

"Sure, that's why I come over. Come on, we'll drive the loop."

The loop was Russell's loop a five and half mile stretch that circled about fifteen hundred acres of land which was composed of six farms. Russell's loop ran right in front of the Oldham and Tatum farms, then wound on the north side separating them from the Jasper and Harry places. Then on the east across Denton Creek, lay the James Spencer Russell farm which consisted of a six hundred acre place, from which the road was named. Mr. Spencer's father was the first white settler to stake a claim in the old Bell County School land in 1870. From the Russell farm, the road ran north to east for about two miles then turned east to south bordering the Trayler farm, next was the Haney's place, then the Blane which bordered the Oldham.

The boys would have about a fifteen minute ride in the new truck. The seats were leather, the interior blue like the body of the truck. It had a six cylinder motor with a column shift, the starter on the floor.

"Let her go, Glen Ray," Elzie whooped. "God dang I never rode in a new pickup before!"

"You have to forgive Elzie, Glen Ray," Jake said, "he has found a new language at the truck stops."

"What's the matter with you, Jake, you never heard nobody say damn or hell before?" Glen Ray asked.

"My mama wouldn't approve," Jake said.

"Neither would mine," Glen Ray said, "but our mama's ain't here and they ain't going to know what we say out here or at school or anywhere else, cept they is with us."

"Then if they are with us, we wouldn't say it anyhow would we?" Jake asked.

"Jake, just quit being a smart ass, and loosen up. Damn," Elzie said.

They boys were in hog heaven riding around the loop with the windows down and their spirits high.

"Hey, Glen Ray, we need to go fishing. Me and Elzie went today and caught ten nice cats on Denton Creek." Jake said.

"We got to have a plan for us to go fishing. You two got your chores, I got mine, Bud helps his dad in the feed store, Billy John helps his dad with cleaning out their trucks all the time. We got to devise a plan." Glen Ray replied.

"We will" Jake said. "But sometimes we can just go the three of us, or me and you or you and Elzie. We can't always get Bud or Billy John in on everything."

Now Bud was Bud Hunter. His folks, Floyd and Leneta Nell Hunter, owned and operated the local grocery and feed store in Sunset. Bud was the same age as Elzie, and Billy John. Glen Ray and Jake were the same age. Bud had three sisters, two grown sisters, Ileta and Janice and had a sister two years younger than he named Nell.

Billy John was Billy John Monroe. His step dad was Bob Hancock. Billy John's real dad had died when he was two. His step dad ran a trucking business in Sunset. It was on one of Bob's trips that he met a waitress in Littlefield Texas. After routing a few trips to Littlefield he had married Dean and took Billy John to raise as his own. Billy John was an only child. His job was to sweep and clean up the trucks once they came in from a run. Billy John usually did this after school.

The trio turned back into the Oldham drive and stopped in front of the house.

"Hey, you wanna get a Dr. Pepper?" Jake asked, "I know we got some."

"Yeah," Elzie and Glen Ray both said. " I hope their good and cold." Glen Ray said.

"They should be," Jake said, "since we got an ice box, we even have cold water."

The boys went inside and each opened a bottle of Dr. Pepper and went out on the porch.

"Glen Ray," Jake began, "next fall is our senior year, can you believe it?"

"Seems like we just started this year and now its almost over," Glen Ray said.

"What you going to do this summer, haul hay, raise watermelons?" Elzie asked.

"Naw, I'm going to work at the Sunset station my dad and Uncle Lloyd own. Buford Miller is running it, but he needs help pumping gas and fixing flats and changing oil. So, dad has offered me a job there to help old Buford." Glen Ray replied.

"I hope you don't start talking like Buford. I think that's where Elzie learned his language," Jake said laughing.

"How's Coop doing in college?" Jake asked.

"Doing good, I think," Glen Ray said. "He says I can probably do like him and get a basketball scholarship to go to school on."

Glen Ray was Sunset's basket ball star. He could dribble the ball up and down the court flying like a wild antelope and shoot from just about anywhere. All the boys played basket ball but not all could play well. Jake couldn't play well. He always felt clumsy at the game and he really didn't like the game that much. His favorite subject in school was biology and his agriculture classes.

"Well, I gotta go," Glen Ray said. "I got to go feed our cows this evening and my folks are having my grandparents over for supper."

See ya Glen Ray the boys called out.

"I think ole Glen Ray has it together, don't you Jake?" Ask Elzie.

"Probably more than we know," Jake replied.

"Hey I hear another truck coming down the road," Elzie said, it's either your folks or your grandparents.

I don't think mom and dad have had time to get back," Jake said.

Turned out, it was both Leck and Ida Lou and Lige and Berthie May. Leck was in the lead truck and Lige close behind.

"Grandpa didn't have to buy any feed today except some chicken feed," Jake said, "so we won't have a big load to unload."

"Good," Elzie said, "I didn't want no more work today or tomorrow either."

Leck and Ida Lou drove on by as Lige pulled his truck into P.D. and Mary's yard.

Lige honked the horn then asked the boys what they were up to.

"Nothing Grandpa, did you see Glen Ray Shelton as you came up? His daddy got a brand new pickup." Jake said.

"And let that wild ass drive it?" Lige said.

"Lige!" Berthie May yelled.

"He drives pretty good, Mr. Oldham," Elzie said.

"If you like flying low," Lige replied. "Now get on the back and ride down to the house and you two can take the truck to the shed and unload the Gal's chicken feed."

"Sure Grandpa," said Jake.

"Why did your grandpa think that Glen Ray drove wild?" Elzie asked.

"Oh, he thinks everybody drives too fast," Jake said. "He even thinks my dad drives too fast. I don't discuss my driving with him," Jake said. "He will ride with me sometimes but usually that's in the pasture."

When they got to the house, Jake said, "Grandma we cleaned you ten nice catfish. There in the ice box soaking."

"Lord, lord," Berthie May said. "The fish must have been biting good. Well now, I'll fry them up and some fried taters and roll out some hush puppies too. I made a chocolate cake this morning before we left for town."

"Elzie you better go see if your mom and dad want to eat too. We can't eat ten catfish."

"Yesmm," Elzie said, "soon as we put up the chicken feed."

"Ok if we drive down to Leck's?" Jake asked.

"Well, I guess," Lige said, "but you boys are able to run down there."

Jake was teasing his Grandpa as he liked to do, because he knew that once they unloaded the chicken feed, he would park the pickup in the open shed.

As the boys drove down to the chicken yard, Jake said, "Now Elzie don't you tell Grandma we drank a Dr. Pepper today, because I'll bet you a dime to a dollar that she bought us some root beer. If you tell her we drank a Dr. Pepper, she won't let us have the root beer until tomorrow."

"I hear you," Elzie said.

The boys unloaded the three sacks of feed and while there checked the chickens feed troughs. Since they were getting low, Jake re filled them, knowing it would help his Grandma. Because he knew directly she would gather the eggs and then go and milk the two cows. Of course he and Elzie could do that, if she would let them.

"Hey Elzie, after we go down and tell your folks about the fish, let's come back and milk for Grandma, ok?" Jake said.

"Aw Jake, I was trying to get out of any more work today," Elzie whined.

"Work my butt," Jake said. "We have played most of the day except the disking we did this morning. We fished, we hunted, and we went for a ride in a new pickup."

Elzie was just laughing because for once he had got one on Jake.

After going down and telling Ida Lou about supper, the boys came back and asked Berthie May about doing the milking for her.

"You want to gather the eggs too?" She asked. "Oh boys, I forgot to tell you that I got you a little treat at Hunter's today. I bought you some Triple X Root Beer."

"Oh, good, Grandma, thanks, I can't wait to have one," Jake said.

"I'll bet you two and Glen Ray had a Dr. Pepper over at your mamas already," she said.

Jake never said a word, neither did Elzie.

"Uh, Grandma we already fed the chickens," he said, "so it's about time to gather the eggs anyhow isn't it?" Jake asked.

"Yes it's time, if you wait too long, too late the evening the chickens will be trying to roost. You don't want to disturb that," Berthie May said.

"We'll gather the eggs, and bring them back to the house, then Elzie and I will go and milk." Jake said.

"Thanks hon," Berthie May said. It was near four in the evening and time she started the supper. She had to get out some hog lard that they had rendered last winter and start it to melting to cook the fish in. Next she took some corn meal to roll the fish fillets in and laid them on a piece of wax paper. Wax paper, she thought, what a wonder. They didn't have that when she was a girl growing up in Alabama. Her parents, John and Eva Sanders came to Montague County when she was ten years old. There were five children and her dad's parents Elihu and Margaret Sanders. Her grandpa died two weeks after they arrived and within a month their house burned down. She remembered it was in March one month after her grandpa had died and how her grandma dragged her trunk out of the burning house. She was barefoot and it was very cold night. It was sure hard back then, she thought.

While the boys were in the house Ida Lou came up to the back porch.

"Berthie May!"She called.

"Come on in honey," Berthie May said.

Ida Lou was a slightly plump woman with graying hair that had once been a dark blond like her own mother. She wore a flower print dress she had bought from the factory she and Mary worked at.

"I thought if you was going to feed us again, I was going to come up and help you cook," Ida Lou said.

"Now, Ida Lou, there is no need, I can manage." Berthie May said.

Ida Lou said, "Honestly Berthie May, you cook all the time for us. You'd think I never cook."

"Look Ida Lou, Berthie May said. I have been cooking for folks just about ever since me and Lige been married. When he and I ran off and got married, we didn't have a pot to piss in. We came back here to stay with his folks until we got on our feet and we never left! I used to help Mrs. Oldham with all the cooking for her family and later on mine too. During the Depression there's no telling how many folks we've fed, folks that didn't have a meal, folks that seemed to be paralyzed by the hard times. They didn't seem to have the gumption to even raise a garden. We did, we always did because we would have starved if we hadn't. Then there was the flu epidemic and Mrs. Oldham came down sick and I never got sick. I cooked for two weeks solid for all the house and for a lot of people that was sick around here. I used to make a big pot of soup and sending it by P.D. to people's houses. I told him to go and knock on the door, leave the soup, we put it in little buckets with lids, and to get out in their yard and yell you left them some soup. I told him you make sure they hear you now, and you make sure they come get that soup.

One day he went up to this house and nobody answered. Finally, P.D. looked in one of the windows and he could see all of them laying everywhere, in the beds and on the floor. He came back home and told me, so I sent Lige and he took his dad with him. They went in and found the whole family had died, all eight of them. It was about the saddest thing we ever did see."

Ida Lou said, "You know I heard my mama talking about that, what happened after they found all of them dead?"

"Well, Mr. Oldham, Lige's dad, went and got a bunch of neighbors, and his brother Uncle Jo and they all went up and dug eight graves at Pleasant Hill. He sent Lige to town and they brought out eight coffins and we buried that family. I think their names was Bottomly, or something like that. They lived over on the old Shanks place over toward Lake Valley," Berthie May said.

"Anyhow, Mrs. Oldham was sick and I cooked for her family and I think that was about the only time she appreciated anything I ever done for her. But, I'm glad to cook for you and Leck and your old daddy. Goodness, him and Lige been together a long time, they walked to school together and they've done a lot of things together and I'm just proud that Jake and Elzie are so close, like Lee and Lige."

"Oh, I'm proud too," Ida Lou said. "You know boys at their age get restless and start complaining about how they want to see the world and want to get away from home."

"Yeah, I used to say that too," Berthie May said as she and Ida Lou were preparing the meal. "I thought I needed to get away from home. I thought my dad was about the meanest man in the world and what did I do but jump right out of the frying pan into the fire."

Right in the middle of cooking the fish and hush puppies, P.D. and Mary came in, followed by Leck and Lee.

"What did the pigs bring?" Berthie May asked.

"The brought eleven dollars each," P.D. replied.

"Lord God!" Berthie May exclaimed, "the last time we sold, they was four dollars. We got anymore to sell?"

"We will have seven more in about two weeks," P.D. said.

"They will probably be down to five dollars then," Berthie May said. "We got fish tonight, Elzie and Jake caught a big mess."

"That's fine Mama," P.D. said. "Mary and I are pretty tired from the trip. I imagine she didn't want to cook tonight."

"We'll have supper in about thirty minutes. You go on in the living room and visit with Leck and your dad," Berthie May said. "Mary stayed in the kitchen and started boiling the tea."

"Where's the boys?" Mary asked.

"Oh, they are out trying to milk my cows," Berthie May said.

"Do they know how to milk?" Ida Lou said. "I don't think Elzie's ever milked a cow."

"Oh yes," Berthie May said, "I've showed the boys several times. They know what to do." "They can do fine if they don't horse play too much."

While they were speaking Elzie and Jake came in the kitchen with two big buckets full of warm milk.

"Do you run this through the separator?" Jake asked.

"Just run one," Berthie May said. "I need one bucket for all of us. Ida Lou, how's your milk supply holding out?"

"We're bout out, Berthie," Ida Lou replied.

"Well, you'll have new jar tonight," Berthie May said. What about butter, are you getting low on butter?

Both Mary and Ida Lou said they were getting low.

"Well, Berthie May said, "I'll churn some tomorrow."

After supper the routine was the same when the two families were together. The men would go into the living room and get out the dominos and play until bedtime. The boys would sit on the porch. However since this was Saturday night and Lige and Berthie May had one luxury that neither P.D. and Mary, nor Leck and Ida Lou had, that was a T.V. Saturday nights everyone gathered to watch Gunsmoke. It was a thirty minute program that came on at nine o'clock followed by Death Valley Days. Jake liked Death Valley Days about as much as he liked Gunsmoke. He liked Stanley Andrews who opened the show with the line, "Howdy folks, I'm the old Ranger." Then he would tell of some tale about the old west that was supposed to be true.

After the two shows everyone was off to bed. There were some chores to do each morning regardless of the day. Tomorrow would be Sunday and everyone would be off to church, everyone but Lee, Lige and Berthie May. They had grown up in a different era when the church was at the cemetery, and was a community church. The same people met every Sunday but the preachers were from different dominations, a different one came each Sunday, or most Sunday's. There were times when they didn't have preachers. Lige's dad used to teach Sunday School and lead the singing, although his brother Joe lead a lot of singing too. Gradually folks moved away, moved into the cities and took factory jobs, the community church went by the wayside and gave way to churches in town and a different church for each belief. None of them catered to the older generations ideas.

Sunday morning the Tatum's would be off to Sunset to attend church at the Sunset Assembly of God, the Hunter's and Hancock's were all Baptist, the Shelton's Methodist, and the Oldham's were church of Christ. P.D. had been converted by Mary who's family had been associated with the church of Christ for over a hundred years. Sometimes Berthie May and Lige would go to church with them. Going to church meant usually going in Mary's car if Berthie May and Lige went. Otherwise the three of them would go in P.D.'s truck.

This morning, it would be Jake's mother and father and himself going to church. Instead of P.D.'s truck, the three of them loaded in the family car, a 50 model Chevy with standard shift. It was an eight mile drive on a red dusty road to town. The church building was located on the north end of East Front street which paralleled the rail road tracks. Usually P.D. would discuss the weeks work needs on the way to town and Mary would want to talk about things the house needed. Jake usually listened and only answered questions his dad might ask.

While the family was gone, the milking done and the chickens fed, Berthie May came back to the house with her two pails of milk. She poured the milk through a cup towel into gallon jars and set them in her ice box. She took out two more jars one from yesterday evening's milking and one from the mornings. The cream had risen to the top of the jar that hadn't been ran through the separator. A separator was a mechanical device that separated the cream from the milk. Since their milk cows were Jersey, almost one fourth of the jar was cream. Berthie May took a wooden spoon ladle and dipped out the cream. The cream was placed into another half gallon jar. The lid of the jar contained two paddles that turned by a handle which was part of the lid. She would turn the paddle for about half an hour. During that time a weak milky liquid, which was called buttermilk came to the top, separated from the butter. The liquid was poured off and discarded into a five gallon bucket kept on the back porch for clabbering and fed to the hogs. Next Berthie would spoon the buttering material out of her "churn" and onto a bowl. There she would take a whipping wire used to make pie toppings and force it through the butter to squeeze out the final butter milk. She would pour cold water onto the butter to make sure all the soured milk was separated from the butter. Lastly she would add some salt and mix into the butter, then place it into a bowl and place in the ice box. Today she would make up some four bowl of fresh cow butter. The final product would be a pure white solid material shaped in the bowl like half a base ball. It would last each family about two weeks. Then, before they ran out, Berthie May would repeat this process as she had done since she was a small girl. The only difference was the use of an ice box.

The parking lot was full of trucks and cars as the Oldham's arrived. Folks were walking in the door as they got out of the car. Both P.D. and Jake were wearing black suits, with white shirts and black ties. P.D. and Jake both wore Stetsons.

The walk way to the door was a long ramp that had been especially made for Avis Cornwall who was in a wheel chair. Avis could not walk well and unless an access had been made, couldn't roll the wheel chair into the building. P.D. and Lige had built the forms for the concrete and tied the steel in order to save the church money. Leighton Hall had worked the concrete and done the finish work. Tony Porter had donated the cement.

The doors to the church were double doors that gave a great squeak when opened. Every person in the building would know when someone else had entered the building. The church building had been built back in 1918. It had fourteen foot ceilings with six ceiling fans to help keep air flow in the hot summers. The windows stayed open during the summer service unless it was raining. Sometimes the trains passing by would interrupt the preacher and he would have to pause until the mighty iron beast had stopped its screaming as it roared down the tracks. The preacher of the Sunset church of Christ was Newby Morrow. He was twenty eight years old, with a young wife, Ruby, and one child with another one on the way. Newby lived in Bowie and worked as a meter reader for the city of Bowie. When he decided to become a preacher, he had gone to a preaching school in Fort Worth. He had been preaching for Sunset the past two years. Folks liked him too. He never preached too long, Jake liked that. Long sermons tended to lose his interest. The longer they droned on, the more his mind would wander back to Denton Creek, where the cool water flowed and the fish swam begging to be caught, and the snakes were always a good target. If he looked like he was daydreaming, his mother would give him a nudge. Sometimes she would nudge P.D. too, as he had the same problem. If the preacher talked too long, he would be out plowing a field, cutting hay, or feeding cows.

Jake knew the routine at church. They always started the morning with a bible class. The kids were divided into classes according to age, while the adults just stayed in the auditorium where Newby taught. Someone would ring a bell warning that the class was over. Five minutes was allowed between class and the formal worship service, what people called "church." Either Matt Flatt or Bill Beachump would get up and lead singing. After a few songs, then the song leader would call on someone to lead a prayer, followed by the preacher giving his oratory skills from the pulpit. It always seemed to Jake that the preacher, and it didn't matter who the preacher was, seemed to follow the same pattern, and that was making a consecrated effort to save the congregation from their sins. Jake always thought that the ones who needed saving were the ones that weren't at church. After a long effort to offer an invitation thorough the preacher's pleas and a special invitation song, like "Just as I am," the members would sit back down. If there were no takers, no one to answer God's call to salvation, the congregation would sing another hymn and partake of the Lords Supper, followed by the contribution, then a last song and a dismissal prayer. The people would then acknowledge one another, men shaking hands as they made their way out the door with a final handshake of the preacher telling him it was a wonderful sermon. Folks told the preacher that whether it was a good sermon or not, but they always told the preacher that it was. Jake wondered if his friend's church service was like his. On their way out the door the men's hats hung on pegs sticking out from the wall. Outside the people would bunch up and visit a minute before departing for their homes where the wives had to cook dinner. Kids would scamper around the yard running and playing for a brief moment before loading into their cars and trucks. They had church on Sunday and Wednesday night, but the Oldham's seldom attended other than the Sunday morning service.

While standing in the churchyard, Debbie Crocket came up to Jake. She was a very pretty girl with olive skin and dark eyes and long dark hair, wearing a dark blue dress, which complimented her dark skin.

"Hey, Jake", she said, "how are you?"

"Oh, just fine," Jake said.

"You ready for school to be out?" She asked.

Jake smiled, "I'm always ready for school to be out."

"What are you planning for the summer?" She asked.

"Well, we got melons and peanuts, and we will cut some native hay before the peanuts make," Jake said.

At that moment Jake noticed his mom and dad leaving their groups of people and joining together and walking toward the car.

"Well, Deb, I'll see you tomorrow at school," he said.

When the weather warmed, the boys had a regular habit on Sunday afternoon. All five of them would gather after church to either go fishing or swimming unless Jake and Elzie were working.

However today they were not meeting to fish or swim. Most likely Jake would spend the day at the house reading or he and his grandpa would play dominos or croquet or thumps. If Elzie didn't come over, then he would go down to his Grandparents house to spend the afternoon, unless P.D. had some chore for him. P.D. liked to have chores for Jake to do. He felt he needed to be busy and productive. That was the way his mama had raised him, so what was good for the goose should be good for the gander.

When they arrived back at the house, there was a note pinned to the door. Come to dinner, it said. They all knew that Berthie May would have the table ready.

Sure enough the table was spread with chicken fried stake, mashed potatoes, butter beans, corn bread, ice tea and a black berry cobbler. Clois was already at the table.

"Mama," P.D. said, "You shouldn't spend all your time cooking."

"What else am I going to do P.D.?" She asked. "You know I don't mind cooking for my family. Besides, we all got to eat. "Lige!" she yelled, "dinner's ready!"

Lige didn't immediately come to the kitchen. He had a habit of going into the bathroom just before eating and washing his teeth and getting rid of his chaw of tobacco. He sometimes was as long as ten minutes before emerging from the bathroom.

The family was well set before he came in and only after Berthie May called him twice more.

Berthie May always fixed Lige's plate and had it ready for him before he sat at the table. Today she had him a cutlet covered with gravy, a piece of cornbread buttered and his tea poured. If he wanted the butter beans he had to dip them himself.

Many times when Jake sat at his grandparents table, he couldn't help think about the time back when he was about five years old. He, his grandparents and Clois were about to sit down to dinner on Saturday. Jake, Lige and Berthie May had all been to Sunset for the weekly supply of groceries and feed. Upon returning, Berthie May had stirred up dinner. This was before Clois was working for the Bar T Donald Ranch. He was living with Berthie May and Lige, but he seldom went to town with them. He would go to town but never with his parents. They wouldn't approve of the company he hung out with. So Jake and Lige were sitting at the table when Clois came into the house to eat.

"Where you been Kid?" Lige said. "His by word for Clois was the Old Kid."

Anytime you asked Clois where he had been, he would immediately fly off the handle. He did that day with a flurry of curses and hateful words in answer to Lige's question. Then Clois grabbed up a stool that was against the wall threatening Lige with it.

Lige, although smaller than Clois, jumped up from the table and grabbed a second stool that usually stood by the wash stand.

The two men were banging the stools against each other and they battled out of the kitchen into the next room which was a bedroom.

As soon as the commotion started Berthie May began running after the two shouting "Lige! Lige!" They all disappeared into the next room leaving Jake sitting at the dinner table. Jake did not move.

In a moment, the three appeared back into the kitchen with Berthie May holding the collars of each men, she pointed them to the table and sat them down in one motion.

"Lige," Berthie May said, "You are a bigger fool than Clois is!"

Lige didn't answer but began filling his plate with food. Clois on the other hand was mumbling complaints, however Berthie May looked at him and sternly said,"Clois that is enough. Eat your dinner or just get out." The storm was then all over. Everyone went back to dinner.

Jake would chuckle under his breath when he thought about the incident and whenever he was at the dinner table at his Grandma's with Clois and Grandpa sitting there, he was often reminded of the incident. He never spoke of it for a long time after it happened to his parents. He was afraid his father might not allow him to stay with his grandparents. However, P.D. understood his brother's hot tempered nature. More than once he had had to calm him down and not know really why his brother would be so upset.

"Was they very many at church?" Berthie May asked.

"Oh, I guess there were seventy five or so there, six or seven visitors," Mary answered.

"Was there any news?"Berthie May always ask.

"They said Vernie Bagwell was home sick and Mrs. Lewis was in the hospital," Mary said.

"Don't look like they had any baptism this morning," Lige remarked, "since ya'll got home about the usual time."

"No, there weren't any baptism," P.D. said.

After dinner, Jake and Lige got out a board to play a game they called thumps. Berthie May had ordered the game from Montgomery Wards, but didn't know what the name of it was. The game consisted of a piece of varnished plywood, with the four corners of the board cut off and pool pockets sowed on. There were twelve green and twelve red wooden washer looking pieces. The pieces were about a quarter inch thick, somewhat like miniature donuts. The board was set up for four players although two could play and each player had a wooden washer that was unpainted. The board had a boarder around it and a square painted in the middle of the board. The twenty four pieces were placed in inside the painted square and the player shot at the pieces with their unpainted piece. The shots were made by using the thumb and middle finger thumping the wooden piece at the red and green pieces. The object was to shoot whatever color one had chosen into the corner pockets. If one had knocked the pieces in the pockets and accidentally shot the shooter piece in the pocket, then a colored one was taken out and placed back into the center. When Elzie came over they would play against Lige and Berthie May. Today Jake would play against his grandpa. To add to the game, Lige had painted one of the extra shooter pieces black. So in addition to all the green ones or the red ones, the last piece that had to be shot in the pocket was the black one.

Around three o'clock Elzie came over. Lige was ready to take a nap, so Jake and Elzie got their poles and headed for the creek.

"Tell me Elzie, what do you all do at your church?" Jake asked.

"What do you mean?" Elzie asked.

Jake explained the "order of service," wanting to know what they did at the Assembly of God.

"Oh, we sort of do a lot of the same you all do. We don't have the Lords Supper each Sunday like ya'll do, and we play guitar's and piano and stuff like that. We have a prayer bench for sinners to go up and pray on if they need saving," Elzie said.

"Do you get tired of it?" Jake asked.

"Sometimes, sometimes I think Brother Charles won't stop preaching, trying to save the sinners," Elzie said.

"Yeah, I know," Jake said, "I know."

The boys hit the creek with poles and some worms they dug up at the barn. It didn't take long before they were getting hits. Jake and Elzie began to pull fish from the water, but Jake told Elzie to just throw them back.

"We had fish the other night and I don't want to clean any," Jake said.

"Was Angie at church today?" Jake asked.

"Now Jake," Elzie said, "I told you what we done in secret, now don't go blabbing that around."

"I'm not," Elze, Jake said, "I just was wondering if the sweet thing came to church today."

"Yeah, she was there," Elzie said.

"Well did she go up to the mourning bench?" Jake asked.

"No, you horses ass," Elzie said, "and I didn't either. We didn't need to and we didn't have too."

Jake was laughing knowing that he had got old Elzie again.

"Ok, Elze," Jake said. "I just wondered."

"Next time I get any, I ain't going to be telling you!" Elzie said.

Around five, the boys started back for the house, when Elzie said, he better go home. Mama wanted me to gather the eggs for her and I got my history final tomorrow, Elzie said.

"Yeah, I've got a math test, and English final tomorrow too," Jake said.

"Yeah, we got English test too, but mine is in the morning. Then Tuesday,

we got our Agriculture final and math, then Wednesday morning our science and geography. Then we're done until September, yahoo!" Elzie said.

CHAPTER 3

Monday morning Jake was out the door and down the walk to his Grandparents house to fetch his Grandpa's truck and head for school.

Jake opened the door and slid in. The key was always in the ignition. He turned it on, mashed the starter and the gas petal and after a moment of turning the engine over the old truck belched a start. Jake carefully backed out of the shed and turned the truck around, to head out the drive way. Lige had come outside and was standing on the driver's side when Jake got the truck turned around.

"Morning Grandpa," Jake said.

"Off to school are ye?" Lige said.

"Just as soon as I pick up Elzie," Jake replied.

"Well, see you boys this afternoon. I imagine P.D. and I'll put a dent in the planting. This morning I got to run the cultivators through the beans. Corn's coming up," Lige said.

Jake headed out the Oldham drive and down to Elzie's house. He imagined Elzie was ready although sometimes he was sleepy headed on Monday morning.

As Jake entered the Tatum home, he tooted the horn, Elzie came out the front door, opened the truck and slid in.

"Hey Jake," Elzie said. "Two more days after today and we're out for the summer."

"Yeah, out for hoeing watermelons and peanuts, hauling hay, then harvesting the melons, if they make," Jake's replied.

"Well there won't be no school books and six weeks test!" Elzie said.

"I bet we get in some fishing and swimming in spite of the work," Jake said.

Things were as usual at the Sunset School. Sunset covered all twelve grades but it was a matter of time before Bowie would consolidate, because Sunset was a shrinking violet. Although in its prime Sunset was larger than Bowie, the Depression of 1929 had decimated the town and it had never recovered. People who had lived their lives in and around Sunset had moved to bigger areas, had quit farming and gone to work in the factories. At one time Sunset boasted four grocery stores, four dry goods, two drug stores, a movie theater, department stores, a hotel, three doctor offices, numerous other business's and three banks. However in 1954, one bank remained, one grocery and feed store and several gas stations and gift shops lined the highway which came through the middle of town. Fortunately for the old timers the bank and store was off the main drag and was on a street that ran perpendicular to the highway. In its heyday Cottage Grove was the main street, but the development of a state highway changed all that.

The school was on the eastern edge of town, a long brick building facing the Forestburg road, which was actually Forrest Avenue. It was a dirt road that ran all the way to the town of Forestburg and to the west, intersected the state highway U.S. 287, crossing 287 and went all the way to Bridgeport. Behind the classrooms was a second building which served as the agriculture and shop building. To the west of the classroom was a separate wooden building that served as the school lunch room and gymnasium. Many hot basketball and volley ball games had been played in the old gym.

Jake pulled into the parking area of the school, which was in front of the gym. Several of his classmates were standing in front of the gym doors. Jake and Elzie got out and walked over to the crowd of people.

Corky Miller yelled out to the boys, "Hey, can we ride in your truck down to Hulet's for dinner?"

"Sure," Jake said.

The first bell was sounding and the kids made off for their class rooms. The home room of each class was also the class room for each grade. Usually one or two teachers taught all the subjects. In the first eight grades there were four teachers, each teacher taught two grades. In high school there was an English teacher for all four English classes, that was Mrs. Merritt. There was a history, government, and science teacher for the whole high school, Mr. Halford, the Agriculture, shop and all sports was Mr. Bankston, and all math classes was taught by the school superintendent Mr. Armstrong.

Elzie headed for his sophomore classroom and a history final, with Jake headed for his Algebra II final.

At lunch the boys headed for the truck and met up with Corky, Glen Ray, Bud, Billy John, Nell, Debra Crocket, and Nancy Shelton. They loaded up in Jakes truck, front and back, to head down the street three blocks but across the highway to Hulet's café which was called Home Away From Home café. However the all the locals called it The Greasy Spoon. Hulet and his wife Ellie were busy in the little eatery when the school kids came in. Several travelers had stopped to eat as well as a few truckers who were fueling at Jackson's across the street. Hulet always waited the tables and Ellie and a hired cook named Ann did the cooking.

Entering the door, Jake saw the bar held four people and all the booths were full, which were set against the four walls of the building. The jukebox was playing Hank Snow's "I'm Movin On." In the center of the room were tables and most of them empty.

"Just find a place and light," Hulet said in his gravel voice. "We got chicken fried steak for the blue plate special."

The gang pushed two tables together so all the students could sit together. The room had an aroma of the kitchen and air was thick with the cooking smoke and cigarettes.

"Ok," Hulet said, "what ya'll have?" Everyone ordered burgers, fries and whatever kind of soft drink they liked. As soon as Hulet stuck the orders up on the order stand, the grease made a loud noise as the raw hamburger patties were slapped on the grill.

The kids were full of chatter and talk of getting out for the summer and finishing finals.

In the seating, Jake had managed a seat besides Bud's sister Nell. He was sweet on her but she paid little to no attention to him. She sat next to Nancy Shelton, Glen Ray's first cousin, who was her best friend. Debra Crocket was across the table sitting beside Elzie.

Most of the time the three girls were together everywhere they went. None of them were allowed to date except in group functions such as school outings, games, or church socials.

"So, how you coming along on your finals?" Jake asked Nell.

"Oh, I'm fine. We had our science and history this morning. We have our English this evening and I've got two more tomorrow but I'm don't have any Wednesday, so I'm done tomorrow," Nell replied, but she ask no questions of Jake nor made effort to carry the conversation further.

"Want to ride up front with me when we go back to school?" Jake asked her, not wanting the conversation to end. All he could do was look into her brown eyes, her light brown hair, and think about her beautiful legs.

"Oh, ok," she said. "But, won't Elzie get jealous?"

"What? Elzie, heck no," Jake said. "He don't mind riding back in the back, he'll be in good company. Course, he could drive my truck and you and I could walk back."

She looked at him for a moment knowing full well he was sweet on her and she had him in her power to do as she wished. She gave a slight smile, and said, "why don't we walk tomorrow?"

Jake drew in a deep breath, about to shout with exhilaration, but with a calmness said, "Sure."

Minutes later the kids were paying Hulet for their lunches, Jake trying to pay for Nell's but she would not let him, then they were all back in the truck.

"You kids be careful crossing that damn highway," he yelled. "These crazy people will run right over ya."

Carefully Jake turned the truck around and watched for several minutes before it was clear that he could cross the highway. Instead of going down Forest Avenue, he went down Cottage right in front of the

Hunter Store. He knew that when he drove in front of the store Nell's mama would see them. She might not approve of her fourteen year old daughter riding with a boy who had turned seventeen, he hoped she wouldn't object.

"You going to work in your folks store this summer?" Jake asked as the drove especially slow back to school.

"Bud is, but I'm just going to keep house for mama," she said.

"You think your mama would let us go to the Drive Inn at Bowie?" He asked.

"Oh, I don't think so Jake, she don't want me going out on a date."

"Well we could take Bud and Nancy and Debra, and Elzie or Glen Ray," Jake countered.

"I sort of think Glen Ray is cute," she said.

Jake's ears glowed red, but he tried not to show any emotion. We could go on "Wednesday night, it is a dollar per car load," he said.

"That's church night, we can't miss prayer meeting," she replied.

"Well, the movie starts when it gets dark, church is well out by then," Jake said.

"I might go if you get Glen Ray," she said.

Jake wanted to die. He was having the moment of his life with a girl he was thinking he could imagine spending a lifetime with and she was torturing him. Take Glen Ray, he thought. No matter, ridding with her in the truck, he didn't want the drive back to school to end.

The trip back to school was over too soon for Jake though. He could have driven that old rattling bucket of bolts to Amarillo if she had been by his side.

After school Elzie and Jake got ready to go home but a few guys gathered at the gym. Glen Ray wanted to shoot some free throws before heading home, and Bud liked the idea. Billy John had left to wash out some truck trailers for his dad.

"Hey," Bud said, "dad's getting one more train car load of feed, figures it will last all summer. It's supposed to be here tomorrow, you and Elzie want to help unload it?"

"Sure," Jake said. "We'd be glad to, right Elzie?"

39

"Oh sure we can," Elzie said. "We are about in the short rows in this book learning for this year, so we might as well unload feed."

"How about we get Billy John and Glen Ray and go camping Thursday night to celebrate school being out?" Bud asked.

"Yeah,"Elzie said, "what ya say, Jake old boy."

"I say, that's a capital idea cousins," Jake said.

Next day, Jake was all ants awaiting for Nell to walk up to Hulet's for dinner. When the noon bell sounded, he dashed from the class room to find Nell.

Coming out of her class room, she noticed him and smiled. "Hi Jake," she said.

"You ready to go down to Hulet's?" He asked.

"Sure," she said, "anybody else going?"

"Yeah, I think just about everybody but I hoped we could walk without them.," Jake replied.

"Well ok, but Deb and Nancy want to walk with us, is that ok?" Nell said.

Jake about wanted to melt, but said, "Sure it is. Let's go."

So, the four of them walked together down to Hulet's. Of course, walking with a crowd killed any idea of trying to talk Nell into a date or a movie or anything else. All the girls wanted to do was laugh at something Jake cared nothing about, or talk about how cute somebody was, but it was never him they mentioned. It wasn't his ideal walk.

All of the gang that ate lunch at Hulet's was walking that day and it seemed they were just a stream of kids, no one in any group. Elzie wasn't ten yards ahead walking with none other than Angie Freeman. Jake wanted to yell out to him to wait up, but he knew that wouldn't be prudent since he had asked Nell to walk with him. He watched Elzie and Angie walking side by side and he couldn't help thinking about the pastor's couch.

The walk back from lunch was just as boring as the walk to, only with a bigger crowd. All the kids walked in one group back. Nell didn't even seem to walk next to Jake, as he had wanted her too. He had lain awake at night thinking about the lunch period. He dreamed that she and he would meet and she would be all smiles and just crazy about him and wanting to walk with him and somewhere along the walk he would make that magical move and slip his hand into hers. God what a thrill! What surge of emotion and power would course through his veins. He would be on top of the world, he had the prettiest girl in school at his side wearing his Ag jacket wanting to walk everywhere with him, wanting to write his name on her notebook and book covers, wanting to whisper to her girlfriends how cute he was. He almost couldn't sleep in anticipation of the moment and it was all lost, it was all for naught, it never happened the way he dreamed it would or thought it should. As far as Jake was concerned, his first date with Nell was a big flop.

Officially school was over on Wednesday with picking up report cards on Thursday and senior graduation was on Saturday night, and the Junior/ Senior celebration was on Friday night. There were fourteen seniors. Jake's class, the junior class had sixteen, unless someone dropped out, or moved, or if someone moved in, they would have the largest class of the last three graduating classes.

The boys could hardly contain themselves until their camping trip. Glen Ray couldn't go because of a trip to Fort Worth the following day with his parents and Billy John had several trailers to wash on Friday. So, it would be the three boys, Bud, Elzie and Jake.

They unloaded the train car on Wednesday and Thursday afternoon's and traded their camp supplies for their labor. Jake didn't take his Grandparents truck on the outing, however Bud borrowed his dad's pickup. The camp out would be at the Hunter's farm about four miles southeast of Sunset.

They would put up their camp beside one of the Hunter's stock tanks that had some nice shade trees.

That afternoon Bud had told Jake he would come by and get him. Elzie didn't ride home with Jake that evening but stayed in town with Bud.

It was getting late in the evening before Elzie and Bud showed up at Jake's. In fact Jake thought they had forgotten him.

He walked out to the truck and said, "Hey where ya'll been?"

"Oh, nowhere." Elzie said, "If you're going, get in."

Jake threw his sleeping bag in the back and slid into the truck. Bud turned around and headed for his dad's farm. Now the Hunter's lived in Sunset, but owned a quarter section of land south east of town. Mr. Hunter always had cows and as soon as Bud could drive, Mr. Hunter had Bud to take care of the feeding.

Jake was riding shotgun, so he had to open the gate at the Hunter farm. Entering the gate was an old barn, in disarray and falling down. The road inside the pasture ran left of the barn. Just inside the gate a fence ran parallel to the pasture road and on the north side of the barn. It was just wide enough to drive between the fence and barn. They drove along side the fence then turned north across the field toward the stock pond. On the west side of the pond were three oak trees that made a nice campground. As soon as the boys pulled up, they got out and began setting up their camp. They had no tent, but would spread their bedrolls on the ground. The big job was to get firewood and build a fire. The site had a picnic table, because Bud's family sometimes came out for family outings. Jake was searching for firewood while Bud and Elzie were unloading the food and soft drinks. Bud and Elzie were laughing, so Jake asked them what was so funny.

"We got a surprise for you Jake ol boy," Elzie said.

"What kind of surprise?" Jake asked.

Grinning from ear to ear, Bud said, "we got a six pack of beer!"

"Beer!" Jake said, "Where would you get beer?"

"That, is a secret," Elzie said, "it's Bud's special secret."

"You going to drink it?" Jake asked.

That's why we brought it out here, Bud said.

"Shoot, Jake, you act like you are so innocent!" Elzie said.

"No, I'm not so innocent, but I don't know that I want any beer. Is it good and cold?" Jake said.

"We got er iced down," Bud said. "Jaxx Beer, ought to be good."

"Let's get a fire going and so we can cook some hot dogs," Jake said.

Elzie began to work the wood Jake had gathered and start a fire. It took several tries, since the boys didn't bring any kind kerosene. Finally Bud found a piece of newspaper in his dad's truck, which made it possible to get the fire going.

"Too bad we don't have some girls out here," Elzie said. "You know to go along with the beer, heck, we could play strip poker!"

"Yeah, I bet," Bud said, "I can just see you stripping for some girl."

"We could roam around Alvord and probably get some girls," Elzie said.

"Naw, let's just enjoy the time out here. Let's don't drive over to Alvord," Jake said. "Girls complicate the issue."

"What issue?" Elzie said, "We want the girls to have a party with."

"If we had some girls out here," Jake countered, "I guess since you are the one with all the experience would have to show us what to do!"

Bud gave out a big laugh and said, "I hear Elzie's been tapping Angie Freeman."

Elzie gave Jake a look, but Jake looked at Elzie with a puzzled " not me" expression.

"Where did you hear that?" Jake asked.

"Oh, I heard Angie was telling it herself. She told my sister and I heard her talking to Nancy about it." Bud said.

"Oh, God," Elzie said. "I hope my Pastor don't find out!"

Both Jake and Bud gave big hoot of a laugh.

Bud looked at Elzie, and said, "what's your Pastor got to do with it?"

That's where the big event took place, Jake said, "In the Pastor's study."

"Well I'll be dang!" Bud said.

"You did bring coat hangers didn't you Bud?" Jake asked.

"Yeah, aren't they on the table?" Bud said.

"No, I don't see them, I'll look in the back of the truck , "Jake replied.

"Have ya'll heard about Sunset school closing?" Bud asked.

Both Elzie and Jake looked at each other in shock. "What are you talking about, it isn't going to close is it?" Elzie asked.

"From what I hear it might. Of course the people got to vote on it first," Bud said.

"I don't want to spend my senior year at Bowie," Jake said.

"Their school's so big I bet that got over a hundred in each class."

No, I don't want to go there" Why I'd ruther go to Forestburg as Bowie."

"I know what you mean, but it could happen," Bud said. "I hear people talking about it in the store all the time."

"Let's hope it's just talk," Jake said.

The boys feasted on their hot dogs and afterward, Bud got out the bottled beer. He popped the top off and gave one to Elzie who had taken a sip before Jake got his bottle. He held it for a moment smelling the soured smell of the liquid. Both Bud and Elzie were taking numerous sips from their bottles.

Finally Jake said, "I can't imagine this being any good, but here goes." He took a big gulp and then spit the liquid from his mouth. Both Bud and Elzie gave a big laugh asked Jake what was the matter.

"Taste awful!" Jake said. "How can anyone drink this, this piss!"

"Oh, did you hear it?" Elzie said, "he almost said a cuss word!"

"If you two want to drink that stuff you can have my share, I'm not drinking that stuff again. I hope you brought some Dr. Pepper's", Jake said.

"We did, because we knew a certain panty waist would have to have them," Bud said.

"You can bob up and kiss," Jake said.

The boys devoured the entire package of Oscar Meyer Franks as they sat around their camp fire. As the night loomed on, even though it was a warm spring night, the fire was inviting giving off its warmth. Bud and Elzie had drunk the six pack, while Jake had downed two Dr. Pepper's. They sat looking into the glow of the fire, when Elzie rang out, Boys, this is the life. "May it never end."

"Amen to that," Bud said.

"I wish we could go camping all the time," Jake said." It is fun to sit out here amongst the stars, enjoy the fire, swatting the mosquitoes, no worries and no work. But tomorrow when the sun comes up, the work demands our time, we can't sit around the campfire then."

"Oh, shut up," Elzie said. "Hey I got to pee." Elzie stood up and went around on the north side of the fire. Since the wind was out of the south, they had sat on the south side of the blaze. Elzie got on the north side in the smoke unzipped his fly and began to pee on the fire. The smoke bellowed up from the urine and so did a great stench.

"What the hell is wrong with you, you dumb ass!" Bud roared.

However Jake and Elzie were just laughing their heads off, although Jake didn't really like Elzie to piss in the fire, but it seemed funny at the time. The madder Bud got the funnier it was.

The night wore on and the three continued to talk and laugh about all the things that went on in their lives. Shortly before sunup they slept perhaps an hour. When they arose, the sun in their eyes, they loaded their stuff in the truck and headed for town. It was Friday morning, no school and no work for them that day. They went by Bud's house and got some breakfast.

Leneta Hunter was still in her house coat when the boys arrived. Floyd had already gone to the store to open up. Originally the store was purchased in 1920 by Benjamin and Hattie Hunter, Floyd's parents. Although they had turned the store over to Floyd, Ben and Hattie still worked in the store. Leneta worked too, but she didn't have to be there as early as her in-laws or Floyd.

"You boys want pancakes with your eggs?" She asked.

"No mom," Bud said, "the eggs and bacon will be fine. We're going out to Amon Carter and fish awhile this morning. We'll be back by noon."

"Well, you boys be careful, don't fall in the lake," she warned.

"We're just going to fish, not swim," Elzie said with a laugh. "May I have some more chocolate milk?"

"Of course, I'm glad to feed you bunch of hungry mob," she said. "What did ya'll eat last night?"

"Just hot dogs and chips," Bud said.

"We had plenty to drink," Jake offered.

Both Elzie and Bud gave Jake a hard stare, but Jake who was good with his puns, never flinched.

After breakfast they headed out to Amon Carter Lake. Amon Carter had been built three years before with speculation that it would take years for it to fill up. However in spite of drought conditions, in October of that year, a thunderstorm struck and filled the lake in one night. It was a marvel to the public, and a pleasure to the city of Bowie as it was the new water supply for the town.

The boys were going to fish behind the dam in the spillway plunge pool. The pool often contained some big fish that had swam through the pipe spill way and had lodged in the plunge pool. Often the fish were carp, but they didn't care what kind of fish they caught. Carp caught on a hook can put up a great fight. The plunge pool was perhaps thirty five feet below the road down a very steep bank. Bud always had a large tackle box and at least three rods whenever he went fishing. Both Jake and Elzie had managed to buy regular fishing rod and reels and shared small shoe box sized tackle box which paled in comparison to Bud's gear. It usually took ten minutes to work ones way down the steep bank to the cemented area that surrounded the plunge pool. Past the pool the water extended into a pure rock bed and on each side of the bank was a rock outcrop that ledged over the water. It was about four feet above the water. The first time Jake and Elzie had come with Bud to fish for carp, Bud had caught all the fish. Jake had trouble seeing his monofilament line and the trick to catching a carp was to watch the line, since the fishing was done on the bottom without a cork. The treble hook was baited with a sweet gummy substance they had bought at Avery's Bait shop in Bowie. Later the boys found a recipe of jell-o and cornmeal in "The Outdoor Life" magazine. They would alternate between the jell-o and the sweet bait. The sweet bait came in two flavors, chocolate and vanilla. Today they were using the vanilla. Jake had met a man fishing at the lake one time using a fly rod. He became fascinated with the technique and eventually bought a fly rod. After several unsuccessful attempts at carp fishing with a regular rod and reel, Jake had tried a fly rod. He tied on a No. 12 treble spring-loaded hook and covered it with the sweet bait. Then he would pull out the fly line and toss cast it into the water. He never used a sinker to weight the hook to the bottom but let the weight of the bait sink the bait. He found that he could see the fly line move when he had a bite and could nail his fish almost every time. As soon as the carp got the bait into its mouth, it would start to swim away, that was the moment so critical in setting the hook. Sometimes on their outings,

Jake would be the only one to catch the carp. However that day all the boys caught fish. They never kept the fish only caught them and released them. One of the last fish caught was by Bud. He hooked a big one and the fish made along run making the drag sing out. After a ten minute battle he brought the fish to the surface. It was at least three feet long. He told Jake to get the net and land the monster. Jake knew from reading the fishing magazines that to net a carp you must not touch the tail, but net the fish head first. He dropped the net into the water to allow Bud to work the fish into the net. Just as he was about to have the big bruit in the net, the hook came out of the mouth of the fish and tangled into the net.

Net him up, Bud yelled, Net him up, don't let him get away!

However the hook had tangled up the net sufficiently enough to prevent Jake from the task. The fish exhausted just floated there for a moment before it got it's wind, then slowly swam away.

Shoot, why didn't you net that giant? I bet he weighed 30 pound, hell 35.

I'm sorry Bud, Jake said. The hook tangled the net, I sort of became helpless.

The staying up all night was wearing heavily on them and they were ready to go home. They gathered up their tackle and started up the hill. However, Jake noticed that Bud had left his tackle box at the bank, but figured he was going back since he was carrying his net and three rods and reels. Neither Elzie nor Jake said anything to Bud about his tackle box until they reached the truck at the top of the hill.

"Bud you left your tackle box," Jake said.

"Why didn't ya'll bring it up?" Bud angrily asked.

Elzie then said, "Hell Bud, our arms were full too, besides it's your tackle box."

"You sorry sonofabitches!" Bud said as he went back down the hill to fetch the box.

Both Jake and Elzie just looked at each other and sniggered.

The eight mile drive back to Sunset was without comment. Neither Bud nor Elzie nor Jake said a single word. When they arrived in Sunset,

Bud parked his dad's truck at the store. He went into the store and got a Coke but did not offer one to Jake or Elzie.

"Come on," Bud said, "I'll take ya'll home." They walked to Bud's parent's house and got Bud's car, a 1950 Ford convertible. All three sat in the front seat with their fishing and camping gear stowed in the back seat. As soon as Bud was out of range of the city limits, he floored the gas and they roared east. When they got to the turn off dust was flying everywhere.

"Hey, Bud," Jake said, "you better slow down or you'll miss the turn."

Bud didn't answer and slowed but little and slid the car to make the ninety degree turn onto Pleasant Hill Cemetery Road. The car fish tailed and wound up in the bar ditch with a bounce. Dust was coming over them and the car came to a stop.

Then Bud began to laugh and so did Jake and Elzie. They laughed until they had tears running down their dusty faces.

"I can't stay mad at your sorry asses," Bud said, "Hell you're my best friends! Shucks!"

He restarted the engine and took it a bit slower down the Pleasant Hill road which intersected at the old Franklin School house where Lee Pariot and Lige Oldham had gone to school. The road then became Russell's Loop and wound down to the Oldham and Tatum homes.

"You want me to take you on down to your house Elzie?" Bud asked.

"Yeah, I'm too tired to walk. I'm going to take a nap," Elzie said.

"Me too," Jake said. "Bud, be careful driving back home. I sure enjoyed our camping and fishing. It was great. Come out anytime and we'll fish Denton Creek or the Jim Harry."

"We'll do it all summer," Bud said.

CHAPTER 4

On Saturday, all the family was going to town. Berthie May had decided to get a new dress for Pleasant Hill, which was coming up the last Monday in May. Lige decided to get a new straw hat for his going to town hat. P.D. and Mary were going to check out Second Monday and treat themselves to a hamburger at the Dairy Mart. The Tatum's had the same thing in mind. Jake had decided to go with his grandparents, because he liked to go with his Grandpa whenever they went to Bowie. Lige didn't like driving to Bowie. He would drive to Sunset at any time, but driving to Bowie was a hazard. The highway from Sunset to Bowie was a paved two lane road. U.S. 287 contained thousands of cars and trucks roaring through town night and day. The hazard to Lige was dealing with people who would run over you if you didn't drive fast enough and he didn't drive fast enough to suit the public. There were always people trying to pass one another and there were always car wrecks, head own collisions and worst of all when a big semi truck was involved. So, when they went to Bowie Berthie May would drive. She was ten years younger than Lige and still felt like she had the reflexes to drive in traffic.

When they got to Bowie, they would drive down U.S. 81/287 until they came to Front Main where they would turn off at the traffic light and find a place to park. The stretch of business's was on both sides of the street and covered the next street over on both sides. The next street over was known as Old Smoky Street because of numerous gun fights that had taken place fifty years before. On the corner facing each other was the First National Bank and the Legion Drug Store. At this corner on any given Saturday, the old men would gather and visit while their wives did the shopping. Lige knew most of the men personally as he either grew up with them or they had played baseball together when they were mere lads. Some were fellows who lived in Sunset, others were people who had lived in Sunset but had eventually moved to Bowie, while others were from Bowie. But in growing up, they had all known one another. When Lige got out with Jake several of the men shouted out, Howdy Lige! Who's that boy you got with you?

Why, that's my grandson, Lige would say, P.D.'s boy.

Today Lige would spend an hour talking with his old buddies before walking down to Perkins and Timberlake's store and look at the hats. He found Berthie May there looking at dresses. They didn't bother each other. Lige let her take care of her business and he his.

"You need a hat Jake?" Lige asked.

"I don't know Grandpa, what do you think?" Jake replied.

"I think a new work hat would do you good. That old one's looking like what Tom Sawyer threw into the Mississippi." Lige said.

After making their purchase and coming out of the store, they ran into Elzie and Lee Pariot.

"Hey Elzie, what you doing?" Jake asked.

"Well mama and daddy are over at Walker's five and dime and I thought I saw ya'll going in Perkins and Timberlake." Elzie said.

Lige then said, "boys how about we go in the drug store and get one of them fountain drinks?"

"Could we Grandpa?" Jake asked.

"Sure, let's go," he said. So the four of them walked back up the street and went in Makings Drug Store. There were two drug stores on Main Street. Jake liked Legion Drug store the best because they had these little tables to sit at that had chairs that were connected to the table that swung out for the customer to sit on.

Makings had only a counter bar to sit at. They entered the place which had a few people shopping around, searching the shelves for whatever. Jake, Elzie, Lige, and Lee sat down at the counter. The woman who worked the counter was wiping the counter top but did not look up at them when they came in nor when they sat down. She did not speak to them. However as she completed her wiping the top, with a scowl she looked straight into Jake's face and said, "Well, I'm waiting!"

It shocked Jake at her rudeness. He had done nothing to the lady, he had said nothing and waited patiently until she was ready to take their orders. Jake looked at his Grandfather for some answer as to what to say. He finally said to his Grandpa, "do you want anything, Grandpa?"

"No, I don't think we want a thing in this place," he said.

"Well why did you come in?" The woman at the counter said, looking dumbfounded as if she had done nothing wrong.

"Lady, we came in to buy something, we got money and we earned it honestly," Lige said.

"Well you people think you're better than us people here in Bowie," she said. "Your nothing but white trash."

"Lady, I'll tell you, I've worked all my life for what I have and I'm proud of what I have. I don't have much but it's mine, it's paid for and I don't owe the bank anything. We have money and we came by it honest and we don't work for nobody either. I'm on this side of the counter and you're the one on that side. But by God we won't be buying a damn thing here. Come on Boys, we're leaving!"

With that they all got up from the bar stools and headed out the door. The customers were all staring at them like there was something wrong with them. As the boys went out the door first, Lige held it for them, then as he turned to leave, he spat a big squirt of tobacco juice onto the floor.

"Here lady, here's something for you to mop up." Then he walked out and they headed down to Legion's.

"Imagine," Lige said, mad as a wet hen, "that old battleax saying that stuff to us. What got into her anyhow?"

Jake and Elzie had no idea but they knew they would never darken the door of that place again.

"Wasn't no call for her to act like 'at," Lee said.

Inside Legion's as they walked in, the owner was behind the counter. Mr. Legion said as they came in, morning folks, come right in. How can we help you?

"These boys want a couple fountain cokes," Lige said.

"Cherry Cokes,"Jake said.

"Cherry Cokes," Lige said.

"And for you sir?" Mr. Legion said.

"I've got a chaw in my mouth," he replied. "And this old man here, pointing to Lee, his mouth's full of my plug tobacco too!"

"Coming right up!" Mr. Legion said.

In a moment a girl Jake's age came out from the counter and brought them their drinks as they were sitting down at the swivel chairs.

"Boy, these chairs are neat," Elzie said as he kept swinging in and out on the stool.

The girl sat each glass down which contained the sweet drinks. She almost blushed at the site of the two boys. Elzie winked at her.

"That will be thirty cents," she said.

It didn't take Lige too long to bring out his coin purse to search for the coins. However before he could, old Lee plopped a quarter and a dime on the counter.

"Keep the change, young lady," he said. "A purty girl like you deserves a little tip"

"Well by God," Lige exclaimed, "that old bandit paid up for once!"

"Sure you don't want one," Grandpa? Jake asked.

"No, no, I'm fine. I'm fine," he said.

About that time Berthie May came into the store. She saw the four and came straight to their table.

"I pretty well knew ya'll be in here," she said. "I got me some material for a new dress. "Did you get your hat Lige?"

"Yeah I got it," he said.

"Well as soon as these boys finish their Cokes, we're going to meet P.D. and Mary at the Dairy Mart," she said.

"What time?" Lige asked.

"Noon," she said.

"Well it's only 11, so we got time to rest, or walk around, or go to Second Monday."

"Elzie where's your folks?" Berthie May asked.

"Uh, they were in the five and dime and said they were going out to Second Monday. When I saw Jake and Mr. Oldham, I told them I was going with them and Grandpa came with me."

"Ok", Berthie May said, "y'all can ride in the back of the truck. We'll go out to Second Monday for a while then to the Dairy Mart. I'm going to have me a hamburger and a malt."

When the boys finished their cokes, they all went out to the truck, Jake and Elzie sitting on the back edge, Lee sitting in the middle between Lige and Berthie May.

"That girl in there likes me, I think," Elzie said. "She winked at me anyhow."

"Oh, she did not," Jake said. "She never even knew you were there, it was me she had her pretty eyes on."

Berthie May started the pickup and threw it in reverse. She always gave the truck a little too much gas when she first accelerated. She back out of the curb parking and zoomed down toward the light and drove down to the railroad track where venders were lined up on both sides of the rail road track. Across the track was a barn that held the majority of the venders, and down on the north end of the track was where farm animals were traded. The area was full of people. A lot of farm people came to town on Second Monday to sell goods or trade.

"Now don't you two wander off too far," Berthie May said. "You watch the clock and meet right back here at the truck at ten minutes till twelve."

"Ok Grandma, but neither one of us have a watch,"Jake said.

"Well you can ask someone that's got a watch," Berthie May replied.

"Hey Jake," Elzie said as they wandered around the booths, "you think that girl in Legion's was cute?"

"Yeah, she was," Jake said. "I wouldn't mind taking her to the drive in."

"But ," Elzie said, "we don't even know her name!"

"I'll bet we could find out sometimes. I'll tell you what, next time we get Grandpa's truck, we'll sneak off up here for a cherry coke, Jake said. And when we do, we'll just ask her what her name is."

The boys had been standing looking at some old paper back books stacked on a counter when a woman with a cigarette hanging from her lip walked up to them. "You gents need some good reading material? The books are ten cents apiece," she said.

"Neither boy spoke but kept looking."

"I'll let you have six books for fifty cents," the woman said.

Elzie found a Hardy Boys mystery book, then he found a book on Buck Rogers, and he found a book called The Practical Guide to Lovemaking (Illustrated). He showed it to Jake, who about died.

"Elzie, put that back, if we're caught with it our folks would just kill us," Jake whispered afraid the woman with the cigarette would hear.

"Now Jake," Elzie said, "our folks would want us to be able to practice the art of love in a proper manner. They sure wouldn't want us to mess that up. You know how your dad is about us doing shit right."

"Shhhhh!" Jake said.

Jake found a Mark Twain book and Moby Dick, and a book on electrical wiring. He took Elzie's three books and his hiding the Illustrated Love making book between and fished out fifty cents.

As the woman put the books in a sack, she saw what they had bought.

"Look around honey," the woman said, "we got all kinds of books. You can get anything you want, and I do mean anything, she said grinning at them." Jake turned as red as a beet, while Elzie just look at her and smiled his big innocent looking toothy smile.

"Uh, do you have the time?" Jake asked the woman.

"It's a quarter to twelve," she said.

"Come on, Elzie, we got to get back to the truck." Jake ordered.

Standing at the truck was Berthie May, Lige, Lee, and both the boy's parents.

"Well what in the world did you two buy?" Berthie May asked.

"Oh, nothing Grandma, just some paperback books to read sometimes when it's raining and there's nothing to do," Jake said.

Elzie then had Jake where he wanted and said, "Oh yeah, Mrs.

Oldham we got some real interesting stuff, you know books to educate and stuff to learn you how to do things."

Jake was about to die.

Then Lige said, "Hummph, best kind of learning is on the job. Books is to entertain, you best learn from someone who's already done it. Come on Gal, come on y'all, he said, them hamburgers be all gone." So Lige herded the group into their rigs and they headed down to the Dairy Mart for a rare treat to a farmer, hamburgers and malts.

On the way home, as expected, they stopped to see Lige's mother. A small and very thin woman with dark brown skin. All the poor old toothless thing could do was sit and grin at them. She never spoke a word anymore, she did not know anyone. Mrs. Brown kept five old women who were in various stages of senility. Two women that stayed there were able to help with the housework, however most of the others seemed as little children. Lige's mother would sit in the same chair all day, or lay in a bed if left alone because she just didn't know the difference. Another woman roamed the room all day calling to a person only she knew. Sometimes she would stop in front of Lige and Berthie and asked them, "Have you seen my Ma? Would you tell her to come and get me?" Berthie May would always tell her she would, however it wouldn't be five minutes before the woman would be back in front of them asking the same question. The last of Mrs. Brown's patients was a woman near 100 years of age who could not hear nor could she see. She would sit in a rocker and rock all day until someone moved her. Jake hoped he never got in that kind of shape.

Lige would sit by his mother and say to her, "You doing all right Ma." But of course she would only smile. Sometimes he would stroke her hair from the top of her head and fight back a tear.

Elzie looked at the whole thing wide eyed. "What a terrible condition for people to be in," he said.

They didn't stay long, they never did. It wouldn't matter as long as Mrs. Brown had what she needed.

CHAPTER 5

While the boys were finishing school, P.D. and Lige finished the planting. They got a nice shower on Monday after the trip to Bowie on Saturday. Then on Wednesday the family awoke to a heavy rain and a violent thunder storm. It rained two inches before daylight.

As Berthie May and Lige listened to the rain and thunder and watched the lightening, Lige said, "I believe that lightening struck something. It was too loud and too close. I sure hope we don't loose no cows. You remember one time, Lige continued, we had lightening to hit the fence and it killed three cows that were standing close enough to the fence to get shocked?"

"I sure do," Berthie May said. "That was a big loss. I remember one time down in Alabama, when I was a child, it came a storm and it rained so much that water flowed through dad's barn and lot three feet deep. The water caused one of his mules to stumble and it drowned right there in the lot."

"Did you ever here of Dave Cantrell?" Lige asked.

"No I don't guess so." Berthie May replied.

"Well, it happened before your folks came to Texas," Lige said. "I remember it, even though I was just a boy. It was about 1900 I think. Old man Dave Cantrell was over at Sunset and somebody asked him what he had been doing. He said he had been out cutting stove wood for hell. And you know what? Lige said. That old man was riding in his wagon going back home that day and lightening struck him right in that wagon and killed him dead and didn't harm his team at all."

About that time they saw a bight light to their west.

"Lord God!" Berthie May said. "You're right lightening has struck something and it's a fire!"

The couple looked on as they could see something burning but not sure what.

"Why that's over on the Jasper place," Lige said. "I better get P.D. and we might ought to go over there."

However before he could do anything, they saw headlights coming their way. It was Jess and Bertha Jasper driving up Jess's old 40 model Ford pickup. The rain was letting up as they got out of their truck. Bertha Jasper had been crying. As they stepped up on the porch, Bertha blurted out, "Oh, Berthie May, our house is gone. Lightening struck it and we just got out and it burned down in minutes!"

"Oh, my God no!" Berthie May exclaimed. Then the two women set to crying.

"Jess, come in," Lige said. "Don't you worry about a thing, we'll figure it out. Come on in, the Gal will get some coffee started. I bet ya'll could use a good hearty breakfast."

For the next few weeks the Jasper's stayed with Berthie May and Lige. P.D. was a member of the board of directors of the Farm Bureau and he got the agent out on the Jasper's situation as quickly as possible. After the insurance was settled, the Jaspers decided to move into Sunset.

"After all," Jess said, "Bertha and I ain't spring chicken's any more. It's time I slowed down."

They found a two acre lot in Sunset which was big enough for a small house, a nice garden, and chickens. Lige and Berthie May insisted that Jess and Bertha stay with them until their house was built.

Lige had two brothers who lived in Sunset and both were carpenters, Jim and Odel Oldham. Lige and Jess went to town every day and helped, but Jim and Odel built the whole house. It took them thirty days from foundation to roof and finishing the inside. Neighbors came and helped with the finishing touches such as painting the walls and planting the flower beds. Lige and Jess built the chicken yard and the hen house. Then the whole town and the community around gave the Jasper's one of the biggest house warming the county had ever seen.

The night of the house warming, Berthie May and Lige came to town with P.D. and Mary. On the way Berthie May wept. "I sure hate to see them move off the old place. Why, Jess's dad and grandparents homestead that place," she said.

"Mama," P.D. said, "I worked out a deal with Mr. Jasper and I'm leasing the place."

"You don't mean it, P.D.," Berthie May said. " Did you buy Jess's cows?"

"I bought the cows, and leased the placed," P.D. said. "Next year we can increase our hay and watermelon production. I'll go see the loan officer at the Production Credit office tomorrow, he said. I'm going to put the cows in Jake's name. It's time he got his start."

Jake and Elzie didn't go to town to the housewarming, but stayed on the place. Elzie's folks had gone to the housewarming too.

The boys were sitting on the front porch sipping a couple of Berthie May's Tripple XXX Root Beers.

"Hey Jake," Elzie begin, when you think we might try to go up to Ligon's and get a cherry coke?"

"Oh I don't know, but if we're going, we gotta get that's girls name." Jake said.

"You can't go out with her," Jake said.

"Why not?" Elzie ask.

"Oh, cause, I hear that Angie Freeman waiting on you to meet at the pastor's couch," Jake said with a chuckle.

"Bull!" Elzie snorted. "You got awful big ears and great big mouth Jake Oldham!"

Then Jake began to laugh and finally so did Elzie.

"Tomorrow, we might ought to check out Denton Creek for fish," Jake said.

A few nights later P.D. came home from the County Farm Bureau meeting. He called Mary and Jake into the kitchen telling them he had something important to tell them.

Dale Bullock, the county president, had told the board that through the Farm Bureau's efforts working with the State Legislatures, a plan to pave certain rural roads was underway. The road from Sunset to Forestburg and the road from Forestburg to Montague, from Montague to Bowie and Nocona were the first that would be funded. They would be called Farm to Market Roads making going to town for farmers more accessible. "The big thing is," P.D. said, "Dale knows the company that will be bidding for the construction to build the roads in Montague County. He said he would help me get a job with the company."

"What kind of job?" Mary asked.

"Operating heavy equipment, building the highway," P.D. said. "It will be extra income for us, but it will put more responsibility on Jake. He'll have to take more of the work share here on the place."

"Jake, P.D. said, "we are going to lease the Jasper place and buy their cows. I've talked to the Production Credit and they are willing to loan the money on the cows. We're putting the cows in your name and the lease is going to be in your name too."

Jake thought about what his father had said. The loan at the Production Credit office would be in his name with his dad cosigning for him. The cows would be his and the calf crop would go toward the note. He knew they would have a heavier work load with the Jasper place. The crop field on the Jasper place was a hundred acres of deep Denton Creek sandy soil.

Jake felt a swelling of pride as his father placed so much confidence in him.

"Wow," Jake thought, "next summer he would be graduated from school and he would be full time in the farm business."

CHAPTER 6

Memorial weekend was always a busy time for the Oldham house. Pleasant Hill Cemetery held its annual meeting and homecoming. People who had lived in the area always came back to see their old friends and the local folks were always ready to see them. It was special at the Oldham house because Berthie May's parents would come for the weekend. They lived in Hedley Texas. They had migrated from Alabama in 1913 to Montague County but had moved west to the sandy panhandle country in 1920. When John and Eva Jane Sanders came to Montague County, John's parents came soon after they had arrived. However John's father, Tom Sanders had become ill and died within two weeks of their arrival. He was buried in Pleasant Hill. The Sander's family had gone to church at Pleasant Hill as long as they lived in the area. It held many fond memories for them plus John always came for the cemetery working and Decoration Day in honor of his late father.

Pleasant Hill began in 1876 as a school, but by 1880 had moved to Franklin. Now Franklin actually is no more than a quarter mile from Pleasant Hill. After the school moved, Pleasant Hill was used as a church and before long the yard on the north side of the church became burying ground. In 1900 Lige's father Henry and his brother Joe organized the community into holding an annual meeting and work the cemetery, which meant that all available hands would hoe the entire grounds chopping down all the grass and repeating the process annually.

On Friday afternoon, Jake spotted the red '51 Dodge coming down the road. He was just as excited as his Grandma because he was very fond of his great grandparents. They pulled up into the lane and drove past P.D.'s house and stopped in front of Lige and Berthie May's. The door opened and Granny Sanders got out eyeing Jake. She was about four foot nine inches tall with white hair tied in a bund on the back of her head.

"Come here you!" she said, "and give me some jaw!" She always said that when she would grab her grandkids and kiss the side of their faces.

John was a head taller than Eva Jane wearing his straw fedora with a chew of tobacco in his toothless mouth, hair white as cotton, wearing kaki slacks and a long sleeve kaki shirt. In his gravel voice, he would shout, "Hey there Jake!"

They were still hugging when Berthie May and Lige came out of the house.

"Mama, Dad!" She yelled as she fell on their necks. Lige and John exchanged hand shakes and Eva Jane would give Lige a squeeze on his arm.

Eva Jane was a jolly person always finding things to be funny about. She and Berthie May were not much alike as Berthie May tended to be more like her dad, more serious minded.

"Where's Clois and P.D.?" Granny asked.

"Oh, Clois is working but he'll be here later, he knows ya'll are coming," Berthie May said.

Before she could say anything else, P.D. and Mary were walking up.

"Here, P.D. give me some jaw," Granny said. She would give a big toothless smack on all her grandkids and it didn't matter how old they were. She would kiss Mary too.

"Mary, are you making P.D. toe the mark?" She asked.

"Not much," Mary said," you don't make P.D. do anything."

"Aw shoot," Granny said, "I can make him walk straight and tall."

"Let's come inside," Berthie May said. "Mama I made you an apple pie. I killed two chickens today for supper tonight and new potaters and fresh green beans, and... "

"Oh, Berthie," Granny said, "quit worrying about the food. We'll get by. We could have milk and cornbread for all I care."

They went inside and sat down in the kitchen. The kitchen of their house was also the dinning area and the living room. The couch and stuffed chairs were on one end of the room separated by the dinning table. On the other side of the dinning table was the kitchen. Lige had two spittoons ready, one for him and one for old John. As they took their seats John emptied his mouth of his tobacco for a fresh chew. He liked the pouch string style tobacco.

As he spat out the old cud, Granny said, "Well there goes a chew of tobacco that went to heaven."

"Why you say that Granny?" Jake asked.

"Cause dad just chewed the hell out of that one!" She said with a roar of laughter. Everyone laughed including John.

Just before supper Clois drove up and came into the house.

He was John and Eva's oldest grandchild.

"Hold up there Clois," Granny called "and give me some jaw!"

"Aw," Clois said, as he bent down and allowed her to kiss his cheek. He grinned a big grin hugging his Granny. He then went over and put his hands on John's shoulders. "Hi Grandpa" he said, only Clois couldn't quite say Grandpa, it came out more like hawhaw.

It was happy night as the family gathered around the Oldham supper table with a spread of fresh garden vegetables and southern fried chicken.

Saturday would be a day of visiting. Folks from around the area who had known John and Eva Jane would come for visits, also a lot of their kin folks would come too. Elzie's family would always come on Saturday afternoon. Lige's brother's and sisters would also come and late in the day Uncle Spence Russell would be brought there by his daughter and son in law, Leslie and Effie McReynolds. Uncle Spence who was James Spencer Russell, was the oldest living person in the area. He had come to Montague County with his parents in 1870 and had received the first granted parcel in that area. He had seen three Indian raids and could remember events of the long ago past. It was a treat for Jake to sit at his feet and listen to his stories. Of course his great grandpa was no slacker regarding stories of the past. John had a photographic memory and could recall the past with amazing accuracy, name dates and places.

Another family that always came to see John and Eva Jane was the Boles family. There were four brothers with their families who would come. Their mother was John's first cousin, although she was considerably older than John and had been dead for two years. The four brothers were Claude, Archie, Red and Vernon. Vernon was the youngest of the brothers. He and his wife Dorothy were expecting their first child. Granny Sanders who was always full of pranks, said to Dorothy, "Honey after having fifteen children, I sure don't envy you fixin to have your first young 'un."

"Why Mrs. Sanders," Dorothy said, "I don't think it will be bad. I don't expect to have any trouble having a baby. Why it will be just like shelling peas."

"I'll tell you this," Granny said, "old girl it will be the biggest pea you ever shelled!"

Memorial weekend was one weekend the family didn't work. P.D. would take care of minimum chores around the place until after Monday. P.D. would meet with ten or so men of his age who would make the final preparations for Pleasant Hill. They would meet armed with yoyo's and level the tall grass in the cemetery and the rest of the grounds. Some of the wives would sweep out the old church house, and the men would repair any of the old benches that needed attention before the Monday meeting.

Sunday was more of the same with people coming and going visiting the Sander's. Mary took Jake to church over his protest, however P.D. stayed home to visit with his grandparents. Several relatives had been invited over for Sunday dinner much to the delight of Berthie May. If there was one thing she liked in this world, it was people to cook and fuss over and to have them brag on her cooking.

On Monday, people would arrive at the old cemetery and visit their relative's graves sometimes placing flowers on the departed. Folks would visit and spend their energy trying to tell each other the tallest of tales, or their version of things that happened in the past. Around 12:15, the women folks would start to spread their food on the church benches. They would turn the benches inward facing each other, there the food would be placed. At the proper time, the president of the cemetery association would call for eveyone's attention then call on someone to say the blessing. Then everyone would dig in and fill their plates. After the meal they would hold a business meeting and take up a collection to have funds for cemetery work that might need to be done. Following the meeting, a short worship service was held with old time gospel singing.

When the church service started, Jake and Elzie would slip out of the old building and distance themselves from the activity.

On this particular Monday the day had begun with an overcast sky. Some were skeptical that the homecoming could be held. The rain did hold up until midway through the worship service. As if on cue, the rain started coming down in sheets, followed by a big clap of thunder. The service was cut short so people could start for home. One thing was certain, when the roads got wet, travel was extremely difficult. The red clay roads would become almost impossible to navigate and sliding into the bar ditch was almost a certainty.

It became a mad scramble as folks were dashing to their trucks and cars where the windows had been left down. P.D. had driven the family car bringing John and Eva Jane, while Lige and Berthie May came in the only form of transportation they had, the flat bed truck. Jake had ridden in the back where his grandmother had boxes of food. Before the devotional service started all the women had loaded their food in the automobiles. Fortunately, Berthie May had placed her boxes of food in P.D.'s trunk. Had it not been raining, Elzie would have rode home with Jake in P.D.s car, but as it was with little room, he had to crowd in his own father's truck with his dad, mother and grandfather.

"Well Pleasant Hill's over for this year," Jake said as the family was leaving the cemetery.

"Yeah, over for this year", John said. "Looks like we'll have to delay our trip home, Evie."

"Well that's all right, dad," Eva Jane said."We sure don't have to hurry home. Since you quit farming, all you have to do is go up to town and sit on your bench."

Jake looked at his great grandmother and ask, Does Grandpa have a bench in town?

"He sure does honey," his Granny said, "and he sits on it all day."

"Oh, I never done no such," John snorted. "I go up to the post office and get the mail and sometimes I sat on that old bench in front of Workers Grocery store and read the paper."

Granny said, "Dad reads the paper like he chews his tobacco. When he's done with the paper it goes to heaven too."

Everyone laughed except John.

By Wednesday, it was dry enough to get out on the county roads. That was the day John and Eva Jane departed for Hedley. It was five hour drive from the cross timbers to the rolling plains and sandy panhandle land where cotton and maze were the principle crops. Depending upon the time of year, one would either see cotton or maze growing or blooming or getting ready to harvest.

Berthie May as always grew teary eyed when her parents left. She would have been happy if they would simply move back and live with her and Lige. But Berthie May's brothers and sisters who lived in Hedley wouldn't hear of it. They would miss them just as bad as Berthie May did.

On Thursday, Elzie and Jake were running cultivators in the peanuts and watermelons. The rain would bring up the careless weeds by the millions. If they didn't get them killed out they would take over a field. Where the crop took weeks to grow, careless weeds grew by the day. In a week they were full adult plants producing blooms and seed and sapping all the moisture from the crop.

Watermelon rows were cultivated and the middles were disc plowed. The final act was to hoe the rows by hand, where the cultivator couldn't reach. By the time they had the fields hoed, it would be time to run the cultivators back through followed by a second hoeing. Elzie and Jake didn't like to hoe, but it was expected of them and they would do it. They didn't even have to be told by their parents, they knew how to tend a crop. Every morning when they were working the fields they would draw up a cool water bucket of well water. They would set the water can under a shade tree with a dipper. As they hoed each time they came back on a row they would get water. The days were long, work was hard, as June wore on, the temperature warmed up.

CHAPTER 7

By the second week of July the watermelons were ripe. That was good for the family as sales would be good with the first melons. Jake and Elzie would help their dad's harvest each morning. P.D. and would walk the rows and examine the melons examining the curl, thumping the melon and looking at its belly. He never liked to be guilty of selling a green melon. Sometimes the curl would be dry, but the melon might not be ripe. Thumping was a good way to determine how ripe the melon was, and the belly was another good test. The belly of a ripe melon was always dull and slightly yellow.

As P.D. cut the melons he stood them up on their ends. Later Leck would drive the tractor and trailer while Elzie and Jake loaded. Sometimes if they thought they could drive the pickup's without getting stuck in the sand, they would take them to the field and save a step. Once the trailer was loaded and brought from the field, they had to pitch the melons from the trailer onto the pickups.

The month of June brought two unexpected but welcomed rains. It was just enough to make the melon crop. By the second week of July they were getting ripe and would peak by the end of July. Today was the second cutting and P.D. found a good supply. They loaded two pickups. Leck and Elzie would take one load and P.D. would take the other. They would take them to the Dallas farmers market that evening.

Around daybreak the buyers would come by and by the loads. They would be back by breakfast.

Jake wanted to go with them but P.D. needed him to check the cows that evening and there was man coming out to look at the melon patch to consider buying the rest of the crop for his store. He needed Jake to meet the man.

Around three in the afternoon, the three of them took off for Dallas leaving Jake to run things. Mary and Ida Lou had gone to town to take Lee to the doctor as he had been feeling low the past few days. Lige and Berthie May had also gone over to town to see the Jasper's. Now what Jake didn't know was that Leck and Ida Lou's granddaughter Lucy Tatum, their oldest son's daughter had come for a few days visit. Lucy's family lived in Chico. She was sixteen years old and coming to bloom. Boys were becoming very interesting to her. She had seen Jake before and had developed a crush on him, though he did not know it. In fact he and Elzie had been so busy the past few days, he had not seen her around.

Shortly after P.D. left a man from Decatur had arrived to look at the melon patch. He had five grocery stores and wanted to see if he was interested in buying the crop for his stores. His name was Delbert Tally. Mr. Tally looked the patch over and told Jake to have his dad give him a call handing him his business card. Jake didn't tell him that they didn't have a phone, but said he would. He knew his dad could go into Sunset and call the man.

It was a hot day, with the work done, Jake decided to slip down to the creek and have a swim. It wouldn't be as fun when Elzie or his other friends were around, but at least it would cool him off. He took a towel from the bathroom and walked down to the creek. Now Jake and Elzie had a favorite pool at the creek. One that had cottonwoods on either side that kept the water shaded and cool. The pool wasn't over six feet in depth, and was usually safe from snakes. It was here on Sunday afternoons that Billy John, Bud, Glen Ray, and Elzie would gather with Jake for that summer swim. The boys would get together around three and run down to the creek. It took them less than a minute to strip down and bale off into the cool water. They had built a rope swing to swing off the bank and fall into the blue bliss. Swimming was a good way to take the stress out of a hot day. All the boys had jobs, either working for their parents or for themselves, like Glen Ray. He had his own melons even though he was working at Buford Millers station.

However, today it was just Jake. He walked down to the creek, undressed and waded into the cool water. It felt so good, so refreshing. He dove under water and swam a distance before coming back to the surface.

As he was shaking the water from his face, he heard a voice call his name.

"Hey there Jake, why didn't you dive in from the bank?"

He looked up at the bank where the rope swing was and to his surprise there was Lucy Tatum. Same age as Elzie even though she was his niece.

"L, Lucy,"Jake stammered. "I didn't know you were up there. Did you just walk up?"

"No, you silly boy," she said. "I was sitting here when you walked down to the creek. I watched you take off all your clothes and stroll out into the water. Jake I'm thinking I'd like a cool swim too. Want some company?"

"Lucy you better go on home, your grandma will be wandering where you are," Jake said.

"Jake Oldham you know good and well my grandma's with your mama and they took Grandpa Lee to the doctor. I think they'll be gone for awhile. There ain't nobody here on this farm but me and you."

Lucy walked down from the top of the creek bank to the edge of the water and started taking off her clothes, never taking an eye off Jake and smiling as she undressed.

Jake wanted to protest, he wanted to run and hide and he wanted her to take every stitch off and stay right there and let him explore all the mystery of women and find every secret. He wanted to forget all the sermons on fornication he ever heard right now. He didn't want his mama to know anything about this swimming adventure. He wanted it not to happen, because he felt the worst guilt a boy can feel about things like that but yet his own body would not listen to his conscience.

Lucy was the first naked girl he ever saw. She might not have been the prettiest girl, but right then it just didn't matter. She was blond like Elzie, although her daddy, Nolan, had brown hair, Nolan's wife Linda Sue, was a blond. Her hair hung down on her shoulders, her developing breast were full and looked to Jake firm as a peach on the tree ready to be picked. After she was unclothed, she started placing her toes in the water letting Jake see her nakedness. Jake was at the peak of excitement, yet afraid of the moment with a sense of dread. She waded into the water and drifted toward Jake. She smiled although underneath she was just as nervous and scared as he.

"The water's nice," she said.

"Yeah," Jake said, Elzie and me swim here all the time."

"Do you like me Jake?" she ask.

"Oh sure," Jake responded. They were about to embrace when the moment was broken by the sound of an engine on the road.

"Oh, good God," Jake said. "Mama and Ida Lou are on the way back!"

Quickly they dressed in haste, and Lucy ran down the creek, climbed the fence and went back to the Tatum home.

Jake tried to straighten his hair and slowly went back toward the house.

He knew Mary would take Ida Lou home first, because they would have to take Mr. Pariot into the house. Or so he thought.

What Jake found was Mary getting out of the car and telling Ida Lou to pick her back up when she was ready to go back.

"Hi mama," Jake said. "Where's Mr. Pariot?"

"He's in the hospital," Mary said. "The doctor kept him and Ida Lou and I are going back up there and stay with him until bedtime. We came home to get Lee's things and to see that your grandparents knew what was going on."

"They went to see the Jasper's and said they were staying for supper," Jake said.

"Well, Jake I guess you'll have to take care of the chores this evening while Ida Lou and I take care of things at the hospital. I'll stir you up some supper before we go back. I imagine Ida Lou could eat something too."

"Sure mama," Jake said. "I'll take care of the chores. Grandma asked me to gather the eggs. She told me to just let the calves have all the milk tonight."

"My goodness," Mary said, "we better check and see if Berthie's feeling all right!"

Jake had to laugh, because he knew what his mother meant. Berthie May was as vigorous as they came when it came to selling and making money. She sold eggs, she sold cream, she sold stuff from her garden, she did everything to make a dime. He remembered one time his father had a big fuss with her because she was carrying around in her bra five hundred dollars. She didn't want to put it in the bank. "

Mama," P.D. said, "someone will knock you in the head for that money!"

"How will they know I'm carrying it P.D.?" Berthie May would say, "I'm not carrying no sign saying look here in my tits, I got a wad of money!"

"Mama," P.D. would say, "be reasonable."

Jake was glad Ida Lou took Lucy with her and Mary back to the hospital. He was afraid she would come back over, not that he would mind it, but he needed time to think about the swimming adventure. He would die if his mama found out. Even though this was his first experience, he knew about the birds and the bees, farm boys knew those things at a very early age.

Not long after the women had left for the hospital, Glen Ray drove up to the house and honked his horn. He was driving his dad's new pickup.

"Glen Ray!" Jake shouted. "Come in."

Glen Ray swung his lanky lean frame out of the pickup. Although tall and agile, Glen Ray was a bit clumsy. Glen Ray wore black rimmed glasses as he was near sighted. He had thin long face like his mama's dad and long hands.

"You been hauling hay today?" Jake asked.

"Oh hell yes," Glen Ray said. "We put up two hundred bails in

Dexter Rater's barn today and there will be that many tomorrow. It is so hot to haul hay and so hot to stack in the barn."

"I thought you were working for Buford Miller at the gas station," Jake said.

"Right after school turned out, Buford's grandson came up wanting to spend the summer with him and work. So Buford asked dad if that would be all right and of course they agreed. I was planning on the melon crop anyhow, but dad wouldn't let me be idle until the melons came off, so I have been hauling hay." Glen Ray said.

"You want a Dr. Pepper?" Jake asked.

"Sure do, I ain't been to supper." Glen Ray said.

"We got supper," Jake said. "Mama fixed some before she left. Ida Lou's dad is in the hospital."

"Oh, sorry to hear that." Glen Ray said." Is it serious?"

"I don't know, but he is sick enough to be in the hospital." Jake said.

"Where's Elzie?" Glen Ray asked.

"He and dad and Leck took two loads of melons to Dallas, be back tomorrow."

"Looks like my melons going to be ready in about two weeks." Glen Ray said.

"There was a man here today looking at ours to buy for his store. You might want to see him to by yours because about the time yours comes off ours will be about picked over." Jake said.

"Man that would work out real good, wouldn't it?" Glen Ray said.

Jake put the plates on the table and he and Glen Ray had the supper Mary had fixed. She had fried some pork chops, warmed up the black eyed peas, and made a pan of cornbread. Glen Ray wolfed it down, hungry as a bear.

"Man that was sure good." There just isn't nothing better than fried pork chops and fried taters." Glen Ray said. "Hey you want to go ridding around for awhile. Go over to Sunset and see Bud and Billy John?"

"Yeah, but I need to change clothes first." Jake said. "I worked all day in these even though I went for a swim, I need to clean up."

"I do too, and I got some clean clothes in the truck. I got them at noon today cause I wanted to come over and see if you and Elzie would go to town tonight. I told my folks I was coming over hear from the Rater's and it was all right with them,." Glen Ray said.

"Well go get your clothes and I'll start cleaning up and you can follow me." Jake said.

Jake wrote his mama a note to let her know where he was in case she beat him back home.

As they headed for Sunset, bumping down the dirt road, listening to the pickup radio playing Hank Williams "Long Gone Lonesome Blues", Jake leaned back against the seat thinking about the events of the day, singing along with the song. He had experienced his fist real encounter with a girl and he decided he liked it.

"Glen Ray," Jake said, "do you ever think about girls?"

"Do I think about girls, does the wild man live in the woods?" Glen Ray said.

"Well I mean do you think about, you know doing it with one?" Jake said.

"Are you kidding," Glen Ray said. "I think about it with every girl I see."

"Why you ask?" Glen Ray said.

"Oh, I don't know, I'm sort of torn between the lust part and the liking a girl part, if you know what I mean."

"Who you trying to like?" Glen Ray said.

"If I tell you," Jake said, "you wont say nothing about it will you?"

"You trying to keep it a secret?" Glen Ray asked.

"I don't know what to do." Jake said. "I don't know if I should tell you or just forget it. I just meant I don't want you going blabbing it to some girl." especially Nancy.

"You like her?" Glen Ray said.

"Yeah I like her, no I don't like her, no I mean, she's not the one I want to like. It's not me doing the liking its wanting a girl to like me" Jake said.

"You sweet on Nell?" Glen Ray said.

Jake didn't answer him. He didn't have to.

"I think Nell would be a hard nut to crack." Glen Ray said.

"Not for you" Jake said.

"What do you mean?" Glen Ray said.

"Well when I asked her about going to the drive in, you know with a group, cause she said her mama wouldn't let her date yet, well she told me if we went with a group, to be sure and ask you, because she thought you were cute" Jake said.

"No kidding!?" Glen Ray said, grinning from ear to ear. "I'll be dad gum."

"Oh, come on," Jake said. "I'm the one wanting to date her."

"You know what, I'll bet she's was just trying to make you jealous, you know talking about me like that knowing it was curling your insides." Glen Ray said. "But on the other hand, if she thinks I'm cute, I better strike while the iron's hot!"

Jake was about to get mad, but he knew he needed to cool down. Besides, Glen Ray was one of his best friends.

"Let's go to Bud's house first,." Jake said.

"No let's go over and get Billy John and then we'll go over to Bud's and hang out. We can see precious Nell." Glen Ray said.

They arrived at Billy John's first. He happened to be out in the yard when they drove up. Billy John was a big block of a boy. He looked like a sawed off stump. He had no neck, his head just sat on his big stout shoulders.

"Hey y'all,"Billy John called out. "What y'all doing in town?"

"Hey Billy John" Jake said. "We're going over to Bud's house and thought you'd like to go. Want to?"

"Sure, let me go tell mama where I'm going. I'll be right back." Billy John trotted to the door off the car port like an African Cape Buffalo and stuck his head in and told him folks where he was going. His mama came to the door and waved at Jake and Glen Ray.

Bud was in the house watching TV when they drove up. Mr. and Mrs. Hunter were sitting in their bed room watching their own TV when the boys came in.

"Well well," Floyd Hunter said. "Look what come in, how you boys doing?"

"Fine Mr. Hunter," Jake said. "We thought we'd come over and see Bud and Nell awhile."

Jake had to slip Nell's name in even though he felt his face flush when he said it.

Bud's room was just off the living room, where he had an array of guns and fishing gear on the wall.   Nell was coming from her room as she heard them talking.

"Hi," she said. "Good to see y' all. Glen Ray what have you been doing this summer?"

"Hauling hay and I'll be cutting watermelons in about two weeks." Glen Ray said.

Bud then said," hey lets go out on the porch and let my folks watch their show."

The boys all went outside and Nell followed. Jake held the door for her.

"Thank you Jake." she said. "I guess you've been busy at your farm too. Have you been to town much?"

"No, me and Elzie's been hoeing peanuts every day. We started hauling melons last week and got the second cutting today. Daddy and Leck and Elzie are gone to Dallas tonight to sell the loads."

"Hey, Nell do you remember in school I asked about us all going to the show sometime?" Jake blurted.

Nell had a way of looking at a boy and melting him. She would peer over her nose slightly look down and up from the top of her eyes. It was a look that would fell any heart.

"Yeah," she said, "have you set something up with Bud and Glen Ray?"

Glen Ray, he thought, "why does she do that?"

"No, I haven't, I just thought about it when I saw you tonight. If you'd rather, I'll just let Glen Ray set it up."

"Ok, if that's what you want." she said. "Bud, she said, when do you want to take us all to the show?"

Bud looked at his sister a moment then said, "The show? What show?"

"Any show stupid," she said. "Just take us to the drive-in in your car."

"I don't care" he said, "whenever."

Well Jake thought that's over and done with. If all three girls went, and Bud went, who would that leave to go with him?

The three boys with Nell sat around on the cement porch reflecting on the summer and school., with Glen Ray and Jake trying to impress Nell. After about an hour, Glen Ray decided they needed to head home.

As they were leaving Bud said, "Hey let's go next Wednesday night to the drive in. Everybody be here at 8:30."

Going home, Glen Ray said, "I think Nell's playing game with us Jake. She wants to pit you against me. Girls like that control stuff."

"You think so," Jake said. "He was so love sick he was miserable."

Jake's house was dark when he got home, which concerned him. The porch light was on at his grandparent's house and the truck was in the shed.

"I don't think my mama's home." Jake said. "Mr. Pariot must be pretty sick."

"What you want to do?" Glen Ray said.

"I guess I'll walk down to Grandma's and see if they know something." Jake said as he slipped out of the truck. "See you later Glen Ray. Hey I'll get dad lined up with the store man have him mention about your melons."

"Thanks," Glen Ray said. "Maybe you and Elzie can help me gather them. My brother didn't come home this summer but stayed in Denton to go to summer school. I think he's covered up in women too."

"Oh, wow," Jake said. "You'll have to save that for the next time we talk."

"Ok, see you later." Glen Ray said as he was backing out the drive onto the county road.

Jake hurried down to his grandparent's house to see what they knew.

The door was never locked, so he went straight in. They were sitting in the kitchen area watching TV.

"Hi Grandma, Grandpa. How was the Jasper's?"

"Oh," Berthie May said, "they were fine. Where you been?"

"Glen Ray and I went to Sunset to see Bud and Billy John."

"Where's your mama?" Berthie May asked.

"She went with Ida Lou, they took Mr. Pariot to the hospital and they haven't come back."

"Lige," Berthie May said, we better go to Bowie and see about Lee."

"Yeah," he said as he spat tobacco into his spit can made from a Folger's coffee can.

They got up and put on their shoes and Lige got his hat. He never left the house without a hat. In the daytime Berthie May wouldn't go outside without her bonnet, but since it was night she didn't need it.

"Jake, you drive." Lige said. "I know you can see a lot better at night than we can."

So they loaded up and headed for Bowie.

When they got to Sunset, the highway was not quite as busy as it sometimes is. They got on the highway without any trouble. They met traffic which always scared Berthie May. If she was driving she would hug the passenger curb with the passenger side of the truck almost running off the pavement. Jake held firm and drove without waver into Bowie. The hospital was located just off Main Street and close to the center of town. It was an old Brick building built in the 1930's. One side of the building was a clinic where doctors saw patients in the daytime. The main entrance was facing the side street that ran perpendicular to Main Street. There were several parking spaces in front of the hospital. They saw Mary's car indicating they were still there. Inside the building was the typical antiseptic smell of a hospital. At the front desk they found what room Lee Pariot was in and walked down the hall to find it. Jake noticed several patients as they walked down the corridor. At one spot a particularly large family was gathered in the hall because the family overflowed from their relative's room. Their faces sad telling the story that so often happens in the hospital.

Finally they reached Lee's room. Ida Lou was standing over her father with the doctor listening to the man's chest. His eyes were closed and his breathing labored. Mary was sitting in one of the two chairs with Lucy in the other. Neither Berthie May nor Lige spoke, but the look on Mary's face indicated it was going bad for Lee.

Mary motioned for Berthie May to come out into the hall, Lige followed.

"I guess Lee had a stroke sometime today. He was feeling pretty bad this morning so Ida Lou and I brought him up here to the clinic. Dr. Louder said he needed to be in the hospital. By the time we got back up here he was in a coma. I don't think he will live through the night. Berthie May would you take Lucy home with you and let her spend the night. I don't think Ida Lou will leave at all."

"I'll take care of Lucy. As soon as P.D. and them get back tomorrow we'll send Leck up here and you can come home and get some rest, if Lee makes it." Berthie May said. "Lige, you had better go in there and tell old Lee good by."

Lige drew a somber breath and went back inside the room. The doctor was telling Ida Lou he didn't have long to live. Ida Lou understood but she couldn't help feeling so alone at that moment. Lige walked over to the bed and took Lee's hand.

"Old friend he said softly, if it's time to go, then you go on and when I get there, I'll bring you a fresh plug of White Tag Tensley's." He then turned to Ida Lou and asked, "Have you gotten hold of your brother's?" She shook her head no.

In 1954 only a few people had phones. Fortunately most of Ida Lou's brothers lived within twenty miles of one another. It would take half the night to go to all of their homes, but Lige knew it needed to be done.

"We better go," Lige said to Berthie May, "Jake's going to have to drive me around for awhile after we take you back to the place."

"We're taking Lucy too." she said.

The truck was a bit crowded with Lucy riding as close to Jake as she could while he drove, letting her hand fall on his leg made it difficult for Jake to concentrate on driving. Before leaving town, Lige had Jake drive up to Stoneburg. Ida Lou's brother who ran cattle in Clay County lived around Stoneburg. Lige knew about where they lived and there was no sense in going all the way back home and having to turn around and come back to the same place trying to notify Ida Lou's family.

"Let's see," Lige said. "Willie Pariot lives just off this road to the west right here. Here Jake, turn left right here."

Fortunately the traffic was light on the road to Oklahoma. Jake made the turn and headed west for about half a mile when Lige spotted the farm. Although it was dark as pitch, the porch light was on, which helped spot the house. The old frame house had a long dirt drive way from the county road. Each side of the drive way was fenced and lined with cedar trees. The house was a typical house of the bygone area a "T" shaped home which usually contained three rooms and big front porch. This porch was about three feet off the ground. Willie had four dogs and they came out barking their heads off.

"Lige," Berthie May said, "you better wait until someone comes out of the house or you might get dog bit."

"Naw, they don't bite," Lige said, "They just like to bark."

He was right too, for when he opened the door and got out of the pickup, the dogs came up with their tails wagging wanted to be petted or fed.

About that time a man in blue overalls who looked a lot like Lee Pariot came out of the house.

"Why God almighty," he said. "Is that you Lige Oldham? And Berthie May, what the world ya'll doing out this late at night. Ya'll get out and come in, I'll get Lillie to get us a pitcher of ice tea!"

"Thanks Willie," Lige said, "but we can't stay. I hate to tell you, but we are bearing bad news. It's you paw, Willie, he's in a poor way at the hospital in Bowie, and he might not make it through the night."

Willie hung his head. "That is bad news Lige, but I'd rather had you brung it more than any other person on this earth. We knowed you growing up out there your pa and ma, and my folks. You and Berthie May is like folks not just friends, he said teary eyed."

"Willie, I don't know where your brother's live. Can you help get hold of them?" Lige asked.

"Lillie and I will do it, Willie said, don't worry about it. My brother Lee Bob lives back yon way close to Bowie and he's got a phone and my other two brothers got one too. Lee Bob can call them."

"Well," Lige said, Can you get someone to get hold of Leck and Ida Lou's kids? Leck is with P.D. in Dallas selling watermelons. They won't be back till in the morning."

"Yeah, my other brother Calvin lives down in Wise County and that's where all Idie's kids live except Elzie. Where's Elzie anyhow?"

"He went with Leck and P.D. to Dallas." Lige said.

"Well Dallas will never be the same, for sure,." Willie said. "Who's the kids you got here?"

"Well that girl is Lucy, Nolan's girl and that's our grandson Jake." Lige said.

"Yeah," Willie said, "I know Lucy now that I can see her. It's kinda dark out here but I can see her now. How you doing Lucy?"

"I'm just fine Uncle Willie," she said, "just sad about Grandpa Lee."

"Well," Lige said, "if you can take it from here, we'll head on back to the place. I'm so sorry about Lee. He and I have been good friends a long long time," Lige said as he shook Willie's hand.

"I know Lige," Willie said, "I know and thanks. Y'all come back in better circumstances."

Jake turned the truck around and headed out of the long drive way. He could see the headlights coming on of Willie's truck as they reached the road. Willie and Lillie wouldn't be far behind them.

It seemed to take a long time to get back to the farm. The place seemed dark and alone.

"Jake," Berthie May said, "you might as well stay the night here too. I don't like the idea you staying all alone in your house."

"I don't mind Grandma," Jake said.

"No you stay here. In the morning I'll fix you a nice breakfast."

"I'll go get a change of clothes," Jake said, as he parked the truck in Lige's open shed.

Minutes later he was back at his grandparent's home. Lucy would get the bedroom in the canning room and Jake would sleep in Clois's old room.

In less than thirty minutes, they were all in bed with the lights out. It would be a short night.

Jake was asleep when he felt a hand on his face. His eyes shot open and he thought maybe someone was trying to wake him because the worst had happened.

However, to his surprise it was Lucy.

"Lucy, what are you doing in here?"

"What do you think?" She said. "I thought we'd pick up where we left off this afternoon."

"Not in my Grandma's house!" Jake whispered. "No, not here."

"Why not, your grandparent's are fast asleep and Jake I've got a hunger that needs feeding she said. Please Jake, just one time."

By this time Jake was awake in more ways than one. When she had aroused him, there was no stopping the need then. He pulled her to him and they made love for awhile. Shortly before time to get up, she slipped back to her room. Jake slept soundly and solidly. He didn't hear his Grandma get up and rattle pots and pans as she stirred up breakfast. In her and Lige's mind, the best meal of the day and the meal that starting a person off, was breakfast. Any other meal was secondary.

She rolled out biscuits with her whiskey bottle she used for a rolling pin. She cooked fresh bacon and ham and she cooked a skillet of eggs. She made Lige's coffee and put the cup in a saucer. She fixed Lucy and Jake chocolate milk. She would take a spoon of Hershey's coco mixed with a couple of spoons of sugar and a slight pinch of salt. She poured boiling water into the glasses to dissolve the chocolate mixture, poured cold raw milk with the cream floating on the top into the glasses. There just wasn't any better chocolate milk than that. She let the kids sleep until eight o'clock before getting them up. Lucy didn't want to rise at first but she did and dressed in the same clothes she had on the day before. Jake had on fresh overalls and shirt. He gladly sat down at his Grandma's table. The breakfast was hardy and he was ready for it. He didn't want to look at Lucy either. About the time he and Lucy were eating, P.D. came in.

"Oh, P.D. your in time for breakfast but go get Leck and Elzie," Berthie May said.

Leck and Elzie had driven to their house, but P.D. went down and got them. They were exhausted from sitting on the market most of the night. Sleep was hard to get on the market.

In a few moments the three of them were back at Lige and Berthie May's house.

"Y'all come in and eat," Berthie May said. "Ida Lou ain't down to home right now. She's in the hospital with her dad."

"Grandpa sick?" Elzie asked suddenly he was no longer in a tired slumber but wide awake.

"Yes hon," she said. "He had a stroke yesterday."

"Now y'all eat and then go home and go to bed and get some rest. Lige and I'll go to town and check on things and when we get back y'all will be rested enough to drive in to town."

"P.D. you get some rest too," Jake and Lige can take care of the chores.

"Dad, that Mr. Tally came out and left his card and wants you to call him. I think he's interested in buying the whole patch. And in two weeks Glen Ray's melons will be ready to pull so that Mr. Tally might find enough melons to supply his store from us and Glen Ray," Jake said.

"If Glen Ray's melons are any good, you might be right," P.D. said. "I'll call the man today."

"Did ya'll sell out?" Berthie May asked.

"We sure did, about five this morning. But it took us an hour to get out of Dallas before we got on the road to home.

They heard a car drive up. Berthie May went to the door. "It's Mary," she said.

Mary came in looking drained from the night's vigil.

"Lee died this morning just after sunup," she said. "Ida Lou and her brothers are at the funeral home making arrangements. Leck, she said for you not to come to town, that she would get one of her brothers to bring her home."

Lucy got up from the table to hug her Grandpa Leck.

Elzie suddenly wanting no more breakfast, tears were falling down his face. He wanted out of the room out of sight ashamed of his grief. He stood up and started out the door.

Jake got up too and followed.

"Elzie," he called, "Elzie, wait."

But Elzie just kept walking but Jake caught up with him. He put his arm on Elzie's shoulder.

"I'm sorry Elzie. It's a sad moment for you and for us all."

Elzie who was never at a loss for words, was at a loss for words. He couldn't stop crying but was afraid to be seen that way. The boys had walked to the barn out of sight of their folks.

"It's ok," Jake said. "Grieve all you want." Elzie sat down under the shed at the barn on one of the milking stools. Jake pulled up the other one.

"I took it for granted Grandpa would always be here," Elzie said. "I should have spent more time with him."

"You lived with him, you saw him every day. You ate nearly all your meals with him. That's more than your cousins can say, Jake said. Just treasure what you got."

For the next half hour the boys just sat there. Their solace was broken by Berthie May coming to the lot to milk.

"You boys get some feed for me and I'll turn the cows into the lot." The two Jersey's were bawling and wanting in the lot so they could feed their babies. They weren't concerned for the sweet feed that Jake and Elzie would pour out in their respective places, nor were they concerned about Berthie May's hands tugging their teats, they wanted their babies to feed. Their calves were kept in the lot so the mammy's would come in twice a day to allow the calves to suck. That was when Berthie May did her milking.

"Jake, if you'll take the other pail and milk Betty, then I can let her and Jul in at the same time."

"Ok Grandma, I'll be glad to," Jake said.

"Jake, I'm going home and get cleaned up and get some sleep. I'll talk to you later." Elzie said.

"Get some rest." Jake said.

Jake could never milk as good as his Grandma, although he tried. She just had a way with getting the cow to let her milk down.

"Saw now," she would say to the cow as she milked her. Sometimes the cow would figet and raise a leg like she might kick, although they never did. Sometimes in the middle of the milking the cow would hunker up and pee. When that happened the milker had to jump back with the pail so that she didn't splatter urine in the milk. Jul was especially bad to do that.

"Oh, saw now," Berthie May said as she had to jump back for Jul's pee break.

Jake chuckled as he was now going to get ahead of his Grandma in filling his pail. Standing from the back, they always milked on the right said of the cow, the calf sucked from the left. Sometimes the calf would try to get the teat one was milking from. Berthie May kept a flat stick handy if that happened. She would slap the underside of the calf's jaw yelling, "Hey! Hey, get back." Sometimes the calf would violently hunch the cow's udder to bring down the milk. This would cause the cow to slightly kick with her back leg but always on the right side where Jake or Berthie May was milking from. The cow never kicked her baby. She would do that later when it was time to wean. The mama always knew when it was time for her baby to wean. The calf would want to nurse, but she would kick the calf off. The calf would just be dumbfounded and not know what to do. Jake thought that was the way it was with humans too. Sometimes the kid didn't know when to wean sometimes they had to be given a gentle push, sometimes they couldn't wait to wean or so they thought. When they hit the real world, they wanted back into their mama's secure arms. But once you leave, you can't come back. Jake liked having the times to milk with his Grandma. They would talk and later in life, this would be one of his treasured moments.

Lee's funeral would be Sunday at the Pleasant Hill church building. Ida Lou's pastor Brother Don Charles would be holding the service. Jake had never been to a Pentecostal service before. He wondered how it would be with the guitar. Since Pleasant Hill had no electricity, they couldn't very well use an electric one.

Lee had died on Friday morning and the family had made the arrangements. Both Lige and P.D. would serve as pall bearers as well as Jess Jasper and the Shelton brothers. That made five men. Jake wondered who the sixth man would be when that afternoon, Elzie came over and asked Jake to serve.

"I want you to do it." he said. "Grandpa thought you were the star of Bethlehem. He told me I couldn't have a better friend and he was right." Elzie said.

"I never served as a pall bearer before," Jake said. "But I know I can do it."

Saturday the Tatum house was covered up with people. Cars were parked all over their place. Some folks were the Tatum and Pariot's kin while others were neighbors and friends who came by to pay their respect and leave food. Always in the rural areas, when there was a death, the folks banded together and did what they could to comfort. People, who might otherwise be on the opposite side of the fence with their opinions, would put that behind them and come to a neighbor's aid. There was always more food than needed, but that didn't matter, it was the kindness, the thoughtfulness that mattered.

Sunday finally came. Jake and his parents went to regular church service in town because the funeral was in the afternoon. Every church announced Lee Pariot's passing.

It seemed to Jake that a lot of the town came out to the funeral. The building was packed full. The shutters were staked wide open for air and the back door was left open as well. Since it was mid July, mid-afternoon in Texas are merciless.

Pastor Don read the obituary and then had a song which a man by the name of Paul Willet led. Paul led all the singing for the Assembly of God church in Sunset. His whole family were musically inclined. His daughter played piano and his two sons played guitar. The two sons were playing as he led the song asking the assembly of people there to sing. They sang Will There Be Any Stars in My Crown followed by Tempted and Tried. Jake noted that the Assembly of God church sang the same type of songs the church of Christ did.

Pastor Don gave his eulogy on Brother Lee as he called him, when Jake couldn't remember Lee ever going to that church. Maybe Jake didn't know.

The sermon tolled on and finally came to a blessed end. It was stifling hot and everyone was fanning themselves, the pastor was wringing wet.

As his sons played Paul sang a solo as folks filed past the body for one last look before that lid was shut. The pall bearers would be the last group to file out before the family.

It seemed to take for ever before the funeral director of the Burgess Funeral home held his hand in a motion to the pall bearers to stand up and he led them to file past the deceased. Lee was dressed in a brand new pair of overalls and clean white shirt. Jake had never seen Lee wear a white shirt. He had never seen the man with his thin hair combed either. The pall bearers filled out of the church followed by the song leader and his sons. Only the family was left now, which numbered about sixty people. One by one they would file out but as the kinship grew closer to the immediate family, the sadness became more apparent. All at once one of Lee's sons cried out in a loud voice, Oh Papa, oh papa. He then began to scream sobs which set the remainder of the family into deep sorrow. He could hear Ida Lou's crying with her brothers. Finally Pastor Don said softly to them, it's time now. He led them out of the building into the waiting crowd. The people stood on both sides of the door in a respectful silence while the family came out. Last was Lee's children and Leck and Ida Lou's kids with their spouses. Elzie was among them, red eyed, tears streaming down his face. That was all it took for Jake who couldn't hold it anymore. He began to sob, his shoulders hunched over him. P.D. had to steady him. "It's all right son." he said.

Then the funeral director called the pall bearers back inside and had them get on each side of the coffin. The metal box was of a deep blue color, with lighter blue corners. In unison they picked it up, which to Jake seemed enormously heavy. They carried the box from the building out the door and headed for the cemetery gate which was held open by the people. Lee's grave was toward the middle section of the grounds where his late wife Roxy Van Stout lay in the lot next to her parents, Hendrick Van Stout and his wife Sarah Lou. They were Germans who had come to Montague County from the Hill country after they arrived in Texas. Sarah was their only child. They had bought their parcel of land from Uncle Spence Russell's father Joseph.

Finally they laid the burden on the stand above the grave. Inside the grave Jake could see a wooden box which lined the inside of the grave. The Pastor made a short message, followed by a prayer before shaking hands with the family. Then the funeral home people stepped in along with some of the Pariot family. They lowered Lee into the ground, and started covering up the grave. The red dirt gave a distinctive thud as it hit against the wooden liner lid that covered the top of the coffin. Finally the grave was finished and the family then was greeted for the last time before departure. Folks began to migrate toward their automobiles.

Jake noticed his Grandpa in his suit. It was a black pin stripped with a vest and white shirt and a bight blue tie. He had not seen him wear one in a long time. He looked like a banker, but Jake was sure he was like a fish out of water.

In just two weeks the process was repeated again. This time it was Lige's mother who passed away. Clarence, Lige's youngest brother whom people called Chick, drove out and told Berthie May and Lige about Caroline being so bad. They loaded up in the truck and were right behind Chick when they left, Berthie May yelling out the window of the truck where they were going. Jake was to tend to Berthie May's chores.

They had arrived at Mrs. Brown's finding Dr. Ligon present. He was listening to Caroline's heart looking very serious. Caroline was laying in bed her eyes shut.

The doctor looked up at the family as they were gathered around the room, Jim and his wife Dora, Odel and his wife Minnie, Lige's two sisters Ella, and Violet with her husband Lester Potter.

"Your mother is about gone," he said. "She has cancer of the liver. I can feel at least five holes the cancer has eaten through her liver. She won't last through the night."

She didn't she died before nightfall.

Burgess Funeral home came and picked up her body, prepared it and brought the body and casket back to Mrs. Brown's home. She offered her home to be used before the funeral. Jake had never been to an individual's house where the dead were laid out. His Grandma told him, however, that in her day it was common practice. It was the best folks could do in the past she said.

The funeral was held at the old Pleasant Hill church. Caroline Oldham was a Free Will Baptist. The local Baptist preacher of the

Sunset Baptist church presided over the service, but Bill Flatt of the Sunset church of Christ led the whole church in accappella singing.

Following the funeral Lige's brothers and two sisters along with their families came to the Oldham farm. The house was full and annoying to Jake. He didn't associate with these kin folks much. They seldom came out here and the second cousins were certainly strangers to him. He heard one of his Great Aunt's daughters say, Is anything in here Grandmother Caroline's. I'd like something.

That was enough to put Jake outside. To his comfort he saw Elzie walking across the field toward him.

"Looks like the house is full," Elzie said.

"Too full, cousin," Jake said.

"Let's get our poles and go down to yon creek. I feel a fishing coming on," Jake said.

"You think it would be all right?" Elzie said.

"Did you never read in the bible after Jesus was crucified that Peter told the disciples he was going fishing?" Jake answered.

"I hadn't thought of it," Elzie said. "Good scripture."

The boys went down to the creek catching some grasshoppers as they went. In a few minutes they were wetting hooks and starting to relax.

"You know, we got some problems," Elzie said.

"What kind of problems?" Jake asked.

"Well we thought Grandpa had deeded the farm to my dad and mama, but what the deed says is that Grandpa deeded to mama her mama's portion of the farm. She's got Grandma's half of the place and one fifth from Grandpa's part," Elzie said.

"What's going to happen?" Jake asked.

"We might have to move," Elzie said.

The statement hit Jake like a ton of bricks.

"No, that can't happen Elzie, you and me we're a team, we can't be separated. You can't go somewhere else!" Jake yelled.

"I think my mom's going to talk to you dad about it after the dust settles.

Two of mama's brothers want to sell the place and they can't just sell one fifth of a house," Elzie said.

Jake felt a sinking doom in his life. Here he was about to enter his senior year, falling in love life with Nell Hunter, unsure of what lay ahead after graduation, and now Elzie is about to move. He sat down on the bank looking totally dejected.

The thing that Elzie told Jake was the truth. Ida Lou came and talked to P.D. and then all her brothers came together and all met again with P.D.

Three nights later, P.D. announced at the supper table what it all had amounted to.

"Well," he said, "with both Mary and Jake all ears, what we have decided to do is buy the Pariot place. We're going to buy each one of the brothers and Leck and Ida Lou's part too. Leck and Ida Lou are going to move out to Willie's. He's got a place with house on it and Ida Lou's brother Lee Bob is going to help Leck get a town job in Fort Worth at the plant where he works."

Jake felt like the world was crashing in. "I just can't believe it," Jake said. "Our best friends in the whole world and they are going to move away. Elzie won't get to graduate from Sunset."

"He might, P.D. said. I told them he could stay here with us so he could go to school in Sunset."

"You think he might?" Jake asked.

"It is entirely up to Elzie,.." P.D. said.

"There is something else," P.D. said. "We have to go to the bank to make this purchase. We've got to borrow a lot of money to buy that old place. We have agreed on fifteen dollars an acre for the farm and an additional thousand dollars for the house. That's thirty four hundred dollars. That means if we make two peanut crops and melons we just about pay for it in a couple of years. But the note will be for five. I want to put the note and the deed in your name Jake. I want this to be your purchase. Now I'll have to cosign the note with the bank, but I won't hesitate to do that."

Jake was silent not knowing what to say. "I'd like that," Jake said. "I really would, if the Tatum's aren't going to live there."

The next day, Jake and Elzie were loading watermelons. Their own crop was about done. Mr. Tally had bought the crop for his five stores and was taking Glen Ray's. Jake and Elzie would be working for Glen Ray.

"Have you thought about where you're going to school?" Jake asked.

"Mama and daddy said I could go to Sunset if I want to, but I don't know. I either got to live with you or transfer from Bowie or I could go to Goldburg."

"You know I want you to stay here and go to school with me," Jake said.

"I know," Elzie said, "I really want to do that but living with you and being under your folks rule is different than me living down the road and working for your dad."

"Well the rules ain't bad," Jake said.

In another week, the boys were helping Glen Ray harvest his watermelons for the Tally stores.

Glen Ray pulled up with the tractor and trailer. "Y'all got the first cutting done?"

"We like one more row," Jake said. " I'll do it while you and Jake load," Elzie said.

"Good enough," Glen Ray said. "Jake you drive the tractor, and I'll load the first two rows then we can switch."

"Sounds like a winner cousin," Jake said.

By noon the melons were hauled from the field and loaded into two pickups that belonged to the Shelton family. Glen Ray's plan was for Jake and Elzie to take one truck and he would take the other in order for them to make the five stores. Mr. Tally had a store in Decatur, Chico, Bridgeport, Springtown and Weatherford. Deliveries were every third day which gave them time to get the ripe melons cut and loaded. Each store took a pickup load, so the boys would have to come back to the farm and reload the truck between stops. It would take longer than they thought.

Next morning they would head for the stores. Jake and Elzie would deliver to Chico, Bridgeport and Decatur, while Glen Ray would deliver to Springtown and Weatherford by hauling on his dad's truck and pulling a trailer.

"If we should have them all delivered by noon," Glen Ray said, "Then we can meet in Decatur and eat dinner."

At six in the morning Jake and Elzie were on the road to Chico. The store opened at seven but someone was there to take deliveries earlier. They would be there before seven. The morning air was cool and for their pleasure the pickup had a radio.

"God dog," Elzie said, "I just don't know how to act around a truck with a radio." Then he turned the volume up above what was comfortable just to make the point.

"Ok, Elz," Jake said, "turn it down some." Elzie obeyed.

They were listening to Bill Mac on KPCN Morning Coffee slurping club. He was about to play Lefty Frizell's tune "I Love You Because." Elzie would sing along in a fashion of sorts, hamming it up with his gestures pretending to be strumming a guitar.

"How you and Angie Freeman getting along?" Jake asked.

"Oh, I see her from time to time. She's a regular at church. She says I'm her favorite boy. Wonder why?" Elzie said.

"I guess she likes making it in the pastor's study." Jake sneered.

Elzie had to laugh. "I went to town with mama and daddy a couple of weeks ago and I saw her down at her aunt's house. Mama and daddy said they were going to be in town for awhile, so I walked down there and found out her aunt was gone to Bowie. She and I fooled around on her aunt's couch."

"Oh, you Casanova you," Jake said.

"You know what, we ain't yet gone to the drive in, like Bud said we would go," Jake said.

"When did he say that?" Elzie asked.

"You remember the evening you and dad and Leck went to Dallas? Well Glen Ray came over and we drove over to Billy John's and the three of us went over to Bud's and we sort of talked about it then," Jake said.

"Today's Wednesday," Elzie said, "when we get back from the melon delivery, let's hit them up and go, with or without women."

"Wouldn't you like to take Angie in my Grandpa's truck and just bed her down in the back?" Jake asked.

"Hell no," Elzie said, "If I go to the drive in, I want to see the show, not make one."

The boys wound back to Decatur past eleven and waited for Glen Ray at the court house square. He got there about thirty minutes after they did. Naturally to the nature of Glen Ray, he had some trouble in Weatherford. He had to wait to unload, he had to unload the melons by himself, he got stopped by a cop, things that could only happen to Glen Ray.

The three of them decided to wait until they got back to Sunset and eat. They wanted a hamburger from Hulet's.

After their dinner, they all went down to Hunter's and hit Bud up about going to the drive in.

Bud was in the feed section of the store, which was the next building that shared the same wall with the grocery store. He wasn't busy and was laying on top of some feed nearly asleep.

"Hey big boy," Elzie said. "We need two tons of range cubes and a ton of cottonseed and fifty salt blocks, delivered today and put it on the credit."

Bud jumped up and said, "Well shoot I thought it was somebody. What y'all been up too, I haven't seen you since the funerals."

"We been busy being farmers," Elzie said, "but we're free tonight and thought we'd take in a show. How about it?"

"Yeah," I said we would go, Bud said. "I'll get Billy John set up and you guys but let's leave the girls at home, there too much trouble."

"That's the truth," Elzie echoed. "They're more trouble than there worth. Besides, we can take em next week."

"Ya'll be at my house at 8:15,"Bud said.

"Sure thing," Glen Ray said.

Jake wasn't too excited about sitting in a convertible with four guys but it was an outing. The show was a real treat as it was a John Wayne western. They all liked John Wayne.

About mid way through the show, Elzie got out of the car and went to the concession stand to go to the rest room.

He was down there for several minutes when on the intercom, the speaker interrupted the movie and asked for Jake Oldham to come to the concession stand. He looked at his friends and thought, what in the world…

On the way down, which was less than a two hundred feet from the car, he worried that something had happened at home or someone was sick.

He came inside the small room where two women were frying hamburgers as fast as they could make them and churning out curly Q French fries. There at the counter was Elzie.

He smiled a big smile and walked over to Jake and whispered in his ear. "I didn't want nothing, I just wanted to have you paged to come down here."

"Get some fries while you're here, there really good," Elzie said.

"You nut," Jake said. "An order of Curly Q Fries, please, and a Dr. Pepper."

On the way home, the boys were feeling the night air in their faces as Bud drove a decent speed down 287. Elzie was singing some song trying to get everyone to sing alone, as he and Billy John and Jake rode in the back seat. With his arm around Billy John who was sitting in the middle, he was patting Billy John's shoulder to the time of his song.

Bud and Glen Ray rode in the front.

"Oh, shut the hell up Elzie," Glen Ray said. "You're not in tune with the song."

CHAPTER 8

Sometimes things are over about as soon as they start. Summer always seemed that way to Jake. Even though when he and Elzie were hoeing their melons and peanuts on those broiling hot summer days and they thought they would never finish the job, they did finish.

Fortunately for them, August brought two good rains which carried the peanut crop. The plans to go to the drive in with the girls never materialized, and Leck and Ida Lou did move, only not to her brother's spare house. They rented a house in Sunset. Ida Lou still had the job at the slack factory and Mary picked her up each day. Leck got a job at Convair in Fort Worth and rode with a car pool. Elzie moved to Sunset too, after the summer was over. Until then he stayed with the Oldham's because of the farm work. He would never go back to the farm life once they moved to town. Elzie's parents bought Lee's old truck from the estate and gave it to him to drive. He could go out and see Jake anytime, which he often did. And Jake bought the Pariot place with his father's help.

September came and it was time to go back to school. It would be different because Jake and Elzie wouldn't be riding together, and Jake would miss that.

Glen Ray and Jake were seniors of a class of seventeen students, consisting of seven boys and ten girls. Senior's had an easier schedule than the other students. They had English, Government, a math class and a science. Both Jake and Glen Ray had Agriculture which consisted of mostly shop work. They learned in Ag. IV to weld, electrical wiring, and minor plumbing. Since Jake's project was his watermelons all he had to do was present his accounting book and he was through with the class. He and Glen Ray would get out around 2:30 in the afternoons. However, Glen Ray was going to work at Buford's Station after school until basketball season. He had to keep up his basketball because he was in line for a scholarship with North Texas State University.

Jake didn't have a single class with Elzie, Bud or Billy John and he missed that.

The fall months were busy for the Oldham's as they prepared to dig peanuts, afterward bail the peanut hay which would supply their cows with winter feed. P.D. had bought ten sows and that would keep things busy during the farrowing time. Then after wean time, they would work on fattening the sholts. Jake's extra schedule would help him from missing Elzie.

There was turmoil in Sunset in 1955. Production in the factories meant secure jobs and a steady income, had caused a few people to want to get a place in the country and move from the big city. A few dozen city folks had bought places in and around Sunset. The first thing that happens after the new wears off is that the people suddenly want the city in the country. They complain about the road conditions, they hate the dust in the summer, they hate the muddy roads after a rain. They find that all the conveniences of the city don't exist in the small rural towns, so they complain. They don't like the services offered. The mail isn't delivered fast enough, the grocery store doesn't have the kind or brands of supplies they wanted and the schools are a joke as far as they are concerned. They don't measure up to the big city, they don't have enough variety, their children were deprived.

So it was in 1955, when a few dozen newcomers began to complain and finally led a petition drive to consolidate the school to Bowie. After all, they said, Bowie offers so much more.

The idea divided the town. The newcomers were leading the charge feeling confident that they could swing the majority to their way of thinking. But there was a core group that wanted to keep the school right where it was. Finally things escalated to a town hall meeting. There hadn't been one in Sunset in fifty years. Letters went all over the Sunset School district advising folks to come out to the school gym and debate the issue.

The matter was no small talk among the Oldham households. Lige announced that he and Berthie May would be going and that P.D. and Mary should too. The meeting was to be held the last Friday night in September. Friday night was football night for people in Bowie and any big school. Until basketball season, there were no sports in Sunset.

Fortunately the weather was cool which would make the meeting more comfortable for those in attendance. On the meeting night, the gym was full to the brim. Folks from out in the country were there as well as the town folk. Every merchant was there, the school board, the teachers, parents and students alike.

Superintendent Armstrong opened the meeting. He was upbeat and friendly welcoming all. He stated the situation as best he could and then opened the floor for the people leading the move for consolidation to have the first speak.

A man by the name of William Tanner, who had moved to Sunset about four months prior to the meeting, was the chairman of the group. He got up and told of all the virtues of a large school, of what it offered to the children, their education, possibilities for their future. The people listened and were polite enough but there were people who followed one after another telling why they wouldn't want it to happen, mostly because the school taxes would go up if they were consolidated to Bowie. However Mr. Tanner tried to refute that point stating that he had spoken with the Bowie School Board and they assured him the taxes would virtually be unchanged.

To Jake's surprise, his grandfather rose to speak. He didn't yell out like some people did but went to the front of the gym and up to the microphone and looked his friends in the eyes.

"Most of you know me, he said, but if you don't, my name's Lige Oldham. I've lived here all my life and I was born in 1885. I went to school out in the country about a mile from my house at a place called

Franklin. Franklin school was open before I was born and stayed open until 1918. When I went to school there, we had one teacher and he taught all the grades, one through eight. We had about seventy kids in that school in 1900. When my sister Violet went in 1918, they had dropped down to less than twenty kids. So folks decided to consolidate with the Huddleston School because between the two districts we could just about pay a teacher. Between the two districts we had forty kids. But the kids from Franklin had to get over to Huddleston. We didn't have busses then, so they walked or they rode the plow mule or somebody took them in the wagon. Sometime in the mid '20's they got an old buss to haul kids to Huddleston. But the kids still had to meet the bus at a common place, because they didn't drive to everybody's house. Then in '41 folks said we needed to consolidate again and send all the kids to Sunset. They had a bus to pick up the forty or so kids out the country and bring them to town."

"Now I said all that to say that every time we consolidated, we lost ground. The community got smaller. I know that the consolidation didn't have all to do with it, but it didn't help matters."

"Now I've seen Sunset when it was in its heyday and I know a lot of you old ones out there like me, did too. We saw a big town with a lot of business right here, be a prosperous place. Then the crash of '29 hurt us and we never recovered from it. But we still got a town here. We need to keep it here. When you move your school, the town will die. We'll loose the bank, the store and someday loose the post office and we'll be like the towns of Uz, New Harp, Dewy, and Pella. We will be a ghost town. I say, to hell with this consolidation mess. We need to keep the school right here. If we need to up the taxes to do so, then by God, do it, but keep it here."

Lige then began to walk away from the front and back to his seat. However the whole gym erupted in applause and people stood, and people slapped him on his back and shook his hand.

Berthie May, turned to Jake and said, "I didn't know the little man had that in him. He has never in his life made a speech. But up there tonight, he sounded just like his dad. That was something, Jake, that was something."

When Lige sat down there seemed to be nothing else to say, so the meeting was adjourned and the petition failed. Sunset kept their school, its store, and its bank, at least for the time being.

The Decatur phone company ran lines out where Jake lived and both Jake's parents and his grandparents signed up for a phone. The State Department of Transportation ran a news article in the papers saying they had been funded to build farm to market roads and they could expect a certain amount in Montague County that fall. Contracts would be let and the roads would be reworked and hot topped. When the contract was awarded, P.D. took a job with the construction company. When P.D. went to work, Jake put in a lot of hours after school. He didn't have much time that year to do anything but work.

In Texas the weather changes about every five minutes. One morning it could be balmy warm and by afternoon a chill hitting the air with a cold front dropping the temperature by as much as fifty degrees. The fall of '55 was a pleasant one. Cool weather set in and it stayed cool until frost. It was refreshing at night to have a gentle cool breeze come though the house. Sleeping was at its best when the weather was like this.

In October the Oldham's dug their peanuts. Before PTO driven implements, a few farmers did custom work for as many peanut farmers that would hire them with stationary machinery. The method was to plow the peanuts up, field hands would walk the field and shake the soil loose from the vines and turn the peanuts upward to dry. Once the drying process had taken place, the vines were stacked in piles, followed by men walking the fields forking the crop on a wagon or a trailer. There the peanuts were hauled to the thrasher which separated the nut from the vine. The peanuts were then sacked and sowed. The vines were run through a stationary bailer where the plant was crimped together and bound up with either twine or wire, depending on the model of the bailer. The hay bails weighted as much as seventy pounds and were stacked on trailers or pickup beds and hauled to the barn. This was some of the richest protein hay that could be found. Cattle wintered well on peanut hay. The peanut crop was a good one that year, and the hay was too.

Jake could expect to make his note payment and the family would have money left for the following year.

Around the end of October the phone rang at Jake's parent's home. Mary answered and called Jake to the phone. It was Elzie.

After a few moments of excited talk, Elzie asked Jake if he could go camping Friday night. The weather had warmed up and it was supposed to be clear.

"We going out Bud's?" Jake asked.

"Yeah, we're all going," Elzie said.

"You mean Billy John, Glen Ray and you?" Jake asked.

"Yeah, and I think a few more might come out for awhile. You know to sit around the fire, eat some franks and drink some cokes, uh no beer either," Elzie said.

"That sounds great. I'll asked the folks and make sure, but I'm sure I can," Jake said.

Friday came and Jake waited patiently for Elzie. Elzie came after Jake in his Grandpa's pickup, the old Dodge truck. Mary had made an apple cobbler for Jake to take.

"Hop in, Jake," Elzie said as Jake was climbing in. "Good to see you Jake."

"Good to see you. Except for lunch we don't see much of each other. I miss you out here Elzie. It's not the same," Jake said.

"I miss it out here too Jake," Elzie said. "I thought going to town would be the greatest thing since sliced bread. I thought everything that went on, went on in town. All I get out of town is noise. Jake you never heard so much traffic in all your days. The cars and trucks roll through Sunset day and night. It's all the time. When I get out of school, I've been working at Comie Jackson's station. I work there all the time and I don't know nuthin and I don't see nuthin. Man, working is the pits. It's all you do, you work, you go home, you sleep, you go to school, you go to work. It's a cycle that never ends, don't ever get in that cycle Jake," Elzie said. "Don't ever move to town."

"Why Elzie, don't you get to see Angie on a regular basis?" Jake asked. "Isn't having her regular worth being in town?"

"Jake would you get that off your mind!" Elzie snorted. "Angie's got her sights on Larry Fox, I'm old news with her."

"Well, at least we can all go out to the camp and not work tonight." Jake said. "Elzie, no pissing on the fire this time."

"Ok, ok," Elzie said, "I wont."

Jake and Elzie drove straight out to Bud's father's farm. They hadn't gone far when Glen Ray was behind them with Billy John. The four of them arrived where Bud was already there along with his sister and her two girlfriends, Nancy and Debbie.

Bud had a fire started and the girls were roasting the weenies on coat hangers. They had several on their wires.

"Hey y'all are just in time," Nell said. "We're cooking your supper for you."

Jake put his mom's cobbler on the picnic table and fished out a Dr. Pepper from the ice chest. He spoke to everyone as if he hadn't seen anyone in a long time when he had seen them all at school that day. However with his schedule of classes and getting out early and returning home to work on the farm, he didn't really seem to have time to talk to anyone. To him, Nell was the most beautiful girl he had ever seen. He couldn't stop looking at her but she acted as though she didn't notice him at all. As the weenies got done, Jake helped them remove them from the wire and place them on a paper plate.

Everyone was happy and joyous that night. The day had been warm, but the fall air turned crisp after sundown. There were no insects to bother them and everyone was relaxed. Bud had his dad's tractor and trailer at the campsite.

"What you going to do with the trailer?" Jake asked.

"We're going on a hay ride after while," Bud said.

That would be nice, he would pull his eye teeth if he could get Nell to sit by him, Jake thought. He would probably end up sitting by Elzie and Billy John.

They all ate with gusto like they were starving, then Bud ordered everyone on the wagon. He was going to drive. Jake made no effort to sit by Nell because he knew or he figured if he tried and she sat somewhere else, he would be disappointed. So there was no use in getting his hopes up, no use in being disappointed. However things fell to his favor. Elzie and Billy John sat on either side of Nancy and Debra sat by Glen Ray. It would fall by fate for him to sit with Nell. His heart was in his throat.

The tractor roared out of the farm and onto the county road. It looked like Bud was going to go down what they called Lover's Lane. It was a very shaded part of a particular county road where people their age took dates, to park. The road would go back some ten miles then hit another road and turn back to the road the Hunter farm was on. It made a rectangle covering some fifteen miles. That would take at least an hour to drive.

It was Nell who spoke first to Jake.

"You know Jake," she said, "even though school has just started, it wont be long until May, do you know what your going to do?"

"You know I'm buying Elzie's folks place," Jake said. "We're leasing the Jasper and the plates full at our house. I have to register in February for the draft. So I might get drafted, but if I do, I'll come back and I'm going to do what we have always done, farm. It's in my blood," Jake said. "In a couple more years, you've got to make the same decisions."

"Oh, I know it," she said. "I'm not thinking about that right now."

"Oh, uh, say Nell, since were sitting here, could I ask you something that's coming up in May?" Jake said.

"What's that, Jake?" She said.

"Well we have our graduation dance and I would really be honored if you would let me take you to it. Nell it would mean the world to me," Jake said almost shaking so bad he thought she could see his hands shaking.

"May's a ways off, Jake," she said, "but we'll see."

Jake couldn't remember a thing more about the hay ride. Her answer put him in hog heaven. He did make one move that she didn't resist. He finally got up enough nerve to hold her hand, and she let him. When he reached over and placed his hand on hers she didn't withdraw it. Then he moved slightly so they could clasp hands and she did so. His entire emotions were on fire. His heart was racing madly like he had run for miles. His sexual arousal was at its zenith. God, he thought he would die, he thought he was in total misery and exhilaration at the same time. He wanted to shout to the world.

"Can we eat lunch Monday?" He asked.

"Of course," she said, "anytime."

"Anytime! Oh my God," he thought, "I am in heaven."

Like the time she rode in his grandfather's truck from Hulet's to the school, the hay ride ended far too soon. When they got back to the camp, the girls were going home, leaving the boys to their revelry.

However before they left, Jake announced to them all a prophetic statement.

"This my friends, is the last good by forever," Jake said.

"What in the hell does that mean?" Elzie said.

"It means, that most likely we will all never again be together like this again in our lifetime. Glen Ray and I will graduate in May, and we have to go new paths. Then next May you three guys will be finishing school and you all will have to find your paths too. This has been one of the greatest nights of my life, but it is one of the saddest."

"Jake, I think you've lost your marbles," Elzie said. "Heck well go camping and fishing and hunting the rest of our lives. We're all best friends and their ain't nuthin that can come between us and I mean nuthin!"

Jake didn't try to argue, he only smiled at the young boy he loved like his own brother, wishing what he said was true.

The girls took Bud's car and went home, leaving the boys to stay up most of the night drinking their cokes and taking turns pissing on the fire.

CHAPTER 9

A few Saturday's later, Bud and Elzie got off early from their jobs. Old Comie didn't like to let Elzie off work, but Elzie bugged the hell out of him until he was glad to get him out of his sight for a few hours.

Floyd was always gracious to his son about working or not working. Most of the time, Floyd could handle the feed store along with the meat market. Besides the heaviest business was always before dinner, afternoon business was always lighter.

Elzie called and asked Jake to go dove hunting with him and Bud. They came out and picked up Jake and headed for their hunt. They would hunt three places. A fellow on Smyrna Road had a milo patch. They would check it first, then they would go out by Turkey creek and sit on the rail road tract for awhile and end up at Jake's sitting on one of their tank dams when the dove come in to get water.

The milo patch proved effective. There were plenty of birds, but Bud was the true shot on flying birds. He could connect on nine out of ten shots. Jake and Elzie were hitting about one out of five. After the boys had decided to check Turkey creek they loaded up and headed west to Turkey Creek. Turkey Creek lays west of Sunset and Smyrna lays to the north east. They were driving in Elzie's truck. However Elzie wanted Jake to drive because if he saw something he and Bud wanted to take pot shots at it. So Jake was driving when he noticed Elzie fumbling with his shot gun. He loaded a shell in the chamber by pumping the action. Then he did a stupid thing. To check the safety, Elzie pulled the trigger. The safety was not on, and the gun exploded in their ears. The cab filled with gunpowder.

"What the hell did you do?" Jake yelled at Elzie.

Elzie looked as shocked and surprised as Jake. "I didn't mean for the gun to go off, I was just checking the safety."

Fortunately the gun was pointed at the floor of the pickup. The shot had gone harmless out the firewall. They hadn't gone far when the pickup began to sputter and came to a stop. It wouldn't start. The opened the hood discovering that Elzie had shot the fuel pump clean into.

"Well Elzie, you got yourself a fuel pump," Jake said.

Bud roared with laughter, but Elzie didn't see the humor in it at all. Jake was just thankful no ones leg or foot was shot off.

"I'm so glad we all still got both feet, even though none of us has an eardrum," Jake said.

"What's that?" Elzie said.

Then the three of them began to laugh, and laugh from their depths relieving the stress of the situation.

"Looks like cousins," Jake said, "we're going to have to walk." The three of them took their shotguns and headed down the county road. They had walked a couple of miles when they spotted a familiar truck on the main road headed north when it turned down Smyrna Road toward them.

It was Glen Ray. He pulled up to his friends and asked, "are ya'll just hunting on the road here or what?"

"The answer is," Elzie said, "choice b, what."

"What?" Glen Ray asked.

"I shot my fuel pump into so we can't move my truck," Elzie said.

"How in the hell did you shoot your fuel pump?" Glen Ray asked.

Jake interrupted, "Glen Ray, you got a chain that can pull us back to town?"

"Yeah, sure but"….Glen Ray was saying but was interrupted again.

"Let's hook up and you take us back to town and I'll tell you all about it," Jake said.

It took only a minute for them to get the truck hooked up to the chain connecting Glen Ray with Elzie's truck. Elzie and Bud rode in the dead truck with Glen Ray and Jake together.

Jake explained what had happened, then asked, "what were you doing out this way anyhow, aren't you supposed to be working?"

"Yeah, but I was going out to the house to get dinner. I forgot my money this morning so I couldn't go get a burger at Hulet's," Glen Ray said.

"Lucky for us," Jake said.

They pulled the truck down to Chambers Garage. The fix it repair shop was run by Cotton Chambers. He was a good mechanic that usually could fix anything.

"Howdy boys," he said as they pulled up.

Cotton was a man in his sixties, balding with a red round face.

"What happened to that old bomb? Did she just lay over on ye?" He asked.

"Well, it had a little help, you see," Jake said. "Elzie mistook the truck for a dove and shot his fuel pump into."

"Haw haw," he began. "You don't know the difference between a Dodge truck and a dove?" He asked.

"Oh come on," Elzie squirmed, "can you fix it?"

Cotton was still sniggering, but said. "Yeah, if I can get a part. Probably have to go to Bowie and get one. I don't have a '49 fuel pump just laying around on the shelf here. Hell."

Glen Ray said, "tell you what. I'll run you up there to get a fuel pump. We'll stop by and tell Buford what we're doing so he won't have a fit cause of me being late from my dinner break."

With that the boys were off except Bud. Bud decided to go on home for the day. Jake on the other hand stayed with Elzie.

They ran up to Boyd's Auto where they knew old Boyd Doughty would have the part. Boyd had started his auto parts store in Sunset back in the thirty's but had moved on to Bowie in the late forties. Sure enough they got the fuel pump and were back in Sunset in less than forty five minutes. It would take Cotton thirty minutes to change it, so the boys went down to Hulet's for Glen Ray's dinner, Elzie's treat.

The jux box was playing another Hank Snow record, "The Golden Rocket" as the boys walked in. Hulet was reading the newspaper.

"Hey boys, what you have?" He growled.

"The usual," they said, as they took a table.

"Three burgers with fries Ellie," he yelled out.

Jake noticed something strange in one of the booths

"What's that hole in the booth there, Hulet?" Jake asked.

"Oh, you haven't heard about that?" Hulet said.

Jake hadn't but Glen Ray and Elzie had, but they had not told Jake.

"Well last Thursday," Hulet said, "this here fellow by the name of Andy Drake came in here and sat down right there where that hole is in the back of the booth. Only it wasn't there when he first sat down."

"Well it seems this here Drake fellow had been plowing with another man's heifer, if you get my drift. It was Colene Jones too. She and this Drake made plans to run off. She was going to leave her husband, Olan and their two kids. Well seems, Olan got wind of it somehow. He found out they was going to run off. I guess Colene told him or something, I don't know. But anyhow Drake was sitting here reading the newspaper, reading the Dallas Times Herald, waiting on her to show up so they could carry out their scheme. Well Olan comes in and shoots this Drake fellow right through the damn newspaper. Killed him deader than a mackerel right there in that booth." "I'll tell you one damned thing, it don't pay to read no Dallas paper in Sunset."

"What did you do?" Jake asked wild eyed.

"Well when Olan came in, I was back here cooking cause Ellie was gone to Hunters to get some cutlets for the blue plate special that day. Ann was off sick so I was running the whole shebang. I had already got Drake a cup of coffee, said he wasn't eating. I was back there at the stove scraping it getting ready for the noon cooking when it took place. I saw Olan come in but before I could speak to him or ask if he wants anything, he pulled out this .45 and let her fly. God dang I don't mind telling you I was scared. I about filled my drawers but what I done was I dove out the back door, with the damn thing latched. I hit that screen door running tore the screen all to hell."

"Olan just walked out and got in his truck and drove off. I ran down to Hunters and they called the sheriff. I had to shut the damn place down the rest of the day until they could investigate. There weren't no blue plate special that day," Hulet said.

"Wow!" Jake said. "I can't believe it. We go to school with them Jones kids. Poor kids, there mama was just going to leave them. I can't imagine that. You know if we have a cow that won't let her calf suck, well, we lot her and hobble her and make her take that calf. When she weans we send her to the stock yards and they make bologna out of her."

"Maybe that's what Mrs. Jones needs, hobbling," Hulet said laughing his course gravely laugh.

After downing the burgers, fries and malts, Glen Ray went back to Buford's to work. Jake and Elzie walked down to Bud's house before going back to pick up Elzie's truck.

The three boys decided to take a ride in Bud's convertible.

The convertible was a bit breezy, but what the heck? The three friends didn't care. They drove around the area of Bud's father's farm, Elzie and Bud in the front and Jake in the back. Spotting a bunch of doves sitting on the highline, Bud stopped and said to Jake, why don't you take a shot at the doves perched on the high lines?

Elzie said, "Me too, I'm going to get a shot too," as he leaped over to the back seat.

"No, Elzie," Jake said, "don't do it, let me have the shot."

"I'm shooting, and if you want a shot get your shotgun up and I'll wait and we'll shoot on three."

"Well, ok, I'm not loaded," Jake said.

"Well get loaded!" Elzie ordered.

Elzie didn't use his shotgun but grabbed up an old single shot that Bud carried in the car. He pulled the hammer back and said, are you ready Jake?

Leaning on Jake's side of the car and scooting Jake to one side.

"Ok, I'm loaded," Jake said.

"Ok, aim, one two," bam! Elzie fired on the count of two instead of three. The dove flew in all directions but not one fell to the ground.

"Oh, oh, man that hurts," Elzie yelled. He turned and looked at

Jake, with his hands over his chin covered in blood. Blood was running down his hands and spilling onto the seat.

"What happened Elzie?" Jake said, trying to move his hands and see what the problem was.

"That dang hammer hit me in the lip," Elzie said. "It hurts like hell."

"Let me look," Jake said.

When he could get Elzie to move his hands he discovered that just below Elzie's bottom lip, was a rough hole where the recoil of the blast had punctured right through inside Elzie's mouth.

Jake took his handkerchief and pushed it against the hole and pressed hard. Then he had Elzie put his hand on it and hold it.

"Bud, we better take Elzie to the doctor. I think he will need stitches," Jake suggested.

"Well hell," Bud said, "can't you shoot a shotgun without messing up the world?"

Bud found a place to turn the car around and sped back toward town. They turned onto the highway at Sunset and sped to Bowie. The clinic had closed for the day, so they had to go to the hospital entrance. Dr. Harris was on call and happened not to be busy at the moment.

"Well well,," the doctor said, "you been playing Wild Bill Hitchcock? Here let me see your lip."

"Um, yeah you sure done yourself up good," Dr. Harris said. He took a roll of gauze and clipped off a piece about a foot long. He then dipped it in disinfectant, then took a small probe and pushed the gauze through the hole, then pulled the foot of disinfectant gauze through Elzie's lip to clean the wound. All the while, Elzie was sitting with his eyes clinched shut slightly grimacing in pain. Then he gave him a shot to deaden the pain and sewed him up, one stitch on the outside and five on the inside of his mouth.

"Now drop your pants Mr. Hitchcock," Dr. Harris said. "Olivia!" He shouted.

"Yes doctor," the nurse said as she came into the emergency room.

"I need to give this boy a tetanus shot," he said. "Draw up a syringe so we can keep this cowboy from getting lock jaw."

Elzie had to stand there for several minutes with his pants and his underwear around his shoes. Jake and Bud chuckled.

"Don't you dare laugh," Elzie tried to say, but it sort of hurt his mouth to talk.

"Oh, no," Jake said, "I was just thinking what my mama always said about having to be in a hospital. She said always put on clean drawers son, you don't want to be in a hospital with raggedy drawers!" Both Bud and Jake let out a laugh, which Elzie couldn't do a thing about.

The nurse brought up the shot and the doctor punched Elzie's fatty cheek then rubbed the spot with a cotton ball soaked in alcohol.

"Now, the doctor said, get your pants up, and get out of here. Report to the clinic next week and somebody will take your stitches out."

As they walked back to the car, Elzie smarting from his wound and probably a little from his pride, Jake said. "Elzie I think Olivia thought you was cute, because she said you had a nice ass."

"Oh, kiss my nice ass, Jake," Elzie said.

November turned cold and Jake spent a lot of time in the evenings feeding cows. In the morning before school started, he check the stock tanks for ice, and in the evenings carry hay and range cubes. Between feeding and school work, there was little time for much else.

Lige and Berthie May were hulling pecans when Jake went over one Thursday afternoon. They were sitting in the kitchen in front of the wood cook stove. A fire was burning inside the stove, the wood giving off a hiss as it warmed the kitchen.

"Well hello stranger," Berthie May said. "We haven't seen you much lately, except in passing."

"When I take the truck to feed, I just get back and park and run home," Jake said. "It's been so cold the past two weeks."

"Normally it warms up between these spells but it hasn't this time. That makes me think about the winter of '31. Don't you remember Lige? We had snow and it was cold for near three weeks," Berthie May said.

"Do you remember when that spell hit?" she continued, "You had driven the team over to Sunset and get supplies. By the time you got back it was sleeting and when you came in the house, you took your overcoat off and it stood up in the middle of the floor. It was frozen stiff enough to stand on its own."

"Yeah, I remember that all right," Lige said. "I thought I was going to freeze before I got home. The last half mile it was sleeting pretty hard and hard to see, but them old mules knew how to get home."

"I had to send P.D. and Clois out to unload the wagon and bring stuff in the house and unhitch the team," Lige said.

"No, your dad went out and unhitched the team. He put them old mules in the barn and loaded them up with corn to keep them warm," Berthie May said.

"How many pecans did ya'll pick up?" Jake asked.

"Oh, we got two hundred pounds to shell," Berthie May said. "We got enough for us and ya'll, and I'm going to sell the rest. I think I can get $1.00 a pound shelled. Mrs. V told me she would buy them for her gift shop. Did you know Elzie's working for her at night?"

Mrs. V. was Venus Lowry who ran a gift shop in Sunset. She had moved back home from Fort Worth when her dad became ill and came up with the idea of a Souvenir shop, since their property lay on 287. She had made a mint in the past twenty years selling chalk made animals, curios and cold cider. Every morning and every night she would put out her display of chalk outside her front porch which, opened with shutters. The chalk animals were dogs, longhorn cattle, ducks and little Black boys smoking corn cob pipes and holding a fishing pole. To help school kids, she hired them to work for her.

"No," Jake said, "what's he doing for her?"

"He puts up her chalk display's, you know sets them on her porch for her. She pays him two dollars a week," Berthie May replied.

"He's still working at the truck stop too isn't he?" Jake asked.

"Yean I think so," Berthie May said. "But she thought he could use the extra money, so she offered him the job."

Jake thought, I see him every day at school and he doesn't tell me he's got an extra job. What's with him?

"Speaking of jobs, how's P.D. making out with the road construction?" Lige asked.

"I think all right, Grandpa," Jake said. "He's been running a bull dozier and said he sure likes running one. He's talking about buying one for the farm."

"Why Lord God," Berthie May said, "What do we need a bull dozier for?"

"Well you know Grandma, we got a lot of ditches we could shape up and build stock tanks on, clear out some timber, plant some more grass, be able to buy some more cows," Jake said.

"We've got enough old equipment around her to keep up without a bull dozier," she said

Jake didn't argue with her, he just sat down and spent an hour or so with his grandparents breaking apart the pecans they were shelling.

"Why don't you stay for supper?" Berthie May asked. "I got some vegetable soup and cornbread and I've got a peach cobbler made from peaches I put up last summer.

Then we can play thumps."

"Sounds good to me, besides mama's not home yet," Jake said.

"When Mary and P.D. gets home I'll call them to come eat too," she said.

Lately they hadn't had the family meals they used to have back when the Tatum's lived neighbors, Jake thought. His mama would come in stir up something and wait for P.D. to get in. If he was going to be late, then she and Jake would eat without him. It was so different these days.

Soon enough Mary came home and shortly thereafter P.D. drove up. Berthie May called them on the telephone and told them her plans. Since it was so cold, P.D. and Mary drove the fifty yards to their house.

"It's been pretty cold," P.D. said. "If we hadn't turned the blower fans around on the dozer's we would have froze, but those fans keep plenty of warm air blowing on you."

They all sat down to the meal, Berthie May wanting to know everything going on in town. "How's Ida Lou and Leck?" she said. "I haven't seen them in several months."

"Leck's liking his job real well," P.D. said. "He told me that having a paycheck every week was like money sent from heaven."

"Well Ida Lou's had that job all this time, he drawd a veteran's check every month. What does he mean?" Berthie May said.

"Well Mama,"P.D. tried to explain, "the veteran's check wasn't enough. You know they had five kids to raise, and they took care of Mr. Pariot. Ida Lou's check wasn't enough either."

"Well I can remember me and Lige not having fifteen cents for three months and we got by."

"But Mama, you didn't have monthly bills, like propane and electricity, and property taxes. You had food from the garden, you had a little supplies from the store and that was all. But it's different now. People have bills all the time and somebody's has to keep money coming in the till."

Berthie May only shook her head. The times were getting past her. Things changed so much in the past fifty years, it was hard to keep up.

In the middle of supper there was a knock at the door.

"Who can that be,?"Berthie May said as she scooted up from the table and went to answer the door.

When she opened the door she shouted, "Why Alf, you all come in!" Leading them back to the table she announced to all, it's Alf Fry and his family, Adilene and their son Lawrence.

"Well God dog!" Lige said as he stood from the table. "What in the world are ya'll doing out on an evening like this?"

Alf said, "Well, we was over at the place in Wise County feeding and on our way home we just thought we'd stop and see ya'll. We hadn't seen ya'll in a month."

"Well sit down and eat with us" Berthie May said. "We got plenty."

They began to protest but it was too late. Berthie May and Mary had their bowls and spoons on the table and were fixing their glasses of tea before they could say scat.

Alf and Adilene lived on their farm about five miles from the Oldham place. It was not on the loop but on the cemetery road leading to the loop. Alf's dad had bought the place back around 1890. When all the kids were grown, Alf bought the place from his dad. He and Adilene had married in 1920, they had one son, Lawrence. He was about ten years older than Jake, but they all were good friends. Jake liked Lawrence a lot but they seldom did things together.

After supper they got the thump board down and Lawrence and Jake played Lige and Alf.

Lawrence said, "I could play this all night. It sure is a fun game."

"I remember back in the thirties the four of us used to play dominos all night," Lige said. "We used to play on Saturday nights all night to pass the time. That was some fun times."

"Yeah," Adilene said, "and bring those boys, Clois and P.D. and they would play around the house and get so tired they would just sleep in the floor."

They must have played five games before Alf said they needed to get on home.

After the Fry's left, Berthie May said, how good it was to see them. Lawrence has just got home from the army.

"He's working in the stock yards and I'll bet he's looking for a wife," she said.

"You think so, Grandma?" Jake asked.

"I'll bet you he marries within a year," she said.

Lige looked up and said, "It's cold enough to kill our hogs. I spoke to P.D. about it this morning and he says we can get ready first thing next Saturday morning. Be nice if Elzie was here to help."

"Well, I'll have to go to town and see." Jake said.

"Wont be necessary, Berthie May said, P. D. can go fetch him on his way home."

That was what P.D. did. He went by the Tatum's and picked up Elzie on Friday evening. Elzie was expected to help because the Oldham's always killed one hog for the Tatum's. Even though the situation had changed with the Tatum's moving to town, P.D. was determined to make sure Leck's family had food for the table.

Elzie and P.D. came in the back door together. He was clad in his overalls, a big blue dungaree and a winter cap.

"You look like an Eskimo, cousin," Jake said.

Elzie just grinned that sly "I'm getting away with something" grin but didn't answer while he removed his wraps.

"If you want, Jake," Elzie said, "step outside and check the air. You might want one of these here caps warming your head. These flaps keep your ears kinda warm."

"Have you had any supper Elzie?" Berthie May asked.

" No, Mars Oldham," Elzie signed, "P.D. picked me up right as I was going in the house from work."

"Well, she said, sit right down at the table, I'll get your plate. We still got tea too."

"Thank ye kindly," Elzie said.

Everyone else had eaten before P.D. came home. Mary would have his supper. Once P.D. deposited Elzie, he went home leaving the boys there, saying he would see them first light.

After Elzie had eaten and they had played a round of thumps, Berthie May took down and extra quilt for Clois's room. Berthie May made quilts most winters, she had several from her mother and grandmother.

They boys would share Clois's room. It was cold without benefit of heat because Lige and Berthie May only heated the kitchen.

Jake said, "I'm sure glad you're here to help with the hog killing."

"Me too, even if it's colder than a witches tit!" Elzie said.

"How do you know a witches tit's cold?" Jake asked as the boys slid under the cover.

"Oh, God", Elzie said, this bed is cold, oh, oh."

Jake had to agree that the old bed was cold and would be until their body heat warmed the sheets. They would shiver for a few moments, then start to feel the warmth.

"You know what" Elzie said.

"No what," Jake replied.

"I always hate the cold nights when I have to get up to pee." Elzie replied.

"Well, just hold it until time to get up." Jake said.

"Yeah, well let's just see how long you hold it." Elzie said. "You can't get up without me hearing you, cause these old bed springs will wake me."

In the night at different times both boys had to get up, but neither heard the other one, the springs didn't wake them.

At the crack of dawn, Berthie May was stoking a new fire in the old cook stove, putting down a skillet of grease and flopping sausages in the hot pan. She pulled the sausages from a jar from sausages they had made last November. It was the last jar. The sausages were always cooked, usually in balls and put in a jar and covered in hog lard. Then the jar was turned upside down, the sausage floated in the melted grease on the bottom of the jar. When the lard cooled and hardened and the jar turned back right side up, the sausage was on the bottom and top was sealed off with the hardened lard.

She would have coffee boiling and rolling her famous biscuits out with her whiskey bottle that served as her rolling pin. She mixed hog lard, flour baking powders, a pinch of salt, and clabbered milk in the bowl. She would flour her hands then start working the dough until she could lay it on her dough board and start rolling and getting the texture she wanted. She had placed a twelve inch glass pie plate on the top of her stove and flopped some hog lard in it to melt. Once her dough was made out to her liking, she began to pinch out her biscuits. As she placed them in the pie plate she would lay the biscuit in the grease then pick it up and lay the dry side down in the grease. She did that until she had made all the biscuits. Over the years she had learned just how much mixture to make to fill the pie plate. Then, the prized bread was placed inside the oven to bake.

By this time the sausages were warmed and all the grease melted, she pulled the sausages out and placed them on a serving plate and put bacon in the skillet. Once the bacon was cooked it was time to cook the eggs and once they were done the biscuits would be ready to come out of the oven. She had boiled a pan of oats as Lige often ate a bowl of them during the winter months.

The smell of the food would fill the house even though the kitchen was shut off from the rest of the house. Lige, Jake and Elzie would be waking up and getting dressed in a hurry as the rooms was dreadfully cold.

The boys slipped on their overalls after they had put on long johns since they knew they would need them in the cold.

When they entered the kitchen, all the food was on the table. A serving plate of eggs, a serving plate of sausage and bacon, a pan full of biscuits, the pan of oats (still in the pan they were cooked in) and coffee for the adults. Lige and Berthie May still drank their coffee from a saucer pouring it from their cups. The boys had fresh chocolate milk, made Berthie May's way. The meal was always topped off with buttered biscuits and some of Berthie May's prized jellies, or sorghum.

When they had finished P.D. came in.

"Have you had breakfast?" Berthie May asked.

"Yes I did Mama," P.D. said. "I done been down and fed the cows, so we can get right on with the hogs."

"Well as soon as I finish milking, I'll be down too." Berthie May said. "Soon's I wash the breakfast dishes."

"Now mama," P.D. said, "Mary will fix our dinner cause she knows you'll be elbow deep in hog."

Berthie May didn't answer but was heating her water to wash the dishes. Even though she had hot water in the house, when she used her wood stove, she would heat water on the stove to wash the dishes.

Although it was cold outside, the wind had subsided and it would be more bearable to work in.

As Lige stepped outside, he said to no one in particular, "Perfect day for hog killing."

"Wish my old daddy was here, this was right up his alley."

"Yeah, P.D. said, "he really liked to kill hogs."

P.D. turned to Jake and Elzie and said, "You boys go start a fire and fill up mama's wash pot. We'll need to fill that old barrel to scald the hogs."

They would be killing three hogs, three hogs they had been fattening for months. P.D. had brought his dad's target and a few shells. He wouldn't need but three shells.

The hogs were pinned up and didn't pay attention to Lige or P.D. as they entered the pin. Lige poured out some slop, which was a mixture of table scarps and clabbered milk. In cold weather it took longer for the milk to clabber. The hogs went straight for the trough and P.D. put the rifle right on the head of one of the animals and pulled the trigger. The hammer fell down and there was a slight pop sound as the hog was brain shot. He never moved but went down on all fours.

The other two hogs paid no attention as they were about the morning feed. Lige and P.D. dragged the hog from the pin and hoisted the hog by his hind feet from a pulley they had rigged under the open section of their barn. Lige took the kitchen butcher knife and stuck the hog to bleed him.

Meanwhile Jake and Elzie were building a good fire and hauling pails of water from the cistern to the pot. It would take a few minutes to get the water to boil. Once it starting getting hot, the water was scooped out with a bucket and poured into the barrel. This would take over an hour. By that time all three hogs had been killed and bled out.

Lige and P.D. would lower each hog from the pulley and place in a wheel barrel and take the hog where Jake and Elzie had poured the hot water in the scalding barrel, as they called it. The wash pot was on the north side of the house but in front of the family smoke house that Lige's father had built. The smoke house was a log structure with one door and no windows. It had a low ceiling and fashioned hooks to hang meet on. Years ago, after Lige's father had died, he had built a room on to the smoke house on the east side. It was where the laundry was done. First before the May Tag, the old wash pot was the staple. However in 1945, they had purchased their first washing machine. The room was added to the smoke house to house the contraption and the three tubs that came with it.

Each hog had to be "rolled" in the hot water, then hoisted again for scraping. Although the water was boiling hot when poured in the barrel, it needed be only warm for scalding the hogs. If the water was too hot, the hair on the hog knotted up and scarping was very difficult. Usually Berthie May did the scraping. Once the hog was hoisted up and hanging by its hind legs, with its face pointing to the ground, she would commence to scrape the hair from the hogs hide. While she scraped, Lige or P.D. would be gutting the animal and saving the liver, placing the warm organ in a white metal ceramic looking wash pan that set on a small table where knives, pans and cup towels lay. The liver was the first fresh meat they always cooked after the hog killing.

The pulleys were brought from the barn. It too had been built by Lige's dad. It was a two story structure with the center section open from both ends. On one side, an open area for stacking hay, and two closed sheds for storing fed. On the south side of the barn were the corral and working pins. The hogs were raised in these pins, the corral used to keep up the milk cow's calves. Inside the corral the barn covered an open area where the milk stalls were which served to protect from wet weather.

In front of the smoke house, Lige and P.D. had built out of pipe a stout rack to hang the hogs where the hard part of working the hogs was done. The dogs would have to be fussed at to stay back as they would want to tackle the entrails. Usually, when the hog was gutted, the entrails were caught in an old lard bucket and taken a distance from the work area to keep the dogs out of their way.

After the scraping done, the hide was then separated from the body in order to trim out the fat. The fat was collected in buckets and placed in the wash pot. While P.D. and his parents were trimming and butchering, Jake and Elzie would be melting the hog fat and keeping the mixture from sticking on the bottom of the pot. When the crackling floated to the top, they had to scrape that off and place in a clean bucket. Crackling cornbread would be on the menu in the not too distant future.

Melting down the fat, scooping out the crackling and collecting the melted hog fat was called rendering the lard. Lard was collected in lard buckets. These were special buckets made in one, five and ten gallon size and store bought at Hunter's. Although they were used time and time again, it seemed they always needed a new bucket now and then. The lard would cool, harden and turn snow white. Women would make almost all their food dishes with the lard which served as a base for everything from pie crust, bread and for frying all foods.

A certain amount of the lard was used for making lye soap. There was nothing better to clean clothes than lye soap. Lye was cooked in that same pot with the lard. The stuff would cook up like cake icing and sometimes colored yellow or left it's natural white. When the mixture reached its desired texture it was poured off into either cast iron cake pans or wooden pans to cool. Once cooled, it was sliced into bars for use.

The meat of the hogs were cut into the cuts, shoulders, hams, bacon and loins. It was rolled in a brown sugar, salt red pepper mixture and completely covered the meat. It was hung in the smoke house to cure. Some people just let this cure and be the final act for their winter meat. However, Lige liked to take oak chips, placed in a smaller version of Berthie's wash pot and kept smoldering for two weeks while the sugar cure did its magic curing the meat. Generally, the curing took two weeks.

Berthie May would take the fresh cuts she wanted and grind the meat in a sausage grinder mixing in salt, sage, peppers until it was mixed to her satisfaction. The sausage was usually cooked and placed in the jars and covered with lard to seal them and used whenever they wanted. Since the family had recently purchased a deep freeze, Berthie May was going to make some tubes of sausage and freeze them to see how that compared to the canned style. Back in Berthie and Lige's early days, the hog entrails were washed and used to tube the sausage, then hung and properly smoked. They would work all day at their task, only breaking for a quick dinner, which Mary had prepared. It was quick and simple, sandwiches and tea or coffee whichever they desired. Then they would return and work until almost sundown to finish.

Berthie May wouldn't let Elzie go home until they had had a proper supper which would consist of cornbread, beans and fresh hog liver. The liver was slow cooked in a skillet covered with onions.

Jake got the privilege of taking Elzie home.

"Well, we'll have a standing of meat in a couple of weeks," Elzie said. "But right now, I don't want to see another hog."

Sunday afternoon, Bud and Elzie were driving up in Floyd Hunter's pick up as Jake was finishing with his feeding. It was still cold but above freezing. Bud honked as he saw Jake.

"What y'all doing?" Jake asked.

"We're going quail hunting," Bud said, "want to come along?"

"Sure, let me get my shotgun," Jake said.

Mary was working in the kitchen when Jake went in. "Is that Bud and Elzie?" She asked.

"Yes mama, they want to go quail hunting," Jake said.

"Well you tell them if they want me to cook up that mess of doves y'all got in the freezer to set a date and let's get them cooked. I want those birds out of my freezer," she said.

"Ok, I'll get them to set a date and we'll have that supper real soon," Jake said.

He grabbed his double barrel and a box of #8 shells and headed out.

"Where we going hunting?" Jake said.

"Oh, we're going all over the place," Bud said, "no place in particular, but everywhere the county road goes, we're going."

"I hope you don't intend on pot shooting any birds," Jake said.

"We're going to drive around and look and listen for them in the brush and then flush them," Bud said.

Since Bud was driving, Jake knew that he and Elzie would take turns riding in the middle. Whoever was in the middle had the least chance to get a shot.

"Elzie," Jake said, "you better leave your shotgun empty, or you might shoot Bud's fuel pump."

"Ha," Elzie said, "kiss my foot."

Usually when the boys went hunting like this, they started in Bud's familiar territory, which were the roads around his dad's farm. He would ride down the road, regardless of how cold it was with the window down. He would freeze out Jake and Elzie. Finally they would demand that he roll the window up for awhile so they could get warm. Bud claimed he could "hear" the quail rustling in the leaves, and that was why he had to keep the window down.

"Hey y'all," Jake said. "My mama said we got to plan our supper and get the dove eat. She wants them out of the freezer. She don't like seeing those dove breast."

Bud said, "I found a recipe, we need to get her to try on cooking the dove. She'll have to get a bottle of wine."

"A bottle of wine?" Jake said. "Where can she buy that?"

"Oh, you dummy, she can buy it at a liquor store in Tarrant County," Bud said.

"I don't think we ever had a drop of liquor in our house in all my life," Jake said.

"Well we not going to drink the wine," Bud said, "just cook the dove in it."

"Hmm, cook the dove in wine." Jake mused. "Reckon it's any good?"

"It's in the magazine, it has to be good," Elzie said.

"Well ok, you better get the magazine and show it to mama. Let's have the supper next Friday, ok?" Jake replied.

"Fine with me," Bud said.

"Fine with me," Elzie said.

"Bud, you tell Billy John and I'll tell Glen Ray," Jake said.

"Let's have tator tots with them," Elzie said.

"Oh, yeah!" Jake said. "I like tator tots."

The run out to Hunter's was a dry one, so Bud turned down toward Union Hill which would take them back through Lover's Lane and it wound them back to Hunter's gate, then they turned back to town. When they got back to Sunset, Bud headed west out on 114 toward Chico, but after he crossed the Big Sandy Creek, he turned north onto Turkey Creek Road. There they wound through the country for an hour shooting occasionally an armadillo, but not finding any quail. They had skirted Park Springs and were almost to Crafton when they spotted a bunch of black birds standing in the middle and on one side of the county road.

"What is that, a bunch of buzzards?" Jake asked.

"Looks like it," Bud said, "but I'm not sure."

When they came up to the flock, it was wild turkey.

"God almighty!" Bud said, "let me out of this truck." He grabbed Jake's double barrel and fired the first barrel. Two turkey's fell over flopping on the ground. The others began to run for hell and some rose to fly. Bud felled one of the birds in flight as it flew over the truck. It almost fell into the bed, but fell just past the back bumper. By then the birds had moved out of range. All three of the boys were excited, yelling and looking at each other. Jake and Elzie grabbed up the first two birds and Bud picked up the one by the truck and threw it in the bed.

As they got into the truck, Jake started babbling about the birds. "Do you reckon they were really wild turkey or somebody's tame birds that got out?" He said. "I never have seen any wild turkey."

"There bound to be wild," Bud said.

"Yeah, but we ain't got no license to hunt the things," Elzie said.

The boys were looking at each other starting to panic.

"We better take these birds home and get them picked and put in the freezer," Jake said.

They turned onto a paved road and Jake was lost.

"Where are we?"Jake asked. "I don't remember ever being on this road."

"It goes to Crafton," Bud said. "Crafton is just around this corner, we'll go up there and turn around and head for your house."

Jake had never been to Crafton before. He had heard about it but had never ventured off into Wise County and drive to it. He had no reason to. The only thing in Crafton was a few scattered homes and a couple of churches.

"This place is drying up worse than Sunset," Jake said.

"Amen to that," Elzie said.

In half an hour the boys were back at Jake's house. They took Berthie May's old wash pot and built a fire to heat water and scalded the birds. They picked feathers for what seemed to Jake, forever. They didn't try to save them as Berthie May always did when she killed a chicken. She used the feathers to make pillows.

Jake had watched his Grandma wash the family laundry in that old black pot many times before she got her Maytag, a ringer washer with three rinse tubs. She said it was heaven sent. Jake liked to watch her wash and put the blueing in the rinse water. Depending on how much was added, it turned the water a rich blue.

He watched his Grandma and his Granny Phane, Mary's mother, make lye soap in that same pot many times too. After hog killing and the lard was rendered, they would mix the lard with lye and make soap. When Jake was very young he thought the soap, as the mixture was poured out on square pans, was cake icing and wanted to eat it. Fortunately, his grandma's would let him.

Once the birds were picked, they took them to Berthie May.

"Lord God, what in the world?" She said. "Did ya'll shoot somebody's turkey's?"

"No, Grandma, nothing like that, these are wild." Jake replied.

"Wild, why we have never seen a wild turkey out here on Denton Creek," she said.

"We shot these on Big Sandy Creek," Jake said.

"Yeah, Mrs. Oldham, the state parks and wildlife department started a release program last year. They are trying to get turkey's started so they have been releasing them down in Wise county," Bud said.

"Well you boys didn't help the turkey population did you?" She asked.

"Will you help us clean these birds?" Jake ask.

"Yeah, I've cleaned turkey's before. We used to raise them from time to time," she said.

"You boys going to take your's home?" she asked.

"Yes, I guess so," Bud said.

"Well, ya'll give me about an hour and I'll bag them up for you," she said. "You bunch of bird slayers."

"Let's get out the thump game and we can play while we wait on the turkey's," Bud said.

"Ok," Jake said. "Come on Grandpa, you be my partner and we'll play thumps."

Lige had been sitting in the kitchen breaking apart some of the shelled pecans when the boys came in, but hadn't gotten a word in.

They got out the game and had a rousing time while Berthie May cleaned the birds and bagged them up.

"We sure thank you Mrs. Oldham," Bud said.

"Yeah, I do too" Elzie said. "I'm coming back out here to eat supper some time. I miss it. After killing the hogs yesterday, I realized how much I miss it."

"Well you come right on, you can spend the night with Jake and I know he always enjoys that. You come anytime too Bud. You boys stay out of trouble, you hear?"

"Yes ma'am," they said.

Bud and Elzie headed out for home content with a great hunting adventure, and a great time that they thought would never end.

CHAPTER 10

Every November, Mary would go to Fort Worth and bring her mother up to spend Thanksgiving and Christmas with her. Jake always looked forward to his Granny's visits. She was a charming witty lady. She was about the same age as Berthie May's mother. They were born of the same era and thought on the same lines. The difference however, between Jakes's two grandmother's was, Berthie May was always planning her business, planning on how to make the next dollar. Jake's Granny Phame spent her time dotting on her family. Her children were everything to her. She had been widowed when she was in her early fifties, and her children were young. She had raised them alone and after they were grown she was devoted to them and they to her.

Whenever she came up and spent Christmas, all Mary's brothers and sisters would come the day after Christmas and spend with them, because it was Granny Phame's birthday. It was one of Jake's favorite times.

Thanksgiving was a great affair at the Oldham house. Both Mary and Berthie May would make every dish under the sun for Thanksgiving and Christmas. It was not unusual for Mary to cook five or more pies. Not to be outdone, Berthie May would cook at least one more than Mary. They always had ham and a turkey. This year the turkey was compliments of Jake. The ham was one of their own from their own hog they killed and cured. The month that Jake's Granny spent with him was always a special time for him. Granny was full of stories of things of the past, of humor and jokes to play on Jake. She and Berthie May got along very well too. Berthie May always called her Mrs. Phame and she called Berthie May, Mrs. Oldham.

Christmas would be a special delight too. Cedar trees would be decorated with strings of popcorn and store bought ornaments. The house would be filled with all the smells of the various foods that were being prepared for the noon meal. There were always a few gifts under the tree, not many, because money was always tight. Jake managed to buy his Grandpa a box of Spark Plug chewing tobacco, his Grandma an electric mixer, his Granny Phame knitting supplies, his mother a cut of material for a new dress and his father and Uncle Clois, a pair of overalls. Christmas morning, the family would open their presents, have a light breakfast and play thumps or dominos. After the noon meal, they would worry about their farming chores. Jake would sometimes just take a walk down to Denton Creek enjoy the air, check for game tracks, and let the day flow at its own pace without worry.

Of course, Jake hadn't expected much from his folks for Christmas. He felt like they had given him a lot already. However, he was pleasantly surprised when Lige and Berthie May gave him a new felt Stetson. His Granny Phame gave him some cash money and his parents presented him with a new pair of boots. He hugged them all in deep appreciation.

The week after Christmas and before school started, Jake and Berthie May would go up to Hedley and spend two or three days with Berthie May's parents. Berthie May would always buy a pickup load of maze from one of her brothers. He would sell it cheaper than the feed store. Saving a nickel was part of Berthie May's life goal.

Jake always enjoyed going to see his great grandparents. In the Panhandle, the sand was deep, cotton and maze were the principle crops, most of the homes were built of stucco, which the residents said kept most of the blowing sand out of their homes. Berthie May always said she didn't like Hedley, she thought it was a tacky little town. Jake never asked her what she meant but he supposed she referred to the stucco homes and the sparse trees. It was completely different environment from the Cross Timbers of Montague County.

The drive took almost five hours. Jake hated the long trip but he and his grandma always had plenty to talk about as she drove the truck. Berthie May would always tell Jake about the failure of the cotton crops in Montague County. How her dad struck out headed up toward the Panhandle and made a deal with a land owner to farm a quarter section in cotton and maze. With ten hungry kids, a wife and his mother living together he had to do something, and four more kids were yet to be born. It was the fall of 1920 they loaded all they had in two covered wagons, with four mules and two milk cows and headed out for Hedley. They followed the Red River until they got to Esteline then turned due northwest until they came to Hedley, picking cotton for farmers on the way. It took them three months to reach Hedley. Berthie May said she cried for days when they left, leaving her all alone in Montague County. She said she would have went with them, but there she was married and had her first child, Clois, by then.

They would drive from town to town and Jake would ask, even though he almost knew by heart, how much further it was, and what towns lay ahead. Berthie May would tell him, well there's Chillicothe, Vernon, Quanah. Then she would tell how many miles it was between each town. She always said, it's twenty mile to so in so, she never said miles.

Recently the Sanders's had moved from their farm to the town of Hedley. Their house lay on a corner block. It was of a green stucco construction with an outbuilding separate from the house which served as the garage. The front of the house had a small porch and a single door entry.

They had not driven up and killed the motor before Granny came out of the house grinning her toothless grin, arms outstretched awaiting for them to get out of the pickup.

"Give me some jaw!" She yelled at Jake. He obliged by hugging her and turning his cheek to her face so she could kiss him.

"Glad you're here Berthie," she said.

"Where's Dad?" Berthie May said.

"Oh, he's gone to town to get me some milk. He'll be right back," Granny replied.

Before they entered the house, John Sanders drove up in his noisy Dodge truck. He pulled inside the drive and parked in the garage. Getting out he held a jug of milk. In his black fedora and kaki shirt and pants, he looked old as the hills. Yet he was not feeble, he walked with a straight walk. His jaw was full of Beechnut. Grinning a toothless grin, he raised his hand in a gesture indicating he was glad to see them. He went into the house by the back door, and they went in by the front.

Entering the house, was a long hall and on either side was a room. The room on the right served as a living room and the room on the left was a guest bedroom containing two beds. At the end of the hall was the dinning room and off the dinning room was John and Eva's bedroom which also contained the bathroom. Off the dinning room was a long room that served as the kitchen.

"Look here, Granny said, I won a brand new gas cook stove!"

"You won it mama?" Berthie May asked.

"I sure did. I won it at the radio station in Clarendon," she said.

"What did you do to win it?" Jake asked.

"I had to go up there, and I had to answer questions from the man that did a program. The contest was on who had the most kids. Well I won that hands down," Granny said laughing.

"I guess so, with fifteen," Berthie May said. "What a nice prize."

"I had to name all my kids and their birthdays but I did it," Granny said.

"Come on Berthie," Granny said, "lets get in here and stir up some dinner for us. You can try out my new stove."

Berthie May and her mama went into the kitchen to cook. They were in hog heaven working side by side stirring up some simple food which would taste like food for a king.

John sat down and spat out his tobacco into a Folger's coffee can. He then pulled a cigar out of his pocket and lit it.

"You want one?" John asked.

"No Grandpa, I don't. I'd take a chew if you don't care," Jake said.

John gave a chuckle and threw out his pouch chewing tobacco. "You better not let your grandma know I gave you that, she'll raise hell."

"Don't worry, I'll get it chewed out before they get dinner ready," Jake said.

A short time later Granny came into the dinning room with plates.

"Jake, go in there and get the silverware," she said.

While she was setting the plates on the table Jake spat the chew into his grandpa's coffee can. He wanted to rinse his mouth, so he made the excuse to go and wash his hands in order to rinse his mouth. He didn't want his Grandma to see him with a chew in his mouth.

Before they finished dinner, one of Berthie May's brother's came by. It was Finis. Berthie May had six brothers and all of them looked like their mother. They were big framed men, at least a head taller than Eva Jane, but all had the block shaped body of Eva Jane. All of them were white headed like their parents except Berthie May who still had dark hair with streaks of gray.

Jake thought his great Uncle Finis was probably the strongest of his Grandma's brothers. He was square built with a bull neck, short stout arms. He wore overalls and a big flat brimmed hat and chewed plug tobacco. His jaw was full.

"I thought ya'll were here," Finis said. "How are you Berthie? How are you Jake?"

"Oh, we're fine," Berthie May said. "How's Dob?" Dob was Finis's wife.

"Oh, she's doing all right," Finis said.

"Jake is this your senior year?" Finis said.

"Yes sir, it is," Jake said.

"Well are you going on to college?" Finis said.

"Oh, I don't know Uncle Finis," Jake said, "I sort of want to farm."

"Well, that will be all right. There's nothing wrong with farming," Finis said.

"It's like playing poker though," Finis said. "Everybody at the table can see your hand and know what your going to do, but you can't see their hand. You're playing against the market, the weather, the operating cost. They all got their hands hidden but your hand is played face up."

"Berthie, you want any maze?" Finis said.

"Well I sure do if you got any?" She replied.

"Oh yeah, I got maze," Finis said. "I got a barn full. Your welcome to all you want."

"How much you getting for it?" She said.

"Oh, I imagine," Finis said, "Two dollars a hundred."

"Well that will be fine," Berthie May said. "We'll take a half ton then."

"Ok, Berthie," Finis said. "They day you get ready to go back, just come out to the house and we will sack it up. Jake can hold the sack open while I shovel it in," Finis said.

That night all of Berthie May's brothers, their wives and their children came out to John and Eva's. Berthie May had only one sister who lived in Hedley, named Grace. She and her husband and five kids came over too. The house was full of people. Jake had seen them all many times but didn't really know them very well. Most of the family was sitting in the dinning room, except Jake and a few of his second cousins. They were all in the living room at the front of the house. Some of his cousin were rowdy and wanted to scuffle with him. He was shy with them but when two of them decided it would be fun to pull his britches off in front of some girl cousins, then he had to stand up for himself. It started in jest, but escalated to a bit of fist fighting. Jake finally got the upper hand when he caught his cousin Johnny across the chin and sent him to the floor. His brother Billy was a bit more scrappy than Johnny. He wanted to get into a real boxing match with no holds barred but before it got out of hand Uncle Finis came into the living room where they were.

"I thought something like this was going on. I'll whip hell out of you boys," he said. "Now Billy you and Johnny ought to know better than to pick on Jake here. Don't let me catch you doing that again," Finis said with a serious note in his voice. About that time Granny came into the room.

"What's happening Finis?" She said.

"Nothing mama, it's all right in here," he said.

Granny then turned and went back down to the kitchen. Some of the ones in the kitchen wanted to know what was going on, but she shook her head no to them.

Billy looked up at Finis and said, "Uncle Finis you don't tell me what to do, that's my daddy's job."

"Well, by God I'll go and get your daddy. You'll just see what he says," Finis replied.

"Hey ah, Homer, Homer come in here a minute," Finis called to his brother.

Homer was a bigger man than Finis. He was a jolly and good natured as any man ever lived.

"What's the matter Finis?" He said with a slow west Texas drawl.

"Your boy Billy here don't think he needs to mind. He kind of wants to back talk me and he said you had the hand, and nobody told him what to do but you."

"Now Billy," Homer said, "if my brother says frog you better ask him how high. He can whip you just as much as I can and I'll approve it too. Don't you ever smart off to one of my brother's!"

"Yes sir," Billy said, "completely humbled by the experience."

"What he do anyhow?" Homer said.

"Oh, him and Johnny were ganging up on 'ole Jake there. I just told them to quit and Billy boy didn't think he needed my advise."

"Yeah but daddy, Uncle Finis said he would whip the hell out of me." Billy said.

"If he whips at all he whips hell," Homer said. "Now you mind yourself. You don't be picking a fight with your cousin here. Jake you are Billy's cousin ain't you?" Homer said.

"Well yes sir," Jake said, "Billy's really my dad's cousin and Billy and I are second cousins."

"Oh yeah, I forgot about P.D. How is P.D.? Probably just working his ass off," Homer said.

"He works hard," Jake said. "I don't work as hard as he does but I'm not lazy."

"I'll bet you have to squat to pee," Billy said.

That was too much for Jake, he sent a right fist straight into the nose of Billy, sending him to backwards into the couch.

Blood was spurting from his nose as his hands went up to cover the pain.

"Here, here now," Finis said. "None of that. Billy you better go to the bathroom and wash your nose. Sorry Homer."

"Oh, that's all right Finis, that smart mouth got him in trouble. I'm sort of proud of Jake there. Johnny you better not be causing no trouble."

"No sir," Johnny said.

The two men walked back to the dinning room.

"Jake why don't you come sit in here with us?" Finis said.

The rest of the evening wore on as the family jested and laughed at stories of the past. It was a delightful evening with the adults. Jake was never sure about his cousins near his age. They seemed all right, but he was not sure how they thought of him. One thing was sure, both them and he adored their grandparents.

Too soon the trip to Hedley was drawing to a close. Berthie May decided to go get the Maze the morning they were leaving. Her dad went with her, leaving Jake with Eva Jane.

She was working in the kitchen on an early dinner so that Jake and Berthie May could start for Sunset.

"Granny," Jake said, "how did you and Grandpa get married?"

"Oh, well you see, me and your granddad decided to get married in the spring of 1889. We planned to marry and a neighbor of ours loaned us his mules and John and I rode over to the Tennessee line in Franklin County. We knew where a preacher lived and we rode up to him to get married. He was an older man but he had a brand new wife. She was a young woman and they had a brand new baby." She laughed and said, "I wouldn't thought that old man could have mustered up a baby!"

"Well he married us and we come back to Alabama and we stayed the night with John's sister and her husband. Then the next day he got a little place close to his parents and we sat up housekeeping. My dad didn't like it a bit. Oh Lord, he threatened to whip John. Why he went over to the neighbor's who loaned us the mules and whipped him. He took a rock and knocked that poor fellow in the head. My dad was kind of high strung," she said. "That's why they called him Blue John."

"Well you sure aren't," Jake replied.

"No, I took after my mama," she said proudly. "None of my brothers did, they was all like my daddy, pure mean. That don't mean I didn't love them, but they had mean streaks in them."

Berthie May and John came back with a half ton of maze loaded in the bed of the pickup. "That will make that old truck ride better going home Jake," she said.

They sat down to dinner and Finis and Dob came in.

"Ya'll sit down to dinner," Granny said.

"No, we just come to see Berthie May off," Finis said.

"But you can eat, we got plenty," Granny said. "You mind your old Ma, Granny said as she pulled on Finis's ear.

Shortly thereafter, Berthie May and Jake were loading up and getting ready to leave. Before they left all her brothers and sister came by. Homer came with Billy and Johnny. They came up and shook Jake's hand. "Hope you come back in August, Billy said, we can go fishing."

"That would be nice, Billy" Jake said. "I'm a pretty good hand at fishing." "Come down sometime with Granny and Grandpa and I'll take you fishing on the Denton Creek."

The cool air was blowing out of the north whipping their old truck all the way back to Sunset. To them the trip home always seemed shorter than the drive up. As much as he liked the visit, it would be good to see home.

CHAPTER 11

Before hunting season ended, the boys would try their hand at deer hunting. Of all things they hunted, squirrel, quail, dove, and ducks, they were the least successful at deer hunting. They would decide on where to hunt, which was usually on over the Jasper and Harry places, spend the night at Jake's, get up two hours before dawn, and march out like a bunch of well armed infantry to their deer stands. Deer stands to the boys meant a board to sit on atop a tree branch, or on a small hill overlooking an opening in the woods, or between two big oak trees leaning their back against the oak, and shiver until dawn. Almost never did they see any deer. Once they saw a buck rubbing his antlers against a tree. Bud saw the deer from his stand but thought Jake or Elzie had a better shot. However they did not see the deer. Finally Bud fired off two rounds from his 6MM Remington but missed. Apparently, the bullets hit a branch between him and the deer. After the second shot the deer ran off.

P.D. used to make fun of Bud and Jake on their deer hunts. He called them "Buck Fever and Deer Slayer." Throughout their entire years together they never killed a deer.

"Let's go get some breakfast and then go duck hunting," Bud said.

"Where at?" Jake asked.

"Well, there's plenty of ducks on the Jim Harry, but I sort of want to go see what's flying on Yonkie Pen Lake," Bud said.

So, they enjoyed breakfast at Berthie May's while enduring the chiding from P.D. and Lige about their questionable hunting skills, then headed out for the Yonkie Pen Lake.

Yonkie Pen was a natural made slew from the overflow of Brushy Creek. As it came down through the south east corner of Montague County headed for Big Sandy Creek, it made a sudden S curve and at that curve the water kept working into a slew before it moved on south to Big Sandy. The slew was covered in Willows making it a preferred sanctuary for migrating ducks. The willows covered all around the slew and right through the middle. If a hunter attempted to sneak up on the ducks they would fly up and just land on the other side of the willows. That was what happened on the day the boys were hunting, but after the boys settled in, the ducks came back over. It was there that the dead eye of Bud connected. Of the five friends, Bud was probably the best shot. Jake had made some pretty good shots from time to time. Once he shot a squirrel from fifty yards. The bullet grazed right across the top of the squirrel's head, enough to kill the animal. Another time they were camping out at Bud's folk's farm and was fishing in the late evening. Light was almost gone. Bud spotted a water moccasin swimming close to shore. He threw out a top water lure close enough to cause the snake to strike and become fouled in the hooks. Bud reeled the snake in and held it at the end of his rod fighting to get free. He told Jake to go to his car and get his shotgun. Jake fetched the 12 gage, walked up within twenty feet aimed and fired. The blast blew the snakes head to pieces, leaving the lure unscathed.

The felled duck landed out in the water. Jake was the only person wearing rubber boots.

"Hey Jake would you get my duck?" Bud asked.

Jake stood there for a moment, but decided to wade in to the cold water and get Bud's duck. However, he found the water much deeper than his knee boots. In fact when he reached the duck he was up to his chest.

"Oh, this is cold, cousin," Jake said.

He carried his shotgun with him and just after he reached the duck, a lone drake flew over not fifteen yards above Jake's head. He led the bird perfectly and fired bringing the duck down. He had to wade over to a willow but fortunately the water wasn't any deeper. He came out with the two ducks and the boys went back to Berthie May's. She was overjoyed at having the ducks. She told the boys she would make them a big pan of dressing.

It was two weeks later and Mary was cooking the dove as she had scheduled with the boys for the fourth time. When she took her mother home in Fort Worth she stopped and bought the particular brand of wine specified in the recipe. She cooked the dove basted in the wine and fried tator tots. Berthie May made the duck dressing, rolls and a chocolate pie.

All five boys were present for the meal which they ate alone. P.D. was gone to a Farm Bureau meeting and would be out until late. The supper time was past Lige's supper schedule. He ate his supper at 5:30 each evening not any later. They were eating at seven. Lige would be into some program, as he called it, something on the TV. He liked to watch Groucho Marx's show, *Say The Secret Word*.

After the supper, the boys rotated partners and played 42 until they were too tired to play. They spent the night making bedrolls in the living room. At bedtime they lay on the floor in the dark of the night each one reflecting on the past few hunting adventures.

"Man that was some duck hunt," Elzie said as he reflected on the Yonkie Pen adventure. "If I had been out there where Jake was, I could have shot three more, at least."

"How's that?" Jake said, "only one duck flew over."

"Well uh," Elzie said, "when you fired a whole flock flew up from the other side of the willows and they came right over where you were. If you hadn't had your head up your back side, you would have got off at least one more shot. You fired one barrel but you could have fired the other one."

"Elzie, you're a big liar. I saw that flock but they flew west. You couldn't have shot one if you had to," Jake said.

"Kiss my ass," Elzie whispered and chuckled.

"Boys," Billy John said, "I didn't fire a shot but there isn't anything better than this."

"That's right," Glen Ray said. "I don't have any better friends and there isn't anything better than us hunting, fishing and camping together. May it never end! You know when we're old men, we'll still be hunting and fishing together."

Jake wondered. He feared that their times were about to draw to a big close in their lives. A new chapter would be ahead and they wouldn't all be in it. In fact there would be five chapters and only one of them would be in each chapter. It saddened him when the moment should have been the happiest time of his life.

The next morning they all enjoyed a hearty breakfast of home made biscuits, eggs bacon, sausage and gravy.

"These are the best biscuits!" Elzie said.

"Well," Mary said, "don't go say a word to Berthie May, she couldn't stand it."

They all looked at each other and grinned but said nothing.

Afterward they went separate ways. Like Jake, Glen Ray had to feed his dad's cows. Bud and Billy John would be working for their dad's that day and Elzie? Well Elzie was going to enjoy the day off. He thought that the hunting and times together were what was to be forever. After a nap, he might go down and see what Angie Freeman was up to.

CHAPTER 12

The Christmas holiday was over and everyone was back in school. Jake always hated the time after Christmas. They would be back in school for two weeks before mid term final exams were held. No one was ever in the mood for the exams after the holiday. He wondered why they didn't have the exams before the holiday. The mid term finals had a schedule of their own. All English classes were at the same time, the math and so on. It also gave breaks between the test times which normally didn't happen. Jake had one test one morning ending at ten, his next class was at one in the afternoon. By coincidence Nell's schedule was the same.

He saw her coming out of her class as he was leaving his. Immediately he walked up to her. "Hey Nell, when's your next class?" Jake asked.

"Oh, I'm out until one," she said.

"Me too," Jake said. "You know we can leave the school ground, would you like to go riding around?"

"Yeah," she said. "Let go."

Jake was on fire. The moment of his life, the time to be with Nell all alone and without anyone tagging along, he hoped they could get to his truck and get out of the yard before one of his or her friends saw them. He opened the door on the driver's side and Nell got in and didn't move past the gear shift.

His luck held as they eased out of the school grounds and headed out toward Nell's folks farm. Jake had an idea where to go.

"What kind of test did you have?" Nell asked.

"Government," Jake said "and this evening we are having our Ag test. What about you?"

"Oh, this evening we are having Math. I'm not worried about it."

"Jake," she said, "are you planning on going to college in the fall?"

"I don't know yet, I can't decide. I know that I want to farm, I know that I like living out on Denton Creek. I like that life and I don't see any reason to do anything different."

"Do you miss Elzie, not being out there?" She asked.

"Yeah, he is like a brother to me and I miss him being there. We did so much together, but he's a town boy now." Jake said with a sarcastic tone.

They were in front of the Hunter farm, Nell looked over at the land. "You and Bud and Elzie spent a lot of time camping out at our place haven't you?"

"Yeah, sometimes Glen Ray and Billy John came too. It has been great times," he said.

Jake got to the corner and turned down the road he wanted to take Nell to. When he drove down the road a half mile, the road turns back to the south, the section called lovers lane. Jake pulled down the road and over to the side and killed the engine.

"They call this lovers lane, you know," Jake said.

"I know, Jake" she said, "I like the spot, but you I are hardly lovers."

"We could be," Jake said. "You know how much you mean to me, don't you? Nell I," but Jake couldn't quite get it out what he wanted to say. He was then looking into her eyes, they drew him close to her mouth. He could feel her warm breath. He saw she was going to close her eyes, so he pressed close and closed his as their lips met. He wanted the kiss to last forever.

When they parted, she looked into him, "Oh, Jake" she said. "Don't say anything else. I just don't know how I feel."

She then just laid her head on his shoulder.

"I don't know what I want in life when I get out of school. I've been right here in little old Sunset, and there is a great big world out there Jake. We need to see it, we need to feel it, or we'll be swallowed up in little old Sunset and we'll never know what was out there," Nell said.

"Do you think we need to know what's out there Nell?" Jake asked. "How many times you been to Fort Worth?"

"Why, do you ask that?" She said.

"Because I think that whatever you see in Fort Worth is nothing more than what is out there all around the world. I think that you can see the good, you can see the pretty, and you can sure see the ugly right down there and you see what it's like to live in a town squeezed together and all their rules and city laws, and you can know if that's for you. I guarantee you that when you finish school and you go off to someplace and get a job and all that. It will be nothing, you'll feel the same because your world wont be any bigger than it is in little old Sunset. You'll be a speck in that big place and all you'll know is what is inside your little circle. In little old Sunset, the circle is bigger because the space is bigger, and you know what's going on in your space."

Nell just looked at Jake like he was talking in a riddle, which he may have been. All he knew that what he wanted in his world, was for things to remain the same. He would have given his eye teeth to have Nell in that world. He wasn't too sure she would or could live in his world. All he could do right then was steel another sweet kiss from her before they went back to town and had a burger at Hulet's.

Soon spring would be in the air. Folks would be planting their gardens, farmers would be getting their crops ready to plant.

In April, Lige was getting ready to plow but he had wanted to change out his plow points. He had the breaking plow hiked up and resting on a big rock while he changed out the pieces.

Jake was helping his Grandpa when Berthie May came down to the barn. She had not been in a good mood, finding fault with whatever Lige did that day.

She saw them working and walked over and started in. "Lige" she said, "you ought to wait until P.D. gets home to help."

"I can change out these plow points, just fine," Lige said.

"Half the time you put the bolts in backwards, you don't do it right, you never have done things right, you just half ass things and then somebody has to do it over," Berthie May snorted.

Lige stood up when she said that. "Did you know Able Blane has a mule he bought down at Jacksboro last week? Able said that mule belonged to a fellow down in Jack County and that him and his wife had been married for forty years. All them years, his old wife had nagged him all the time. He never did one thing right. Well a couple of weeks ago she was making a fuss over something he hadn't done to suit her and after a half hour of listening to her, he got up and walked down to the barn and hooked up that mule, the very one Able bought, he hooked that mule up to the plow and started plowing the field. Well after he had made a round and come back to where he had started from, his old wife was standing there and she waded in on him just chewing him up and down one side and the other. All at once that old mule hauled off and kicked that old woman in the head and killed her dead! Well Gal, I'm thinking about going and trying to buy that old mule from Able."

Berthie May jerked her head backwards and snorted "Well!" She turned on her heels and marched back to the house slamming the porch screen door as she went back into the kitchen.

As she marched off, Lige spat a wad of tobacco juice behind her. He didn't say a word for a moment, then looked at Jake and shook his head and said, "By God."

"Grandpa, is Able Blane really got a mule that kicked somebody in the head?" Jake asked.

"I don't reckon, but it was a hell of a good story. Hell of a good story," Lige said laughing.

"You know Jake," Lige said. "There's enough pain in this old world without having to make some. Jake, I hate to tell you this, but the secret in life is to learn that that is women's purpose in the world, make pain. They look plenty sweet when they are young but as they age, they just become the biggest pain in the ass that you ever saw."

Jake and his Grandpa sat down on a log beside the tractor.

"Grandpa," Jake said, "do you think I can take over some of this land when I get out of school and farm for myself?"

"Oh, you probably can, Jake, but you ought to go to school and not be a farmer only." "When I was going to school there wasn't much to encourage you to go. I quit after the fifth grade. I just started farming with my dad, even though I never could farm like he thought we ought to farm, or do it the way he wanted things done. I tried not to do P.D. that way, I sort of showed him and let him try and make his mistakes and learn from that. He could handle a team better than I could, but he never could plow very straight. Clois could make a row straight as an arrow but the trouble was getting him to do anything was always a big hassle."

"This place will be yours someday, Jake but by then you might not want it. It won't be the same place. It wasn't the same place after my dad died, and when me and the Gal's gone, it wont be the same for you either. Life just doesn't stay the same you see, it's always changing and the changes are sometimes hard to take. Change is sometimes welcome, sometimes necessary, sometimes needed, but a lot of the times change is the last thing we want. It is the painful part of growing up. We don't even know it when we are growing up, we just find out toward the last of things. About the time we are wise enough to know what is going on, well, no one is willing to listen, and we are about spent by then."

P.D. walked up while they were sitting and said, "Hey, dad, mama said you needed help putting the plow points on the plow."

"Sure son," Lige said, "I am all thumbs today, so go ahead?"

"Sure dad," P.D. said, "I'll take care of it."

Lige winked at his grandson, and the two of them walked away from the barn and looked down on the bottom fields.

"When I was a boy, we plowed that with a team of mules. Sometimes the mules weren't agreeable to work and it made a long day. Everything we done with this field, we done it walking the ground behind a mules butt. Today we fret riding a tractor because we think that it's wearisome.

I guess I better go take my licking at the house, Lige said. We'll see if the Gal has cooked any dinner, by God."

CHAPTER 13

May came with final exams, graduation and the senior party. Not being able to understand the nature of girls, Jake failed to get a date with Nell. She agreed to go to the celebration with Glen Ray. That sort of got under Jake skin, but he didn't let it show. He asked Debbie Crocket who readily agreed to go with him. Some boys were afraid to ask Debbie out on account of her father. He had a reputation in town as being a bit strange and people who don't know or understand strange behavior are prone to avoid them. John Crocket was such a man. However, Jake had seen him many times in his own yard, had spoke to him on a few occasions. He wasn't sure what the man did for a living. He knew that Deb's mother worked at the slack factory like his and Elzie's did. Deb was glad for Jake to take her to the party, but he would have to ask her father.

It was like a lawyer's grilling but the man finally consented.

The night of the event which was held in the school gym, was clear and warm. Jake came in his Grandpa's old truck to pick up Debbie. Both Jake and Debbie were wearing their Sunday clothes.

When they arrived at the gym, many of their classmates were already there.

Before they went in, Debbie took Jakes arm and said, "I am sorry I'm not the date of your choice. I know you wanted to take Nell, but she had other ideas. I want you to have a good time tonight, but I'm sorry I'm not Nell."

"Debbie, you and I have grown up going to church together. Sure I like Nell, but she's not the only girl in school. I made a choice tonight of who I wanted to take to the senior night, and I wanted it to be you. Now let's just go in there and have a good time."

They got out of the truck, Jake hoping that his slight lie would make Debbie feel better. Debbie was a wonderful bright and beautiful girl. Jake's problem was his attention was turned elsewhere. He was going to do his best to show Debbie a good time.

Elize was coming in the door himself with none other than Nancy Shelton.

Hey, cousin, Jake said, that's not the same girl I saw you with last night.

"Aw, kiss my ass," Elzie whispered to Jake.

Inside the gym, which the junior class had spent the day decorating, there were some thirty class mates of the junior and senior class. The school superintendent and most of the high school teachers were the chaperons. Usually the parents stayed home and let their kids practice being adults. This was their night and the highlight of their entire high school time besides graduation.

Glen Ray was beaming like a bolt of lightening as he stood with Nell holding to his arm. Bud was there with a girl named Linda Wilson, a sophomore. Jake didn't know her too well. She was a pretty girl though. It was Bud's first date. Billy John was there without a date. Of Jakes circle of friends, Billy John was the true bachelor.

"Hey, y'all," Jake said, speaking to his entire group of friends.

"Tonight the big party, tomorrow night graduation, you got your speech ready Glen Ray?" Jake asked.

Glen Ray was graduating valedictorian, head of the class. A class mate by the name of Meridian Connell was second in the class and Jake had managed to come up third in the ranks.

"Yeah, I think I'm ready to make a speech. I've never made a speech before, but I'll try to do it," Glen Ray said as he put his hand on Nell's hand which was on his arm.

"You'll do fine, Glen Ray," Jake said, "you are never at a loss for words."

The school had a group from Decatur come up and play music for the kids. The music was a mixture of Bob Wills and Hank Williams. It was perfect ball room dancing music. Even though most of the kid's churches frowned on dancing, and none of them professed to know how to dance, somehow they managed to two step and waltz like they had done it all their lives. About a week before the event, a few teachers had coached the kids on how to dance.

Jake was a bit nervous about it at first, because he had never danced and neither had Debbie, but she was willing, very light, agile, and could stay with the time of the music. As they danced, Jake held her close to him, he could smell her hair. He wanted to kiss her ear, but he dared not. He didn't want his friends see him do something so crass and anything that was seem inappropriate.

Later here came Elzie asking Debbie if they could dance. Good old Elzie broke the ice that got people to dancing with others besides their dates.

Jake got to dance with Angie Freeman. He couldn't help thinking about the pastor's couch and she and Elzie making quick love on it.

"Angie, are you and Elzie still dating?" Jake asked.

"We never have dated," she said. "I see him at church whenever I go. We ate at Hulet's together a few times. But, we have never gone out. Why do you ask?" She said.

"Oh, nothing just that Elzie said you were the cutest girl in Sunset," Jake said.

"Did he really? Honest?" She said.

"Honest," he said. "Elzie and I are like this, and Jake held up two crossed fingers. He tells me everything. You know like the church picnic, the pastor's study."

Jake let that slip out, he couldn't help himself. He was so curious about it.

"Oh, God," she said, "you don't know about the pastor's study?"

"No, I've never been to the pastor's study," Jake said. "Man that was a good dance, and you dance perfectly Angie. Keep old Elzie in your sights. After while they have a Sadie Hawkins dance, you can asked him to dance. Then he'll know you like him."

"Thanks Jake," Angie said.

As Jake danced with different girls, he asked them all to dance with Billy John, because he knew Billy John was too shy to ask. Before long he was dancing on the floor and into the music. A broad grin was across his big round face, Jake knew he was having a good time.

Jake would dance with most of the girls in his class and would wind back up with Debbie. They would dance two more dances together before the Sadie Hawkins dance.

"Debbie," Jake said, "you can ask any guy here you want to dance with when they announce the Sadie Hawkins dance."

"Oh Jake," she said, "I don't know, I thought I'd just ask you."

"No no, Debbie," Jake said, "I think the rules are you can't ask your date. You have to ask someone else."

"Ok," she said. "But you're my first choice."

"Mine too," Jake said, "but rules are rules."

Sure enough the band leader announced the Sadie Hawkins dance and that the rules were the girls had to ask someone other than their date. The dance was a waltz.

Jake had started for the punch bowl because he didn't feel like any girl would be asking him to dance. When he had gone around the room, he had a couple of girls to turn him down, so he didn't expect to be asked. It was amusing to Jake when he saw Debbie go up and ask Glen Ray for the special dance. Of course he obliged.

"May I have this dance?" A familiar voice said.

"Jake turned to face Nell. Do you really want to dance with me?" He asked.

"You wouldn't go to the party as my date?"

"Yes, Jake you're my choice for the dance." She said. "Glen Ray asked me to go to this two weeks before you got around to it. I couldn't go with you because Glen Ray already asked."

Jake did not remind her that he had asked her months ago. He just let that slide.

Jake found when he had learned to dance that he liked to waltz.

He liked the feel of the dance the movement of the feet, the sudden time to whirl around the room. As he took Nell around the room, it seemed to him the crowd moved out of the way and cleared the floor. Like everything else he did with her, the dance would end too soon.

"Is it alright if I ask you to dance one with me?" Jake asked. He had not asked her to dance at all.

"Yes, of course," she said.

Later that evening, Jake walked outside while Debbie was powdering her nose. The gym was getting warm and he wanted some air.

He was looking at nothing but looking out away from the gym when he felt a hand on his back and then slip up to his arm.

"What are you doing out here?" Nell asked.

"Just getting some air. It's getting warm inside." He said. "Have you had a good time?"

"Oh, yes, it's been nice. I get to go again next year and the year after. I'm someone's date tonight, next year I'll be the junior class that host the event, and then the next year I'll be the honoree," she said.

"Some people have all the luck." Jake said.

There was nothing more to say, but Jake didn't want to go back inside but he knew he had to go back inside. He turned to go back but he was brought up face to face with Nell.

God, he thought, why is she so beautiful? He pulled her close to him and kissed her in the longest kiss he had ever had. "Nell, Jake breathed, Nell, I, I love you. I want to spend my life with you."

"Don't Jake, don't say it. I can't make that commitment right now," she said.

They drew back from each other and Jake said, "We had better get inside."

Jake let Nell walk ahead of him and waited for a few more minutes before going inside. He thought he had just risk his entire life and had seen himself go down in flames. He must be a big fool, he thought. The biggest fool in Sunset. He wondered if the kids inside would be lined up waiting for him to come in and they all applaud him as the dunce of the town. Oh, they would laugh they would all laugh.

Debbie met Nell at the door and said, "Nell have you seen Jake?"

"Oh, I think he was standing out by his truck," Nell said. "He was probably just getting some air."

Debbie walked out to toward the truck. She was feeling a little hurt when she saw Jake. She couldn't help thinking that the two of them were out there together.

"Hey, Deb, I just went out to get some air. The gym was getting warm to me. You want some punch?" Jake asked.

"I had some Jake," Debbie said. "I think I would like to go home."

"Go home?" Jake asked. "Its still pretty early, don't you want to hang out with all your friends, and classmates? You know my bunch graduates tomorrow and this is the last senior celebration for my class. This group won't ever be together like this again."

"I thought I was your date," Debbie said. "I thought I might have meant something to you. There's not another boy in this school I would even consider going out with but you, and you don't even care."

"That's not fair Debbie," Jake said. "It's not like that. You and I have always been good friends, but we never talked about being more than that. I took you here tonight because you are my friend. You're going to be here two more years and your going to go to two more of these party's and your own graduation. Your whole life is before you and you can do just about anything you want to do. You're not limited, you can have any boy you want too."

"You're just saying that," she said.

"No I'm not," Jake said. "I can prove it too. Come on, let's go inside."

She obeyed him, walked by his side, with Jake holding her hand. When they entered the gym, the lights were on as the band was taking a break.

Jake didn't find the crowd waiting to line up and laugh at him either.

"Hey everyone," Jake said. "Listen. Tonight has been a special night for us seniors. You juniors have made us all feel special. I want to say thank you, thank all of you. We probably haven't shown it, but we are grateful for the dedication of our teachers who've tried to make us learn. Thank you."

"I want all of you to give my date a hand tonight. I think she has been the bell of the ball. Don't y'all?"

Jakes question evoked the response he needed for Debbie. To give her that moment in her life she needed the encouragement to feel special. Elzie started the applause, and all of Jake's friends followed suit. Debbie seemed to glow.

The lights dimmed and the band geared up for the final round of music. They would play Faded Love and Maiden's Prayer, My Confession and several others until the final call for the last dance. Jake did not change partners once during the final session but danced every dance with Debbie. He wanted more than anything in his life to have held Nell the way he was holding Debbie, but couldn't and he wouldn't hurt Debbie for all the tea in China.

The night was over and the kids were filing out of the gym, some excited, some were laughing, others just savoring the moment, dates holding hands as they walked to their automobiles. Jake and Elzie were walking four wide with Nancy and Debbie, Glen Ray and Nell were following behind and behind them was Bud with Linda. Instead of going to their own trucks, they all came to Jake's.

"It was a good night wasn't it?" Jake asked.

"Sure was. You made us all feel good. The band was sure good. You can't beat country music," Elzie said.

"I'm glad we can all sleep late," Glen Ray said.

"Yeah, I don't have to help at the store tomorrow," Bud said.

"Will we want to get together tomorrow night after the ceremony?" Glen Ray asked. "Let's have some kind of party somewhere."

"I can sweep out the barn loft," Jake said. "We can ice down some cokes and we can fix sandwiches, and we can play all the music we want. Glen Ray got a new portable stereo and all of us can bring our record collections."

"Yeah, let's do that," Elzie said.

"Ok, so after graduation, we all go out to Jake's and we have a party in the loft," Bud said.

"I'll come out tomorrow and help get the barn ready," Bud said.

"I'll come too," said Elzie, "How about you Billy John?"

"Sure," he said. "I've got all of Earnest Tubbs records."

The group then broke up, Jake wondering just who would show up at the barn tomorrow night.

He and Debbie drove to her house which wasn't five minutes from the gym. Their house was a fancy old Victorian style home that had been built before 1900. It had a big front porch, three feet off the ground.

"I had a good time," Debbie said. "Jake I just want you to know just how special you made me feel tonight. I'll never forget this night."

"It was special for me too Deb," Jake said. "Everything was special. Are you going to come out to our place tomorrow night?"

"I don't know no, Jake, I'm not sure my father would let me. I'm sure it would be fun. I'm going to call Nell and Nancy and see what they are going to do, because I don't want to be the only girl there."

"It wouldn't hurt to be the bell of the ball," Jake said, "But, well, we'll work all that out tomorrow."

Then Jake kissed Debbie. He was sure he was her first kiss because she was tense and not sure of herself. They got out of the truck and Jake walked her to the front door.

Good night Debbie, I'll see you at graduation.

Good night Jake, she said. Then he took her one more time into his arms and kissed her with all the passion he could muster.

Saturday was a full day. Jake and his dad had to take care of all the regular farm chores that know no special days, nor holidays, nor even Sunday's. About ten that morning Elzie, Glen Ray, Bud, and Billy John were all at the Oldham's house. Jake had told his father what they wanted to do and he gave his permission. Besides P.D. thought, he would get the loft cleaned out in the process. The barn loft was big enough to drive the tractor in, if the tractor could have been winched up to the upper loft. It took the boys only a couple of hours to sweep out all the loose hay, and make the area presentable. They hung lanterns for extra light. P.D. had wired the barn for electricity, there were two plugs in the loft. It was perfect for playing the stereo.

"Well I wonder if any of those girls will come out?" Jake said.

"Sure they will," Bud said. "Nell is coming and she's got Debbie and Nancy lined up and Elzie asked Angie Freeman to come."

Glen Ray said, "I called all the girls in our class and they are coming out and Corky Miller, Ronnie Love, George Hubberston, Luke Brewer, Tan Wanning and his sister Annie, they are all coming. It's probably our last night together," Glen Ray said.

The day wore on and the night of the Sunset Graduating class of 1955 commenced. The gym was full of admiring parents and grandparents. The senior class marched into the gym single file and took their seats on the stage. Superintendent Armstrong opened the service with a welcome and extolling the virtues of each student. The special guest speaker was the Mayor of Bowie, Franklin Underwood. Mayor Underwood encouraged the young adults to go far in their lives and never take a second seat. Then it was time for the head of the class to address the audience, followed by the salutary address. Both were nervous but they got through it. Then they passed out the diploma's, followed by the class filing down off the stage and standing at the front of the gym, and dismissal. Parents and family came forward to congratulate their own, but would shake hands with all the class.

Jake's parents, grandparents including Granny Phame, and Berthie May's parents were all present. In fact Berthie May's brother Finis and his wife Dob had brought them. Granny Sanders yelled out to Jake, "Give me some jaw!" He hugged her as he had all his life remembering when he was little, hugging that little round woman and now he stood a head taller than her. but still hugging and allowing her to kiss his cheek. Gradually the gym emptied out and folks were headed home.

Bud said, "I'm bringing five girls with me out to your place," Jake.

Most of the class was going out to the Oldham farm. When they left it looked like a funeral procession.

Arriving at the farm they parked their cars near the barn. Everyone was eager to get to the loft, start the music and have a coke. Mary had called Francis and Lenetta and Ida Lou. They had fixed sandwiches for the group. Chips, sandwiches and iced down cokes with the stereo playing one LP after another of their favorite music. Some of the kids danced while others sat on hay bales and enjoyed the moment.

Jake was torn as to how to deal with the situation with two girls he liked in the same room visible at all times. He wanted to spend it all with Nell but she had plenty of company. Every boy except Bud was trying to vie for time with her. Jake decided he would just let them enjoy the night with everyone and not try to cater to any girl. He would talk with all of them, but he decided the safest route was to sit down and drink a Dr. Pepper with Elzie.

"Hey this is all right," Elzie said. "I may not get any from Angie tonight but were getting tight."

"Oh yeah," Jake said. "Well keep in mind we don't have a pastor's study out here. And you're not using my mama's couch."

"Oh, kiss my ass, Jake," Elzie said. They both laughed.

"You know," Elzie said, "tonight was yours and Glen Ray and all the senior's shinning moment. But come Monday you're all history. You will be the people that used to go to school, and chug by in your old pickups and go down to Hulet's an eat burgers and now you all are the grown ups. You have to start acting like the grownups."

"Oh Elzie," Jake said, "Why don't you kiss my ass?"

Soon the party was over and people were going home. Elzie had rode out with Billy John but decided to spend the night.

The second story of P.D. house had two bedrooms one for Jake and one for company. Jake always considered the second bedroom Elzie's.

Jake and Elzie were upstairs getting ready to go to bed.

"Elzie," Jake said. "What you said awhile ago, that was the real truth. When you finish school, everybody expects you to be grown up and act like a grown up. I don't think I'm ready. I still want to be a kid. I still want to count the minutes until I'm fishing or hunting birds or something. It's coming too fast."

"Yeah, I know," Elzie said, "I know it too well. When we moved to town and I started working at the truck stop, it came home hard. I can't just go fishing or hunting or nothing without planning it. I have to work around my work."

"That's the way it will be for the rest of our lives too," Jake said.

"What a terrible thought," Elzie replied.

CHAPTER 14

J ake registered, as required by law, for the draft. Somehow he drew
a high number and wasn't called for a physical for almost a year.
He was able to make the second crop and bank note payment before
the letter came. He had to report to the bus station in Bowie and
there he would be taken to Dallas for the army physical. It was the
first time in his life he had ever gone anywhere without one of his
parents or grandparents. He thought the people rude and the treatment
disrespectful. No one cared who he was, who his family was, nor where
he came from. Jake did not particularly like the experience.

He passed the physical and was called for duty about a month later.
He was bused off to Fort Pope Louisiana, and from there he went to
Germany and finally in South Korea. He was discharged in the fall of
1958. Coming home was a great reunion and joyful time. He never
wanted to leave again.

Glen Ray won a basketball scholarship at North Texas State
University and got a student deferment. After graduating with a degree
in business, Glen Ray went to law school and became a corporate
lawyer in Dallas. He married a girl he met in college but never had
any children. Fifteen years later, his wife would leave him for another
man and Glen Ray would never remarry. He spent many years devoted
to his practice.

The year Billy John, Elzie and Bud all graduated from Sunset and would be the last class. The next year the town folk did consolidate the school with Bowie. Bud and Elzie were both drafted, but Billy John did not pass his physical.

After returning from the Army, Jake devoted himself to the family farming. He paid off the Tatum place ahead of schedule. However, farming became very difficult the second year. Drought had reduced pastures to little or no grass. They sold most of their cows and relied on their hogs for long term cash. They didn't make a peanut crop nor watermelons that year either. They lost the crop to dry weather. The one thing that saved them was P.D.'s road construction job. From that job he bought a dozier and fixed the erosion problems on their farms, afterward he had started hiring out doing custom work. He taught Jake how to operate the dozier. So, the two of them worked together in farm activity and doing custom dozier work for the public.

Billy John worked for his dad's trucking business and bought a station in Sunset. He started providing a flat fixing service at the station and oil changes. The business grew and he added a tire shop. Later he would buy his dad's business and became very successful for a number of years. Billy John never married.

When Bud came home from the service, he ran the store with his parents until they retired. He married the girl from Bowie that worked in at Legion's drug store and they made their home out on the Hunter farm near Sunset. He and his wife would have three children.

Elzie came home from the service and went to work in the Bridgemon Brick Yard in Bridgeport Texas. He started as a yardman and worked his way up to plant superintendent. He finally married Angie Freeman and they had four children.

Debbie Crocket won a music scholarship to North Texas College, graduated with a degree in music and became a public school teacher. Later she married a man who was a physician and became a minister and they worked for many years in the missionary fields. They had two children.

Nancy Shelton would marry a local Bowie lad, whose father owned a carpet shop. Nancy worked for her father in law and her husband

Brad Pitcher eventually bought out his father. They had one son who also grew up in the family business.

Nell would marry a local Bowie boy named Doug Cunningham. She married him shortly after she graduated from Bowie High School. However, she found Doug abusive and one night after he had struck her, she got in her car and drove out to Jake's. Jake remodeled the Tatum house and was living there. He was inside going over his feed bills when he heard the car drive up.

"Who can that be?" He thought.

He went to the door, and was surprised at seeing Nell.

"Nell, come in, what happened to you. He could see the bruised eye and another on her chin.

"Oh, Jake," she said, "I probably shouldn't be here, but I didn't know what else to do. I just couldn't tell my parents."

"What has happened?" Jake asked.

"It's Doug" she said. "He got angry tonight and he hit me a couple of times."

"Has he ever done this before?" Jake asked.

"Yes, she said, he has. I'm afraid of him. I've got to get out of the whole thing."

"Well, tomorrow, I'll help you find a lawyer." Jake said.

They spent the biggest part of the night, talking and soul searching. Jake felt that feeling he had always felt for her. Why couldn't she feel the same for him? He wondered.

Jake showed Nell to his guest room sometime late in the night. He had a hard time going to sleep for what was left of the night, knowing he had work to do the next day. Well if need be the work could wait.

Next day, he called his dad to tell him the situation and that he needed to help her in what way he could.

P.D. warned him that he better be very careful. But, he understood the need.

Jake took Nell to Decatur to a lawyer's office. He had done dozier work for the man and he was a divorce attorney. The lawyer advised Nell on what to do and she made the decision to file for divorce. The attorney would take care of the paper work, after she paid his fee. Nell didn't have any money, so Jake paid it for her.

Two days later, a car drove up in Jake's yard. It was Doug Cunningham. When he got out of his car, Jake met him outside.

"Hey you sonofabitch." Doug, said, "You got my wife out here?"

"Yes, she's here and she's staying here as long as she wants, and your not." Jake said.

"Yeah?" Doug said, "I'll teach you a thing or two."

However that was enough for Jake. A right jab to the face and a left hook sent Doug to the ground.

"Now you get up and you get the hell out of here," Jake said. "If you ever come near Nell again, if you ever lay a hand on her, you will answer to me."

Cunningham got up on his feet, blood pouring out of his busted lips. He was breathing hard.

"I'll kill you Oldham," Cunningham said.

He started to get into his car but he made a suspicious move that alerted Jake. Cunningham was reaching for a pistol that lay in his car seat.

Jake hit Cunningham in the jaw that sent him sideways in the seat. He then reached inside and retrieved the gun. He emptied the shells and threw it back into the car.

"Now, I said get out, Cunningham and don't ever come back out here."

Cunningham shut the door and started the ignition. He backed out and drove off spewing gravel and dust.

Nell was then standing on the porch. She ran to Jake and held him tightly.

"Oh, Jake," she said, "I was so scared."

"Ah," Jake said, he's all wind. " Nothin to worry about."

That night after they had gone to their separate rooms, Jake heard Nell walking in the house. He figured she was going to the kitchen for a drink of water, but to his surprise she came into his room.

She didn't speak, but she let her gown fall from her and she slid into his bed. She began to kiss him passionately. Jake surrendered to her wants willingly. It was the best night of his life.

That morning, Jake had to tend to neglected chores. He had cattle to check, he had some dozier time to put in. He quietly dressed and left Nell sleeping in his bed.

He thought about the night and thought about the future. He couldn't wait for her divorce to be final.

Around eleven Jake came back to his house finding Nell's car gone. Inside, he found a note from Nell which read: Jake

> I can't thank you enough for what you have always been to me, all these years. You have been and will always be my Knight in shinning armor. Last night was something we both needed and wanted and I will never forget it. But, I must make changes in my life. I must get away from this town, this county and start a new life. I must find myself. I'm sorry if this hurts you and it does hurt me, but I have to do this. Forgive me. I will always hold a special place for you in my heart,
>
> Love,
> Nell

Jake was stunned. He could have been knocked over with a feather. How could someone have so much passion and walk away from what was going to be given? He would never understand it but he sure knew what his grandfather meant when he had said, that women seem to just hurt men.

It was a full year before Jake heard from Nell. She had gotten her divorce easily from Doug. She had gone to school, was working on a degree in nursing and was working in a hospital near Dallas. She was dating a doctor. Later she would marry the doctor and they would move to Vicksburg Mississippi.

Thirty Five years later, Jake operates his farm business. He sees Bud and Billy John anytime he goes to Sunset. Sunset lost its school;

its stores, the bank closed, and all the stations after U.S. 287 moved and skirted the town. All the fruit stands and curio shops closed and the town's population declined. Jake's grandparents were all gone, his mother, Mary had died and P.D. now retired helped Jake as best he could.

Jake saw Elzie occasionally because Elzie came every Sunday to church in Sunset. Sometimes Elzie would drive out to the farm and the two would walk out across the pasture and go down to Denton Creek and fish for hours. They didn't even care if they caught a thing.

Jake was now a grandfather. He had met a young lady named Lois Belew working at an insurance office in Wichita Falls. Jake had gone there to meet the manager who had hired Jake to do some dozier work on his farm. Lois was a very attractive girl with deep set blue eyes, long brown hair and when she smiled she had dimples. He was struck. He made excuses to call the office pretending to look for the manager, when he knew the manager wasn't there. He finally got the courage to ask her out and after six months of courtship, they married. They would raise two sons who would bless their house with three lively grandchildren who loved to go down to Denton Creek and fish with their Grandpa.

Jake never left his beloved farm, but he had to endure changes over the periods of time. Sometimes the changes saddened him and sometimes he fiercely resisted them. Most of all, from time to time he had to fight an urge to wonder how things were in Vicksburg Mississippi.

BOOK 2

CHAPTER 1

J ake sat in the chair that he was told to sit in as his two sons and
daughters in law lined up beside him and took their respective seats.
With a signal from the funeral director, the preacher Dave Preston
began, "My friends we are here for the final part of this service, this
memorial to our beloved sister Lois Oldham…"

At that point Jake's mind took over as he pondered the events of
the day and was thinking of how he and Lois had first met nearly forty
years prior.

Jake was operating a dozer as well as operating his farm when Earl
Cleveland, a lawyer from Wichita Falls had purchased a place near
Forestburg and was needing dozer work. Jake's name had been given
to him and Cleveland had hired him and as Jake had finished some of
the work, he drove up to Wichita Falls to hand Mr. Cleveland his bill.
Lois Belew was Cleveland's secretary. She was bright, she was friendly,
had a great smile, beautiful hair and eyes and Jake was glad he had
chanced to meet her. He kept making excuses to go up to Cleveland's
office and one time had an appointment with Cleveland but went early
to ask Lois if he could take her to lunch. She accepted and he got her
number and later would call her for another date, which would be a
real date, not just a lunch, but a night meeting where they went to
supper and took in a movie and spent time talking and getting to know

one another. Lois had ambitions. She was finishing her junior year in college, getting a general business degree with a minor in accounting.

When she and Jake talked she asked him if he had gone to college. "No, I went in the army and when I came home, I went right back to what I knew, farming." He had told her. And so it went, they dated like that for some six months and one evening Jake just asked her to marry him and before she could think, she was kissing him and telling him yes, she would marry him. But she wanted to finish school and he understood that meant one more semester and one course in the first part of the summer. So, they planned a wedding for September when she was finished with school and had given thought to what she would do once they married and settled in to the rural life, something she knew nothing about.

Jake remembered the first time he brought her home to meet his folks, his parents and grandparents. He had driven on Sunday morning to pick her up and get back in time to go to church and meet up with his parents, only that day his grandparents came to church too. They got there as the first song was being sung and there wasn't the chance to properly introduce her until after the service. His Grandpa nudged him in the side saying "Boy she's really pretty." Jake turned a little red but was beaming with pride at his Grandpa's compliment.

His Grandma had prepared a lunch for all and it was a full table. They had all been unusually quiet as they ate unlike the usual chatter at the table, but they were all eying Lois and wondering if she liked the food that was prepared. Of course she liked the food they had prepared. She had never had such home cooking but had grown up in a house where everything they ate came from a store, from the butcher's section and the canned section. These people were eating food they had grown.

"This is really delicious," Lois had said to no one in particular.

Bertha May glowed from the compliment, saying, "Why hon it is nothing, just some things I threw together."

"We don't have a garden," Lois said, "we never have."

"I'll bet not," Bertha May replied.

The afternoon they spent mostly outside Jake showing her their farm, the livestock, the garden, the orchard, and then walked down to his sacred place the creek.

"My best friend Elzie and I spent a lot of time down here, either fishing or swimming." Jake said. "It is my favorite place on this farm."

"It's nice," Lois said, "you know we have a park at Wichita, where a little creek flows through and people like to walk the banks of it."

"I bet so," Jake said, "And I bet there has been plenty of young men wanting to stroll you around that creek in the park."

Lois wasn't sure how to take that. Yes she had had her share of boyfriends and suitors, but it certainly wasn't because she was a girl of a bad reputation.

Finally, after thinking on what Jake said, she countered, "I bet you've had few girls out here at your creek and your own park."

Jake almost blushed thinking about the incident many years back when Elzie's niece had caught him skinny dipping in that very creek, but said, "Uh, no not so much, a time or two but mostly Elzie and me and few more of our pals hung around out here."

Lois only smiled, she suspected something else had gone on but knew Jake would never admit it. He was trying too hard to make an impression.

"Have you always lived out here?" Lois asked.

"Yup," Jake said, "all my life, and I plan on staying right here."

"Seems like you like being way out, away from it all," she mused, "Just how often do you make it into town?"

Jake was catching the sarcasm in her voice, feeling like she was poking a little fun at him at his expense.

"Why," he finally said, "We gets to town about once every six months, likely."

"You're being silly," she said.

They slowly walked back toward the house, Jake taking initiative to hold her hand. He felt a thrill at that, like he had when he had been with Nell.

The evening wore on, back to church before taking her back to Wichita Falls. They didn't say much driving back but as they got near Lois's home, she expressed how much she enjoyed the day and meeting his folks. She could see the relationship blooming into something serious. As Jake walked her to the front door, they stepped in and had a light conversation with her parents before stepping back out on the front porch and Jake for the first time built his courage and kissed her goodnight. He could sense their relationship going somewhere.

And thus it was, they bloomed, they grew to love one another and finally planned to marry. She had no idea how they would live in their rural setting and how that would be, but she wanted to do it. She wanted to spend her life with this charming young man. Was he dashing, no not really, was he handsome that he took your breath away, no it wasn't that either. There was just this common sense of goodness, a common core of values and the way he considered her, which influenced her to love him.

The wedding was simple, held at her parent's home church, The Faith Baptist, held as a family affair with only the closest of friends and their respective families. Of course Elzie was best man, but Jake had included Bud, Billy John and Glen Ray as guest. His grandparents, his Grandma's parents, and his mother's mother were all there all beaming with pride.

They took a little trip to Corpus Christi, something Jake's mother planned for them. She told them about a time in her past when she had gone there with her mother to visit her ailing grandmother how struck she was with the scenes. So they were booked into a hotel that overlooked the gulf and they were driven to Dallas to take a new company's peanut fare flight to Corpus. It was whirl wind and overpowering to Jake. The gulf was ok, but he was really anxious to get back to his own familiar grounds.

When Jake knew that he and Lois were going to marry, as a present to Lois, he tore down the old Pariot house he was living in and built them a brand new house to start their life together. It was slightly behind the Pariot house, a three bedroom affair with modern kitchen for that time. The year was 1960.

By 1962, their first son was born, Philip Dwayne, named after Jake's dad. This was the first grandchild and great grandchild for Jake's family. Lois's family were just as thrilled though Phillip was not their first grandchild. Three years later, Elijah Owen came into the world, named after Jake's grandpa and Lois's father. The name fit well and all were pleased.

Before long Phillip was starting school and in no time two rowdy boys were getting on the yellow school bus and all going to school.

Though Lois had easily adapted to the rural life, to canning garden vegetables and fruits, cutting up chickens, gathering eggs, she longed to use her college skills. So, when the kids started school, she approached Jake about working as an accountant. She had kept the Oldham books right from the start of their marriage, but she wanted to be a bread winner, she wanted to earn her own money and utilize her training. Jake couldn't object to whatever Lois had wanted. He never did, he never would have, he loved her too much. He never wanted to do anything that would cause them to even disagree.

Lois got a job at a local real estate agent and started by keeping the accounts for the agent and before long was keeping records for other businesses in Bowie. She eventually opened her own bookkeeping business and until her illness, had been very busy and successful.

The years went on; the kids finished high school, and went to college in different directions. Phillip became an engineering architect. He would meet a girl in his office, Julia, and they would marry and bless the family with twin boys.

Elijah, who was called Ely by the family to distinguish him from his great grandpa, while studying business in college and working at an oil change place, ended up buying one and within a few years owned five such businesses. He had married a girl from Fort Worth, named Susie and they had one daughter, Mary Elizabeth whom they called Leeza.

One day in the shower, Lois had discovered the marble size lump in her breast. She decided not to tell Jake but made her own appointment with the local doctor. He had suggested removal of the small lump. She then told Jake and told him it was a cyst and not to worry. However, upon removal, the doctor sent it in for a pathology and when that came back he sent Lois to an oncologist who had her take a pet scan with radioactive dye. The doctor told Jake she lit up like a Christmas tree, that the cancer was very advanced and in her bones. He gave her six months and suggested no treatment. Lois lived six weeks. She was home and under as good a nursing care that was available, kept as comfortable as possible. The morning she died, she called Jake in their bedroom where she lay in the hospital bed; she took his hand and told him she wouldn't have traded one thing. Right before she could say I love you, she stopped in mid sentence and she was gone. The six weeks had been a very heavy load on Jake. His father had died the year before, his grandparents some time before that and his mother had died before his father. It was just too much and Jake had mourned many times since the doctor had given him the sad news and that moment when Lois breathed her last, a flood gate of sadness gushed from him. His children had been there that weekend and he had sent them all home and now he wished to God he hadn't and now he wished to God they were all there.

"My friends we hallow this ground where we bring our good sister's remains to be turned back to the earth but make no mistake about it, she is not here, she is like our dear Lord Jesus, she is risen. Now, let us pray..." And Brother Dave began his short prayer for all this family. He took his boutonnière from his coat and lay it on top of the casket reef, and slowly walked by each son and daughter in law to briefly shake their hands, but when he came to the end of the row his sadness broke as Jake rose to stand and hug, the preacher cried as much as Jake.

The preacher had been at the Sunset church of Christ for about seven years. He had come to know the Oldham's, come to respect them, come to recognize Jake as a church leader had personally suggested to the other men that he should be an elder and they all had agreed. As the elder Jake had helped and advised Dave and had helped him in his ministry. Dave was the first preacher they had ever had that was a full time minister. He had come to their church looking for a job when he had finished his studies in college from Henderson Tennessee. He was single and some of the church members were hesitant about that but Jake had convinced the congregation to give Dave a chance, reminding them that the Apostle Paul was never married. Dave had become a good preacher, a good community person and a much respected man of the community. He finally went back to his hometown of Brownsboro and married his high school sweetheart and brought her back to be his helper in Sunset. And Lois had been nothing but help to Alberta and to Dave as well. He looked at Jake and Lois as secondary parents. Jake's loss had hit Dave hard and though he had carried himself well through the funeral service, seeing Jake rising up to thank him and knowing the sadness, it was just overwhelming.

The service over, people by the hundreds filed by to pay their respects to Jake not excluding Bud, and of course Elzie. Glen Ray was off in Canada when Lois had died and was unable to be there and Billy John had died the year before. All of it had been emotionally strapping to Jake. He was overwhelmed with all the kindness but the boys, the guys he had grown up with; having them there by his side at that moment had emotionally drained him completely. Jake felt almost numb. He was on an emotional high overwhelmed by the kindness, visibly shaken by other's outpouring of grief, and simply without words to communicate. It seemed they were at the cemetery for hours. Jake took a long look at the row where Lois was laid. To her left was Jake's parents, his uncle Clois, and to the left his grandparents and to theirs, Jakes great grandparents from the Oldham side. There was some from the grandmothers in different spots in the cemetery but the Oldham line was a solid row for four generations. Even Jake's great great Grandparents were buried there but not in the row with the rest of the family.

Phillip touched his dad's shoulder and asked Jake if he was ready to go back to the house. He was, he wanted to lie down, he was spent.

After Jake's mother died, Jake noticed his father starting to have health problems and so he and Lois took up living in P.D.'s home and for two years their home was empty. After P.D.'s passing they decided to just remain at his parent's home and were preparing to rent out their own home. Jake wasn't ready to do that as much as Lois was. If they were going to rent the house, he wanted to do some work on it and he strung that out for a couple of years and then Lois became ill.

After Jake's grandfather had died and after his grandmother's health began to change, P.D. had insisted she move in with them. Shortly after his Grandmother moved into P.D.'s home, Jake tore down his grandparent's home. It was an old home, like the Pariot's and most difficult to remodel. He hated to take it down but knew it was for the best. One of the reasons Jake did not want to rent out the old house was every time all the kids came, they had enough beds for all to stay and renting their old house would certainly change that.

Lois had died on Tuesday and the funeral had been on Thursday a week before Thanksgiving. Jake had already told the kids that if they needed to go home not to stay over the weekend. They all had agreed to leave after lunch Friday. But they were all concerned about leaving Jake there by himself.

However, Elzie had asked Phillip what their plans were because he wanted to come and spend time with Jake. Since they were all going to leave after lunch Friday, Elzie would come out that Friday afternoon and he was going to stay all weekend.

Back at the house, Jake sat down in his recliner and dozed off. He never made it to his bedroom. In spite of the noisy grandkids in and out of the house running and playing, he was in a deep sleep. He was dreaming of his youth, and he and Elzie were going to the creek to fish but when he got there Elzie wasn't there and he found himself swimming and there was Lucy Tatum, she was embracing him in the cool water smiling and coaxing him and then Elzie is yelling out "What are ya'll doing? I thought we was gonna fish." Jake whirls around and Elzie is laughing and pointing a finger at Jake saying "Shame shame Jake Oldham, I'm gonna tell your Grandma what you did."

"Dad," a voice is saying, "Dad." It was Ely looking in the face of Jake as he opened his eyes. "Did you get a good nap?"

"What time is it?" Jake asked.

"About 5 in the evening." Ely said. "We got supper warmed up; I thought you might want to eat something."

"Five, good grief, how could I sleep so soundly?" Jake pondered.

"You were worn out, dad, you needed that. We just let you sleep and wondered how you could with our noisy kids." Ely said.

"They didn't bother me none," Jake answered. "I just can't believe I slept the afternoon."

"It was ok, dad, we handled all the folks who came by here after the cemetery. They all understood." Ely said.

Jake got up and went to his bedroom and pulled off his suit and slipped on his usual attire, his overalls. Then he came back to the dining room. They were all seated but waiting on him to sit at the head of the table and say a prayer if he wanted. He did, though it was hard and a few times he had to choke back his grief, and then they had supper which started with reserved talking that escalated into normal and lively chatter. It was as if at the beginning they were wanting to talk but were walking on eggshells. But Jake sort of said something amusing that broke the atmosphere.

After supper Jake and his boys went to the living room to sit and talk while the girls cleaned up. Jake who was usually jovial and a conversation leader just sat in silence thinking his sons were wanting to talk to him.

"Dad," Phillip said, "Are you going to be ok with all us going home tomorrow?" "Because if you're not, I am at least prepared to stay, stay all week if necessary."

"I need to go home and check on things at the business, but I can be back in two days, if you need me." Ely said. "I am wanting to talk to you about Susie and me making a change, moving back here if we could."

"Well that's a big change, Ely, Jake said, "Have you really given that some thought, what does Susie think, and what about Lezza, wouldn't she object?"

Phillip spoke, "Dad, we all have some things to talk about and we will but we will when we come back up for Thanksgiving, ok?"

"Fine with me," Jake said.

The rest of the evening was quiet and all went to bed. In spite of Jake's nap, he slept solid and well that night. It was the first time in a long time that he slept in their room alone. He had sat up with Lois during her illness and had not slept all night in a good while. But, he was too tired to think about that.

He woke a few times in the night; he could hear the wind picking up howling at times. At the cemetery he could sense the weather was changing as the weather people were saying a cold front was coming in and sure enough it was, and it came in gale force in the middle of the night. Jake could appreciate a warm bed and a warm house as the wind howled, he would settle deeper into the bed and covers.

Jake didn't really hurry getting up that morning. It was overcast; the wind was gushing from time to time, the trees shaking, leaves on the ground stirring.

He wanted to go and pick up a round bale and take it to his herds but he didn't want to be gone and all his kids leave. So, he waited. He got dressed and came into the kitchen where he could smell coffee brewing. Jake never drank over one cup and he liked to saucer it just like his grandpa did.

"How do you take your coffee?" Julia asked.

"Oh I have to doctor it some," Jake said, as he fumbled for the sugar and cream.

"I thought we'd have a late breakfast or early brunch, and then we are all going home." She said. "In a way, we all feel bad to leave."

"No, there's no need to feel that way." Jake said. "I'm going to be just fine."

"In fact, the sooner you all can get gone, the sooner I can get the hay out to my cows."

"Oh you don't need to worry about that, Ely, Phil and our boys have gone out to take care of that already."

"What!" Jake exclaimed, "I'm not helpless, I can take care of the cows."

"No one is saying you can't," Julia said, "The boys are just wanting to help you a little before we leave."

"I suppose they know there are three herds and we need to take one round bail to each herd."

"Yes," Julia said, "they got it."

Soon the two boys returned. As they were coming into the house they were talking and laughing about something they had done when they were kids.

Ely said, "Hey dad, we took three round bales to the cows, one bale to the cows on this place, one at the Blane, and one over at the Jasper's. We counted and there was 160 cows and 145 calves."

"Well," Jake said, "Ya'll done good. Thanks for thinking of me. But I could have took care of them after ya'll went home."

It was about 10:30 that morning and all the family was present,

Julia had trimmed up a ham that had been brought to the family and made a ham salad for sandwiches and everyone dug in and soon they were all packing to head home.

By noon they were all driving out and Jake was standing in the yard deciding to walk down to the road and check for mail. Both the boys were looking back in the mirror as they saw the lonely figure standing by the driveway, feeling so sad for him.

Jake figured the mail carrier should have come by now. And he had, there were a number of sympathy cards and other mail including the Bowie News. As Jake was looking at the post he heard a car driving down the road. It was Angie and Elzie.

CHAPTER 2

They pulled up to Jake at the mail box. "What ya'll doing out here?" Jake asked.

"Yesterday, your kids told me they were going home today and I told Angie to bring me out cause I'm going to spend the weekend with you." Elzie said.

"Get in and ride with us back to your house. Besides its getting cold." Elzie said.

Jake got in the back seat of their nice Honda Accord and rode up to the house, not saying a word.

Elzie got out with his suit case and Angie bid them goodbye.

"Where's Angie going?" Jake asked.

"Oh she's going back home, she's got housework and things she wanted to do. She's going to catch back up with us on Sunday." Elzie said.

Jake looked at Elzie. His best friend since they were born, his almost brother and the very person that growing up meant more to him than anyone. They had spent a large part of their lives together growing up on neighboring farms, they had worked their fields together, hoed peanuts, melons, they had hunted the land and fished and swam that same creek together many times. But when Jake was seventeen, Elzie's family had to move off their place, and Jake's family bought the place. Elzie's parents decided to move to town as Elzie's dad was going to get a job and it changed life for both boys. Then after they were both out of school, and married, they saw less and less of each other. Sometimes Elzie would drive out after church on Sunday and the two would go down to the creek or they would just sit on the porch to visit. Sadly, as they got older, they had seen less of each other.

"It's awful nice of you to think of me to come out and want to stay." Jake said.

"When I talked to Phillip at the cemetery, and he said all of them was going to try to go home today, I just couldn't stand the thought of you out here by yourself." Elzie said. "I just couldn't Jake, It had me all tore up."

"Come on in and let's get out of this north wind. I'll give you your old room upstairs. And I'll put myself in my old room up there too." Jake said.

The men shuffled inside and for the time being Elzie just put his belongings in the living room and they sat down in chairs that faced a nice gas log fireplace with the fire going.

"Oh that fire is nice and inviting." Elzie said, "When did you put this in?"

"Oh about fifteen years ago," Jake chuckled. "Don't guess you ever came out much to visit during the winter."

"Naw, don't guess I did," Elzie said, "I should have. Lord knows I've wanted to come out here more than I have. This is really home you know."

"What year, did your Grandpa die?" Elzie asked.

"It was 1970." Jake said. That morning dad and I had a dozer job but we was finishing up and he and I went over to it and it was down to dad finishing and I was moving my dozer back to the house at noon. When I got home, Grandma told me that she hadn't seen Grandpa since mid morning. He'd gone down to the barn to work on building some laying boxes and there it was dinner time. And you know Grandpa was like a clock about wanting dinner at a certain time. So I went down to the barn and Elzie, he was just sitting there against one of the post and I called out to him and when he didn't answer I touched him and he was dead. He was cold. I picked him up and carried him to the house and laid him out on the bed. We called the sheriff cause when somebody's dies they have to send the justice of the peace out. Me and Grandma changed his clothes cause he had soiled them, we cleaned him up before they got there. I tell you Elzie it just broke my heart, I just couldn't stand it. Grandma was stronger than me; she didn't shed a tear but she had to just about hold me. I had to go and get dad though and brought him back to the house and by then the justice of the peace come. I told I had moved him and brought him up there and the justice of the peace was understanding. Then the funeral home came and took him up to Bowie and got him ready. I know why you are asking cause you was gone then on your job out on some training school and out of state as I remember."

"Yeah, I was and I sure hated that." You know my folks didn't even tell me Lige had died until I come back home from that school. That sure made me mad; sure hurt me not to have been here. Ya'll had the funeral out here at the cemetery at the old church didn't ye?" Elzie said.

"Yeah, and you know we had Grandma's out here too." Jake said. "She lived about fifteen years after that and spent the last five living with dad and mother. They added that back room where she had a big bedroom, living room like space. I tore Grandma's house down after she moved in with dad and mom."

"We had mama's funeral over at Sunset at the church." Jake continued. "She was a good strong solid Christian woman. She died two years after Grandma and it sure changed my dad. He began to change, not have much will to go on. I tried to keep him busy with our dozer work but he was wanting to quit that long before and he sure shut down after mama passed away."

"I know what you mean," Elzie said, "After my dad died, why mama just gave up and before I knew it, she was in bad health and with my brother having health problems and my older sister living out of state, why it fell on me to take care of her. I say fell on me, Angie was a big help taking care of my mama."

"At least I was here and able to go to your folks funerals and was proud to serve as a pall bearer." Jake said.

"Our folks are all gone, and we are about what's left." Jake said.

You know I sure hated when Billy John died. He was your age, a year younger than me."

"Oh I know it." Elzie replied. "It was a shock but he had been having some heart problems for awhile."

"Yeah but our mortality hits home when some of your own friends die." Jake said.

"What ever happened to your niece Lucy?" Jake asked

"Oh she's fine," Elzie said, "she been married a couple of times, lives down in East Texas somewhere, I don't rightly know the name of the town. Did you know her that much?"

"Well no, not that much, but she was up here staying at your house when your Grandpa Pariot had that stroke and died. You remember you and your dad and my dad all had gone down to Dallas with the pickup's loaded with watermelons and I had to stay here. I never told you this but after I had took care of feeding Grandma's chickens and I think I had gathered the eggs, you see Grandma and Grandpa had gone off to visit the Jasper's at Sunset and I was here alone, so I thought, as mama and your mom had taken your Grandpa to the doctor. Well I decided to go down to the creek and have a little swim, cool off; you know it was real warm. And dad gum, if I wasn't swimming and had one time even dove off the bank when there Lucy was sitting over calling out to me. She was watching me and me with not a stitch on and she saw me. Well she come down to the water and she got naked as I was and let me tell you cousin, she got plumb tempting and all of a sudden we hear a car coming. I sent her packing to your house and I got my clothes on and sure enough it was my mama!"

"Of course she had no suspicion of anything; if she had I would have died after the beating." Jake said, as he and Elzie cracking up with laughter.

"Well you know your mom and mine went back to the hospital and by then Grandma and Grandpa had come home, and Lucy was left to Grandma's care. After we went to the hospital ourselves and come home and late that night when all was asleep, even me, Lucy come to my room wanting to finish what we had started down at the creek."

"You don't mean it!" Elzie cried. "Oh my God, your Grandma

would have crapped the bed full had she knew it!" And both men had a big laugh.

"You know I never told that story to nobody before." Jake said almost serious. "Nobody."

"Well, shoot, Jake that was near fifty year ago, you think you're in danger now?" Elzie said.

"I might be," Jake answered, "I doubt my church would be very pleased with that story."

"Oh good grief, Jake," Elzie said, "You always worry about too many things that won't make a hill of beans."

Jake didn't answer because he sort of knew that was right.

Elzie asked, "How come you and Nell never connected? "Lord God, I know myself, I know how you was so crazy about her back then."

Jake was looking down and he looked up, looked Elzie in the face and said, "I guess we were not meant to be, you know I thought when she was going to get a divorce she was going to be mine and that then was all I ever wanted. You are right back then, I was crazy in love with her, but she left, and I have never seen her except at her daddy's funeral but we never even spoke. And when her mama died Bud said she and her husband were off in Europe and couldn't get back for the funeral. After she left and got her divorce, I met Lois and we had sweet love, she was good to me and probably better to me than I was to her, but I sure tried to be a good husband and I was faithful too. I never looked at another woman. I just tried to provide for her and be a husband and father to the boys."

"I think ya'll had a good life." Elzie said. "I don't doubt a bit, that you loved Lois and she you and I know you and she were always happy."

"Have you been happy?" Jake asked.

"Oh yeah, most of the time, sometime I wander what I might have been like had I been with someone else, but sure most of our time together has been good, real good. We've had a few problems with our kids, and who hasn't? Our oldest boy been married twice and our youngest girl has had some problems and has recently divorced and that kind of stuff worries you and it sometimes wears on your own marriage." Elzie said.

"I got no business asking this, but have you been faithful?" Jake asked.

"Well yeah mostly." "You know working like I have for some time you are off on business trips, you try to impress people and get different deals for the company, sometimes you are in situations that if you aren't strong, well, things can happen, you know sort of…" Elzie stammered.

"Jake why you asking me that? What about you, you been faithful, true blue?" Elzie asked.

Jake just sat there, looking at space, not really looking at Elzie, sure not wanting to show any kind of disapproval. Finally he said, "I've known a few guys and a woman or two for whatever reason, thought the grass might be greener on the other side and mostly to find out it wasn't. Except for some time thinking about things I probably shouldn't, I've been or I was faithful to Lois."

"I've been pretty lucky about my kids. My boys got fine wives and good kids and I think they are all doing well with their jobs and things you know. That youngest one though said he was wanting to talk to me about moving home. I supposed he meant him and his family. I'll know more about that come Thanksgiving, which by the way is next week." Jake said.

"You know Jake," Elzie said, "I got some hard hitting news the other day. They come told me they were going to retire me at the end of the year. It don't matter what I think, what I feel, they are going to buy me out, I'll be out, no job, retired."

"Oh wow," Jake said, "You and Angie got plans? You going to go on a long vacation or something or what?"

"Well," Elzie said, "I'm sure not wanting to retire and live in Bridgeport, not that it is a bad place or anything, cause it ain't, but it ain't home either. I'd give my right arm if I was living out here."

"Well I imagine you could live out here and keep your right arm." Jake said.

"What do you mean?" Elzie said.

"After my mama died, me and Lois had to move up here and live and take care of my dad, so I got a house down there that we haven't lived in for some time. Our kids use it when they come up, but we could do something else." If you want to live out here, you and Angie can just live there, rent free. I'd love for you to be back out here, to finish our lives out here, to die out here cause I'm going to die out here." Jake said with a certain air of authority.

"I couldn't do that," Elzie said, "I'm not looking for some kind of charity, a hand out, not that I wouldn't love it and I think Angie would like it, she's like me we are just there where we are now. We own our home, I imagine we can sell it all right but you could sell me a little spot and we could just build us a little place."

"Well why would I need to? I'm telling you, you can live in my old house, the house I built on YOUR GRANDPA'S land, where I raised my kids, you can live there as long as you want and I'll put that in writing and attach it to the deed of that property!" Jake said almost getting loud.

"You getting irritated at me?" Elzie asked.

"Elzie," Jake began, "if you never knew this, if you have known it and forgotten it, then hear me now. There was never anyone that was more like my own brother, a brother that I never had, if there was ever anyone that I loved more as a brother as a friend, than you, they don't exist. If I can't do this for you now, and do it as I want, then I'll do it any way shape form or fashion, whatever it takes if you want to live out here, I'll move heaven and earth to make it so. The easiest thing to do, is sell or rent your house out and move in and live there as it were your very own just like it is yours because if you will do it, as long as you or Angie is alive, then it is yours to have to use to do whatever you want and I mean that from the bottom of my heart!"

A big tear rolled down Elzie's chubby cheek and the two men just looked at each other then embraced and patted each other on the back. Elzie didn't say another word about it.

"Would you look!" Jake said, "it has got dark, what do we want for supper?"

They had used up the afternoon and the day was getting spent.

"Got any baloney?" Elzie asked.

CHAPTER 3

Both men woke early as was their tradition. They were dressed almost at the same time.

"Did you have to get up much in the night?" Jake asked Elzie.

"I think three times maybe four." Elzie said.

"Old man's syndrome." Jake said.

"What you hungry for breakfast?" Jake asked.

"Coffee and oatmeal." Elzie replied.

"Grandpa and Grandma always called it oats." Jake said, "They never said oatmeal, but something like, I'll have a bowl of boiled oats."

"I remember." Elzie said.

"Well then, I'll have me a saucer of coffee and a bowl of them boiled oats." Elzie said.

Downstairs the fire place had come on and was humming heat looking like a real log fireplace. Jake turned on the light as he went from the living room to the kitchen which was the next room. There he filled a coffee pot and fixed the portion and then poured the water into the coffee maker. He then took a cooking pan, added some milk, some vanilla and then came the rolled Quaker Oats and let it come to a good boil and occasionally stirring. As soon as the consistency was there, he took it off the heat, added butter and sugar.

"You cook that like you've had practice." Elzie said.

"I watched my Grandma and my mama do this so I'm an old hand at it," Jake said.

"You got any plans today?" Elzie asked.

"Well, we need to drive out and look at my cows even though the boys fed em yesterday, I want to make sure everything's all right. I won't need to feed them until tomorrow afternoon; after church." Jake said.

"Then we'll take a run over to Sunset, maybe give old Bud a yell and if wants to go with us, when it gets dinner time, we'll go over to Lindsey for some good German Bar B Q."

"Hot Dog!" Elzie said rubbing his hands together. He was putting a little salt in his poured coffee, setting it in a saucer and getting ready to pour it in a saucer.

"Just the way our grandpa's drank it." Jake said as he poured his own cup. They both made a gesture as if they were toasting each other with their saucers as they took a sip.

Elzie was studying Jake. He noticed Jake was a good fifty pounds heavier than their youth but so was he. He was looking at Jakes white hair that once was blond, and thought of his own gray hair what was left of it as his was most thin. He thought about Jake's offer on the house. It was really a good deal, if Angie wouldn't object. He knew she wasn't any more fond of living in Bridgeport than he was, it just so happened to be close to Elzie's job and Angie's since she had gone to work at the local hardware store. But in just about forty days, he was going to be out of a job. Living out here would be a dream compared to living in town and besides he and Jake could run around together as he knew Angie wouldn't mind him being out from under her feet.

As Jake was eating his "boiled oats" he was studying Elzie. He thought Elzie must be sixty or more pounds heavier than they were as boys, but then who wasn't heavier? And of course, Elzie didn't have much hair anymore and what he had as old man's hair, gray. Jake thought how he would like for Elzie to be back out here.

As soon as they finished breakfast and had a quick pee, they were out to the shed and in the work truck. The morning was clear, crisp, cold and frosty. The wind had died down. Jake still kept a one ton flat bed for most of his farm work, with a hay fork on the back. At least he wasn't going to need a bail right then but would get one and have it ready for tomorrow. The diesel cranked as soon as he had held the key to warm and then it cranked. He checked the cows in the pasture by the house first and then went to the Blane hollow where he had built a dam and drove across and through a cattle guard.

Elzie was seeing this dam for the first time. "Did you build this?" he asked.

"Yup, sure did, about six years ago. It sure helped this old hollow. Gave us water and checked a lot of erosion." Jake said. Most of Jake's cows were Angus but he had several white face crosses.

The cows thinking Jake was feeding came to the truck bawling and even running to the truck.

"Your old cows look good, fat, and healthy." Elzie said.

"My Grandma used to say, "You can't starve a profit." Jake replied.

The men looked at all the cows, many with white faced calves, a contrast to the solid Black Angus mothers. The few white faced cows, Jake's replacement cows, had three quarter cross calves that were white faced and sometimes had more Herford look than the Angus.

"You keep em on a white faced bull." Elzie observed.

"I've always liked the angus Herford cross," Jake said. "They are usually the top market makers."

"Most of your calves born in the fall and winter?" Elzie asked.

"Most, yeah." Jake said.

After driving around the old Blane place, they headed out to the Jasper which was down the county road.

"Jake you own that old Blane and the Jasper?" Elzie inquired.

"Yeah, after we bought ya'll's old place, we leased the Jasper for about ten years but when Mr. Jasper died, Mrs. Jasper and her son agreed to sell it to me and the same happened with the Blane. Between all of it, I've got a thousand and forty acres." Jake said.

"You've come a ways since we was kids when ya'll had a hundred sixty acres like Grandpa Pariot." Elzie said.

"The Lord's been good." Jake said. "And hard work."

The Jasper farm although lay just across the county road from the Pariot, was entered from the south west side which was around the county road about one mile. It was as Jake thought, one of the prime farms in this part of the county. Of the four hundred acres, a full hundred lay on the old Denton Creek bottom. Except for occasional drainage problems during flood season, the bottom soil was rich and fertile and usable. In the past he had raised a few very good and rewarding watermelon crops but of late, the bottom was now Coastal Bermuda which provided a lot of good grazing plus at least two cuttings of hay. Some ten years ago, he had converted twenty acres to a pecan orchard which provided an additional income to the farm. The upland was a mixture of heavy oak timber and open spaces that were in native grasses. Jake had added to the open areas by taking out sections of the timber yet keeping enough in a pattern to provide for the deer and turkey.

Right off the county road was a narrow lane that entered the Jasper place. Jake liked having cattle guards but because of poachers and thieves, kept a locked gate at the entry. He handed Elzie the key as he got out to unlock and open the gate. "Shut it after I pull in," Jake said, "But don't lock it."

Elzie obeyed and soon they were headed down to where the old Jasper home had once stood. Jake well remembered the early morning hours that after a four year drought, they had a heavy thunderstorm and the Jasper home had been struck by lightning and the place had burned down. The Jasper's immediately came driving up to Jake's grandparent's house and they stayed there until they bought a small acreage in Sunset and built their new residence. When they made that change, they soon decided and offered their place for lease to the Oldham's and Jake's dad wisely accepted the lease but had it in Jake's name and it was Jake who worked to pay it and worked the place and would eventually be rewarded by getting to purchase it. Driving down the lane with fences on each side of the narrow drive always made Jake think about the privacy the Jasper's enjoyed contrasted to the Oldham's home being right on the county road. The lane ran a slight descent and then the homestead that overlooked the bottom, to Jake was like a small kingdom. Jake really liked this place, always thought it was much more of an artist picture of a true farm than anything they ever had. This morning he could see the cows down in the bottom and drove toward them. They were around a ringed bale of hay pulling at the round bale. Small calves were idle and some were nursing while some were butting heads with one another and some were kicking up their back heals responding to the crisp morning.

"Look over there," Jake said, there's a cow that has freshened I would say just yesterday.

Elzie observed her swollen bag and evidence of shed afterbirth which indicated she had calved likely the night before. Usually a new mother would hide out her newborn for a couple of days before she would let it join the herd.

"You going to look for her calf?" Elzie asked.

"No, I imagine it's alright." Jake said. "They usually are."

After spending some time as they had with the other herds, Jake studied his cows, and mentally counted them knowing most if not all were accounted for. Most cattle people knew their stock. They learned each cow individually, knew her personality, knew if about when she was due to calve, knew if she was sick, knew if she was in trouble because each cow is a margin of profit and loss. So Jake like his father before him and his grandparents before that had the knowledge of generations of practice, studying the herd, counting the cows and knowing if any were missing. If even one was missing, he would go and search. Searching the bottom was easy and normally if one or two was not there, they could easily be spotted in the bottom. If they were not in the bottom, it may entail a painstaking walk throughout the woods. Sometimes an owner would be too late, that the cow was having birthing problems and had died as well as the calf. Then again by searching, might save both. Today fortunately, all the cows were accounted for.

Jake then drove to the north end of the bottom to show Elzie the pecan portion. They had been planted on thirty five foot spacing and were a perfect checker board pattern. No matter which direction or angle you looked at the trees, they formed a row.

"Wow," Elzie exclaimed, "How many kinds of pecans you got."

"Oh we have four paper shells and then about five acres of native trees." Jake replied. "Last year we made over three thousand pounds to the acre and let me tell you it is like manna from heaven, it is a great gift when everything else is going well, but it is a God-send if you're having problems with say calf prices or if you have had to sell because you didn't have the grass or low on water, the pecans can sure be a nice help in the cash department."

"How do you harvest all these?" Elzie inquired.

"Oh, I have a man that has the equipment, you know he has a shaker, and he lays tarp down and he has a vacuum to gather them and clean them." Jake answered. "Then we bag them and off to the sheller's we go. I wish I had a sheller and keep a thousand pounds or so to shell and retail myself. When we sell these, we get around $1.20 to $1.35 a pound, or that was what we got last year. It can vary from year to year. But if I had a sheller, I could sell shelled pecans for $5 a pound or maybe more, just depending on the market."

"You sure have developed a business head." Elzie said.

"An old man told me one time, when you stop chasing women, and start thinking business, and then you begin to make money." Jake said.

The men had to laugh at that one.

"I'm really doing things like our folks did. We didn't just do one thing, if you remember, we had some cows, we had hogs, chickens, we milked, we sold eggs and cream, we raised several kinds of crops. Some farmers just do one thing, you know like run mama cows and nothing else and if that don't make any money, what then?" Jake said.

"So, I raise hay, I have pecans, we have our cows, and I have a pretty good dozer business, so I'm doing what they call diversity in our farming." Jake said. "It pays I think." "And I could get additional income if I was a mind to; lease out some of this land for hunting, good money and all I have to do is put an ad in the newspaper and people come out of the wood work and will pay top dollar for hunting."

It was getting on to ten in the morning when they pulled out of the Jasper gate and headed back to Jake's house.

"I thought we was going to town," Elzie said.

"We are only we are going in my go to town truck, not the feed truck." Jake said.

"You got a go to church truck too?" Elzie joked.

The truck was a late model Chevrolet with an extended cab, loaded with power windows, air, tinted windows. It was a nice truck.

"Yeah I do but it is the same one as the go to town, since church is in town." Jake said as they scooted inside the truck.

"Well, what about a stepping out truck? You got one for that?" Elzie was saying it joking with a slight sarcastic twist.

Jake just looked at Elzie with a slight smirk on this face and a roll of his eyes.

As they were approaching the paved Farm to Market highway, Jake said with a grin, "Do you need me to stop to pee?"

CHAPTER 4

Jake and Elzie arrived in town about 10:30. As they entered town, Jake said, "You know Sunset is so different from our young days. We had business here then, a good school and now it is dying town. There's no school, there's hardly any business, only a post office."

"Yeah, even the stations are gone, the gift shops, the old café. About all that's left is some houses and churches." Elzie said.

"Sadly, that's true." Jake said. "Wasn't no one to even want to take up Billy John's business after he passed. You know I did all my business with Billy John."

"It's getting to where I hardly know who's a living here." Jake said. "I'm becoming a stranger in my own town." "And you know what? The majority of the people who come to church here are people who live somewheres else. I know that for a fact at our church and the Baptist, what about yours?"

"I think that is probably right, that last two years, Angie and I have been going to church at a church in Bridgeport." Elzie said.

"No kidding!" Jake said, "What brought that on, you used to be one of the pillars over there at the Assembly of God."

"Well we had a new pastor and he pretty well wanted his own people in his corner so he worked to get the ones in there out and brought in who he wanted and like you said, he brought people with him who will drive up to Sunset from as far away as Rhome, Saginaw, or Justin just to be with him and serve him and it was like we didn't even matter." Elzie said.

"Why, I never knew, Cousin," Jake said. "I can't imagine that."

"Well imagine it, cause it is true." Elzie said, "However, that preacher has now moved on, somehow the Lord has mysteriously called him to another church and all his flock have about went out with him. They are in sort of a rebuilding the church now, trying to get old ones back, and keep some of the better new ones and me an Angie might try to go back."

"We got a real good preacher at our church." Jake said. "He came here seven years ago just out of college. He went to Freed Hardeman in Henderson Tennessee and he is well grounded. But at the time he was single and a lot of the church didn't want to hire him but I argued that that wasn't a criteria for hiring a preacher and I won out and the church is glad I won that argument. And as soon as he got established with us, he went home and married his sweetheart and she came and jumped in with both feet. About six years ago I was installed as an elder but I know within reason that now that Lois has died, they will expect my resignation as one of the church pastors."

"I can sure see you as a pastor," Elzie said, "You always was trying to steer me in the right direction and all of us back then."

Jake chuckled a bit and said, "Well in the church of Christ, a pastor is not a preacher but he's an elder, or a bishop and the term pastor is also applied because it means to shepherd the flock."

"Well isn't that what the preacher does too?" Elzie asked.

"I suppose he does, but he also proclaims the word and a teacher of the word or the gospel and the elder or the bishop or the pastor, he is the guidance to the flock but he might not necessarily be the preacher."

"Like I said," Elzie said, "Isn't that what the pastor/ preacher does?"

"Uh, Jake," Elzie said, "How come you think the church will want you to resign because of Lois passing away?"

"Oh, the qualification for an elder is to be the husband of one wife, so if the wife has died, as in my case, some will likely think that disqualifies me to serve as an elder." Jake said.

"Don't sound right to me," Elzie said, "You can't help it that your wife died, how does that make you not qualified to be an elder?"

"Just some people's traditions" was all Jake would say. "I'm not going to rush in and volunteer to resign, I'm going to wait and see what the attitudes are."

For a few minutes the men just drove around the town looking at the condition of the community. There were old falling down buildings, a few abandoned old homes, then there were homes where people were living but to Jake he knew few of the people who were living in homes of people he had known in his past. Downtown Sunset was empty and the old Hunter store was a pile of rocks and broken lumber. Across the street, the old Sunset Guaranty Bank building was still standing but the windows had long been bashed out. The rest of the street was empty, the buildings of Jake and Elzie's parents were long gone and had not they seen that same business as children, there was almost no one to even know they had existed.

"Boy this is a sad state." Elzie said.

Jake made a face but said nothing. Jake drove back by the old school but hit the road on the west side of the school property and headed out of town where Bud lived, on the Hunter farm. Bud's parent's home in Sunset continued to be empty as far as Jake knew and he wondered why it was that way. Jake wondered why, but had never asked since Bud was a very private person, rarely discussed his family matters or private affairs.

At the Hunter farm, Bud's house lay off the county road by about a hundred yards. It was a fine one story brick structure with a large front porch that faced the county road which was now called Sunset School Road. It so happened Bud was in his yard picking up pecans from under a very large pecan tree. He looked up as they pulled up and as they got out of the truck, he started over to them.

"As I live 'n breathe," he said, "Elzie Tatum. How are you doing Jake?"

"Doing ok, considering the circumstances." Jake said. "Me and Elzie are going to drive over to Lindsey for dinner, wondered if you would like to go with us."

"Let me go in and tell Patty where I'm going," Bud said "And we'll be off."

Bud shot in the garage and into the door off the garage, which went directly into the kitchen. Jake figured Patty might be in the kitchen. She came back out with Bud to pay respects to Jake and to rib Elzie a bit before the men were off.

Bud, looking at Jake's truck said, "Hey lets go in my new truck, it's a four door and we will have more room. Jake you need to go look at the new trucks, those four doors have better riding room in the back than the extended cabs."

"I may have to do that," Jake said, "But right now I haven't had a lot of need for my back seat, but am glad I have it when I buy groceries."

Bud backed his new tan four door GMC Sierra out of the garage.

"He loves that truck more than me," Patty joked.

Jake couldn't help thinking about her when she worked in the old Legion pharmacy serving those wonderful cold fountain cherry cokes. He and Elzie had had an argument over her one time thinking she was interested in dating them when she didn't even know them. Now she's been a good wife and a mother to her and Bud's children, and now a grandmother. She was still a very attractive woman.

Jake and Elzie got out and had to decide who was going to ride in the back and who was going to ride in the front and it was like school boys again arguing over shotgun privileges.

Starting out Jake got the back seat and preferred it and let Elzie and Bud spin yarns as they headed to Lindsey. Lindsey was in Cooke County completely north of Montague by way of going through Forestburg and either Saint Jo or around Hardy to Lindsay.

Lindsay is a German town, clean and well run. There are two restaurants there both serving German barbecue but these guys liked the Smoke House over Dieter's even though Dieter's was really just as good and actually having more variety on their menu but Jake preferred the Smoke House's sausage over Dieter's.

Soon they were there and were anxiously waiting for their food. They all ordered brisket sandwiches with onion rings and lots of tea.

"Oh God," Elzie said, "We will never get home without having to stop and pee a dozen times."

"It is all back roads, so that shouldn't be a problem." Jake said.

As they chomped down their sandwiches, Jake was studying Bud. "He's heavier than our school days," he thought, "and his hair is all salt and pepper, not that raven black as it used to be."

Bud was looking at Jake thinking how he had aged from the days of their youth, heavier than those days, and white headed. And Elzie too, he was heavier and a lot less hair.

The guys had a great meal and a great time and even kidding with their waitress but giving her a generous tip for putting up with their foolishness.

"You know," Jake said, "When I was a kid, my grandparents would treat once in a while a hamburger at the Dairy Mart, but would never have thought about coming to a place like this."

"Or a steak house, or anything else that wasn't less than two dollars." Elzie said.

They all three nodded in agreement. Their folks came from a different mold, and they would consider eating out like they were doing that day as something frivolous and even wasteful. Yes, times had certainly changed.

As they were starting back home, this time Jake rode in the front.

"Did Elzie tell you he was retiring at the end of next month?" Jake asked.

"No," Bud said, "How about that!"

"They are going to move out to live on Elzie's grandfather's farm too," Jake said.

"I guess we'll have to plan some fishing and hunting. I'm probably going to retire by the end of the year myself."Bud said.

"That'll be ok," Elzie said, "But you have to carry your own tackle box!"

Jake turned and looked at Elzie and then at Bud then they all three had a big laugh remembering the time Bud had left his tackle box on the bank of the fishing hole and thought Jake or Elzie would or should go back down to the spot and get the box. But they did not.

The ride back to Bud's was jolly, jovial and fun and helped take Jake's mind off of his recent loss.

It was near three in the afternoon when the boys got back to Bud's house.

"Ya'll come in," Bud said.

The men obeyed and went in Bud's house entering through the kitchen.

Patty kept a spotless place, nothing out of place with her floors shinning. Jake noticed the fine kitchen bar and dining table.

"With ya'll's kids, Jake said, I guess you fill up this here kitchen."

"It gets lively with three married children and eight grandchildren," Patty said.

"It is hard to believe we are grandparents," Jake said. "It just seems like yesterday we were all in school thinking about going down to Hulet's for burgers and listening to the jukebox playing those old hits."

"And those runs out to Lover's lane," quipped Elzie.

"Shut up." Jake said.

Patty had a fresh baked chocolate cake. She got saucers and sliced each one a generous helping.

"Patty," Jake said, "You remember when you worked at the drug store in Bowie? Me an Elzie and my grandparents all came there and me an Elzie argued about which one of us you thought was the cutest."

"Well good Lord," she said, "That was a long time ago, I can hardly remember you two coming in there for a cherry coke. I was awfully shy back then."

"You couldn't have matched yourself any better than Bud Hunter for being shy," Elzie said.

Then they all laughed with Bud turning red.

It was after four and Jake said he needed to get back and feed their chickens. He still kept a dozen hens for him and Lois and got anywhere from five to seven eggs a day. It was enough for him and Lois and would be more than enough for him.

Jake and Elzie drove off but headed out south to go back home instead of through Sunset.

"Going to take the tour route I see." Elzie said.

"Well yeah, it won't hurt, we can just see some of this country and what kind of shape it's in." Jake said.

It made for good conversation and wondering who was now living on what place they had known in their youth as so many of the families they had known were now long gone. Some farms where the homestead was, was gone and the land was used for cattle but no one was living on the places.

"You know I've seen a complete turnaround from our days," Jake said. "Back when we was young boys, they was somebody living on about every eighty acres, usually share cropping. Some of them folks was rough too, lived rough, acted rough and was rough. Some I was glad to see leave this part of the country to become someone else's problems. You remember them Rivor twins? One time them two rascals caught me coming around a corner at school and just about beat the living tar out of me and did it just cause it was fun to them. After they got me down on the ground they was kicking me all over when Glen Ray and Bud came up and stopped them. I was in no shape to take revenge that day but a while after we caught them two and I got a cut of 'em one at a time and they began to beg off saying they was just funning not meaning nuthin but I took great pleasure in whipping holy hell out of them two. I was glad within a few months that family left out of here and I never knew of them since."

"I sure remember that," Elzie said. I got there after the fighting had stopped and helped you to the bathroom to wash all that blood off ye. I was so mad about that but you told me to let it go right then, they would be a better day."

"And there was," Jake said. "After school, no teachers around and we was out walking out to Gamers Bridge just to throw rocks and when we got out there, there them two was and me and Bud, Glen Ray, Billy John and you. We got down there with them. They thought was just going to have nice little friendly playing around but I told Bud and Glen Ray to hold one of them and I took off my shirt and was starting to push old Scott Rivor and he just dropped to his knees saying he didn't want to fight and then Todd Rivor said the same thing. Only I didn't care, that day they hit me I wasn't thinking about fighting either, but right then I was in a real mood for it."

"You had them two crying and crapping their pants," Elzie laughed.

"Well when I got done, it was them that had to go and wash blood off," Jake said. "I never was one to try to fight or cause trouble but that was one time I wanted to fight the other time was when Doug Cunningham came to my house looking for Nell."

"I never heard this story, tell me what happened," Elzie said.

"Oh she came out to my house looking for help her face bruised up and I had to do something. She stayed with me for a few days and old Doug drove up about half tight and thinking he was God almighty. I put him on his butt and threw him in his car and sent him home. He even had a gun but I took it away from him and emptied the shells so he was harmless. It scared Nell pretty bad but I told her it was nothing. She wasn't out in the yard when I busted his lip and knocked him to the ground. He didn't come back."

"Why did she marry that creep?" Elzie asked.

"I don't know, I think because when she dated him, he told her that when they got out of high school he had big job waiting for him in Kansas and she always had this roving eye thought she just had to get out of LITTLE OLD SUNSET as she put it. And old Doug had sure enough interviewed for a job in Kansas but they didn't hire him but that was after they got married. I bet she was disappointed. Then he got to drinking more and more and when he drank he got a little mean and took it out on her. One day she had enough. I helped her and paid for her lawyer. But she left the day after old Doug came to my place. Except at her daddy's funeral, I have never seen her since but heard from her one time. She went down to Dallas and got into nursing school and she ended up marrying a doctor and they moved down to Vicksburg Mississippi and I guess are still there. I never ask Bud, I just can't ask." Jake said.

When they got back to Jake's, Elzie insisted on going with Jake to the hen house. He wanted to relive his days as a big kid helping out from time to time picking Miss Bertha's eggs. Elzie had a great fondness of memories of his youth and really thought a lot of Lige and Berthie

May. He remembered the many fine meals he and his family had had at her table. So, going back to her hen house was just a good memory.

That night the men feasted on some of the leftover food from the funeral. Jake said it would be the last time he had it because he just couldn't go another day of the left over's.

"Hey," Jake said, "You remember our old thump game?"

"Oh yeah," Elzie said, "Why you ask?"

"Cause I still got that old board, and all the pieces, you wanna play a round or two?" Jake said.

Jake got the old board out and the twenty five wooden shaped washers, twelve red, twelve green and one black and the two natural unstained for their use. He put the twelve green and red and the one black in the center of the board. Elzie decided on red so Jake was the green and they started thumping the natural washer into the crowd of red and green until they had some singled out and started trying to hit them by their thumping the natural colored washer to hit the green or red and shoot it to the pocket.

"Ow," Elzie said, "that hurts your fingernail, all that thumping and not used to it."

"Come on you sissy," Jake said, "I'm going to whip you good."

"We'll see," Elzie answered.

The played only one game as it did make the middle fingernail sore, and because they hadn't played in years, didn't want the finger hurting all the next day.

"Man we sure used to have fun with this old game. Me, you, your grandpa and whoever was around to be his partner, but we played a million games back then." Elzie said, sort of looking off to the distance.

Then they sat in the living room for a few hours before turning in for bed.

Jake asked Elzie about church and to his surprise Elzie's plan was for him and Angie to visit Jake's church and then would take Jake to lunch before Elzie going home. Jake told Elzie that tomorrow he didn't want to go to the bible class but just go to church. Elzie called Angie to tell her to meet him at the Sunset church at 11 for church. She said she would see them tomorrow and hung up, then the men turned in for the night.

That morning Jake wrote a thank you note to the church for all the things they had done during and after Lois's illness and death. Someone could read that to the members that morning when they made announcements.

Elzie loaded his bags in Jake's go to town truck and he and Jake headed to church. Angie had just drove up when they did. Others were too and were getting out some looking at Angie, Elzie and Jake. Jake of course was nodding hellos and greetings to different ones as they walked in and took a seat.

The preacher noticed Jake and came over to speak to him and to acquaint himself with Elzie and Angie.

"Two of my dearest friends," Jake said to Dave as Dave was shaking their hands.

"And where are you all from?" Brother Dave asked.

"We live in Bridgeport, but we were both raised here at Sunset." Elzie said.

Before Dave could press where they went to church and all, Jake interjected, "Uh Dave, please don't call on me to lead a prayer today or wait on the table, if you don't mind."

"Oh, of course, I understand." Dave said. And he was then off to greet other people before the service started.

The service went smooth, the singing was good, and the three young men handled the serving of the Lord's Supper without any problems. One of the church's elders Archer Fuller made the announcements including reading Jake's thank you and the welcome of all visitors. Archer was acquainted with Elzie and so made special mention of Elzie and Angie at their visit.

Dave's sermon was about faith and obedience and nothing about what was wrong with the way the Pentecost church believed, for which Jake was thankful.

When the service was ended, a number of brethren came by to wish Jake well and to see how he was doing. Of course Jake would say he was fine but the truth was he was like a raw nerve, overly sensitive and tender.

Jake asked Angie what was their pleasure on lunch, where was it she wanted to go.

"I decided to cook at home, I want you to come to our house for lunch," she said.

So, Jake and Elzie rode together to Bridgeport to Elzie's house. Jake had never been there and needed someone to guide him there anyhow.

Elzie had a nice gray brick home on a corner lot with big oak trees in the front and back for shade. Around the border of the house, Angie had a good assortment of flowers and bushes, even though the flowers were naturally not in season in November, but the bushes were evergreen's always green with leaves.

Inside was a small foyer leading to a large kitchen den, nicely kept. A couple of deer heads mounted the wall.

Jake looked at Elzie and said, "Did you bag those deer?"

"Yeah," Elzie said, "The Company has a deer lease down in south Texas and I've gotten several over the years but these were real trophies and I had them mounted."

"When we was kids," Jake said, "You couldn't have hit one of those with a Sherman tank."

"I sure could." Elzie countered, "It was you that was always a poor shot. Bet you aint' never even shot a deer."

"Truth is cousin," Jake replied, "I never did cotton to killin one, cause then you got clean the thing and I wasn't interested."

"And you just come from church," Elzie said, "that's the biggest windiest tale I ever heard."

About that time Angie called the men to the bar for lunch. She had a nice pot roast with carrots and potatoes, roast gravy, hot rolls and she had made a coconut pie for desert. She had even poured their tea.

"You want to say grace?" Angie asked looking at Jake.

"Sure," Jake said. And he bowed his head taking Elzie and Angie's hand offering a prayer of thanks and thanks to the good friends they were and for a moment having to choke back a tear.

The three had their lunch with conversations on family and the up and coming holiday.

Jake looking at Angie told her about his and Elzie's conversation, not sure that he wasn't stepping into something that he might not should but he wanted to know if Angie would want to live out at their farm.

Angie listened to Jake with her big blue eyes, gray hair that once was dark brown, yet still maintained a youthful figure in spite of having four kids. When Jake had told her his offer, she said, "That's so nice of you. To tell you the truth, if Elzie wants to live out there, I am fine with it. He and I have a good life together and I didn't care if we were here or yon, Bridgeport Texas or Bridgeport Egypt, if I was with Elzie, I'd make a home. I know he has roots there and mine was in Sunset too, and going back there is ok. I could make home here, we've been here over twenty years, the house is paid for, but if Elzie wants to move, then we will move."

Elzie had remained silent in the conversation. He was giving it serious thought and he and Angie would decide after he had been officially retired. He was interested to see what kind of buyout his company was going to offer him. He knew one thing, that he and Jake would certainly be good company for each other.

Shortly after that Jake decided it was time for him to head back, he did need to feed the cows today. So, he thanked Angie for the fine lunch, and thanked Elzie for thinking of him and coming out for the weekend. It had really meant a lot. And with that, he was out the door, into his "go to town, church and stepping out truck," and on his way home.

It was a twenty minute drive to Sunset and another fifteen to the farm. It was arriving at the farm, and entering the house, he realized that he was really and suddenly all alone. Lois was not there to greet him or ask him about his day. She wasn't in the kitchen or sitting at her sewing machine or in her favorite chair watching TV, she wasn't there and she was there somehow yet. When Jake and Lois moved in with Jake's dad, his dad had moved himself into the part of the house he had added for Berthie May. It was a room on the end of the house, the full width of the house that made it a comfortable bedroom and a secondary living room and bath to give her privacy. It afforded P.D. the same luxury for the final part of his life while Jake and Lois took over P.D's bedroom. Jake figured if Ely was moving here, he would move into this part of the house like his grandma and father had, only he was not figuring it to be the last thing of his own life. Jake was thinking about building himself a new home a replica of his grandparents home but more modern.

The house was very quiet. Jake tried not to think about that as he changed out of his Sunday attire which was not his normal Sunday wear. Instead of wearing a suit that day, he had gone to church casual like the majority of the men now days and Elzie had as well. Usually Jake wore a suit and tie but he didn't today. But for feeding purposes, he slipped on his most comfortable clothing and the clothes he wore every day of his life, overalls. The wind was calm and he didn't feel he needed a jacket but he carried one in case, just in case he stuck his truck, or the truck died and he had to walk.

At the barn he loaded in his dispenser cubes and at his hay pen he would come back for a bale when he went to the Blane. He had put a bale on when he parked the truck Saturday. The diesel came to life and he was headed to the first area to feed on his family's place which joined the Pariot. He saw the cows were actually on the Pariot so he met them half way as they saw him coming and headed to him. He led them to where the last round bale had been left with the hay ring and let the bale down and drove away from it with his hay spike easing out of the center of the bale. Next, he cut the binding and kept the string, never leaving it on the ground as he had noticed some did, leaving a mess and something that sometimes an animal could get tangled on their hoofs. He tilted the hay ring and then let it fall around the new bale. Then he lowered the feeding shoot and left out a trail of cubes for the animals. The cows usually hurried and rushed for the cubes even though Jake kept out some liquid feed, they had wheat every three days to graze and always bales of dry hay, they still rushed for the cubes pushing each other away from them to get more for themselves. While they grazed, he counted them and studied them to make sure there were no problems.

Jake repeated the process on the Blane place with that herd and then over to the Jasper. Jake kept a hay pen over there for the ease of feeding. Otherwise he would have to pick a third bale at his house and carry over to the Jasper. Since he baled hay at the Jasper he always kept what he needed at the Jasper instead of bringing it from his house. By the time he had finished, it was time to gather the eggs and feed the chickens. Today he would get six eggs. It was then past time for going to church but Jake didn't mind, he really didn't want to go back to Sunset and come back after dark. There was something about coming home to an empty and dark house.

In the house, he was thinking about supper. Angie had made him a plate to take home, so he didn't have to cook, only warm what he had.

He turned on the TV to catch the end of some football games and to think about what he was needing to do tomorrow.

CHAPTER 5

One thing about being on a farm, you never knew exactly what your schedule might turn out. You might be planning on one thing and a dozen other events happen that change everything and before you know it the day is gone and you never got to do what you planned.

One thing Jake decided to do was to change rooms. For now, Jake was going to move his belongings into the room at the end of the house off the kitchen. For Jake it was about just being closer to the kitchen besides if his youngest son and his family were going to move up here soon, they would have to stay in this house and he could be in that part and out of their way. He could even shut the door and really be out of their sight. That was going to be tomorrow's project right after breakfast.

Jake woke early as was his habit, got up to shave and brush his teeth and then a hot shower. He dressed in his familiar blue overalls and headed to the kitchen. He cooked some oatmeal and made coffee and then went down to his shop to fetch his two wheeled dolly. He would pick up the chest of drawers and move the whole thing in one move and move the empty one to the master bedroom. The bed in the master bedroom was a king size and he was not going to move it, didn't need it and the one in his grandmother's old room was a regular size bed, which would be more than adequate for him. But, it took a couple of hours to move and empty the closet. Fortunately the closet in the new room was empty as after Jake's father died, Jake had removed all his father's clothing and items he didn't want and donated the clothes to hospice. He would have to deal with Lois's things later.

It was mid morning and Jake was going to check his fluid levels in his tractor when the phone rang.

It was an attorney in Bowie named Lance Linger. He had represented Mrs. McReynolds and her estate. Her estate was the old Uncle Spence Russell spread that was across the creek from Jake's family farm. Mr. Russell had come with his parents as a small child to Montague County just after the Civil War. The Indians were still wreaking havoc over the county and the Russell's laid claim to some six thousand acres. Over the years most had been sold off. The current acreage was two sections. The original house from Uncle Spence's family was still part of the homestead. Uncle Spence had died in 1957 at the age of 98 years just shy of his 99th. He had only one daughter Effie and she had married Leslie McReynolds and they had continued in the cattle business up until a few years ago. Mr. McReynolds had died about ten years ago and since then, Jake had assisted Miss Effie as she called with her operations but she finally leased out the place to Jake. She liked Jake as she had never had children and she always thought him a good boy. She was especially fond of Berthie May and Lige. Miss. Effie had died last year and her place had been in probate since. The lawyer was calling to tell Jake the probate was now all settled and he had some accounts he needed to go over with Jake. Jake made an appointment to meet after lunch that very day.

He had really no idea what the lawyer was speaking of. After Miss. Effie's death, Jake had operated the place but had sold all the cattle and was cutting hay on the hay field and letting the native grass have a rest, what ranchers called deferred grazing.

The appointment was at 1:30 and it was now eleven. Jake decided to drive in to Bowie and just have lunch there, that way he hadn't messed up the kitchen any more than what he had done at breakfast.

Jake arrived in Bowie at 12:30 and went to restaurant called The Texas Longhorn. They usually had buffet style food and he wouldn't have to mess with a menu. He took a plate and made his selection of salad and fried chicken and a couple of vegetables. The waitress took his tea order and he was ready to feast when he looked up Glen Ray Shelton was sitting down at his table.

"Well my God," Jake said. "When did you get back from Canada?"

"Yesterday," Glen said, as he sat down with a plate full of food twice the size of Jake's."

"How was the food up there?" Jake asked.

"Oh it was ok, nothing to run foot races for. Why you asking? Glen said.

"No reason, just making conversation. I don't know a thing about Canada, so I just wondered if they fed you ok up there." Jake said but under his tone there was sarcasm. He was poking fun at Glen Ray but Glen Ray to his nature was sometimes the last to catch on.

Jake studied his longtime friend and fellow classmate. Glen Ray was like the rest of his friends heavier than their youth days. Glen's hair was very thin and he wore glasses just like he had worn in high school only a more modern style.

"Jake," Glen Ray said, "I am so sorry that I was out and not able to get back for Lois's funeral. I really grieved at that."

"It's ok," Jake said. "I got through it and am coping. Hey, you will never believe what has happened in the past few days. First off, my kids went home Friday and Elzie came out and spent the whole weekend with me, and then he and Angie went to church with me and then we went over to their place for dinner after church. But Elzie is being forced out at his job into early retirement, not really too early cause next year he'd be 65, but he's having to retire at the end of December. Well, anyway, I'm going to let him and Angie move out to my old house and live. Lois and I moved into my dad's house after mother died to look after him and we just stayed."

"You don't mean it?" Glen Ray said. "Are you selling him back part his Grandpa's old place?"

"Naw, just going to let them live there as long as they want. They can pay their own bills, and that's all they got to do." Jake said.

"That's a pretty good deal, I'd take that." Glen Ray said.

"I hope they do." Jake replied. "We can be good company to one another. Might even play some thumps sometimes."

"I remember that," Glen Ray said, "Made my middle fingernail sore too."

"What are you doing up here? Jake asked.

"I flew in to Dallas last night, wanted to come up visit you but I had some client work to do on some oil leases and had some other business to take care of. My youngest brother, you know Morgan lives here," Glen Ray said.

"I'd forgot that," Jake said, "I just haven't seen him in a long time. He still in the oil business?"

"Oh yeah, he's a partner with me and Cooper. But he also has a big car rental service in two airports and he has the home place and keeps cows but he lives in Bowie."

"Well I sure hope I'll see more of you before you dash back down to Houston." Jake said. "Right now I've got an appointment to take care of and then I'll be at my place. Come see me." Jake said.

"I sure will." Glen Ray replied.

Jake had finished his meal and it was close to the appointment time. Leaving, he paid for Glen Ray's lunch.

He arrived some ten minutes early at Linger's office.

Linger had bought and converted an old house into his office. Several attorneys in the area had done that. Jake entered the foyer and was looking straight into the face of the secretary. Behind her was a small room for files and copiers and behind that room was Linger's private office. He usually didn't have clients in that office but in his conference room which was the big room off to the left of the Secretary's office. She led Jake into that room and said that Mr. Linger would be with him shortly.

Jake thought he could hear Linger on the phone and he was sure of it when he heard him say "Ok, goodbye."

Shortly the very young youthful attorney came in the conference room in his shirtsleeves and tie loosened. He shook Jake's hand very vigorously, and motioning Jake to sit back down.

"As you know," Linger began, "I was Mrs. McReynold's attorney for several years. ("How could you," Jake thought, "You don't look over 16, how long you been shaving anyway?") "She was very astute and she conducted her business in a professional way. She has no linear heirs and her late husband has some but Mr. McReynolds left his estate to his wife, which really was some cash assets since the ranch was her father's. So it is or was hers do whatever she wanted."

Jake had not said anything because he was not entirely sure why he was there.

"Well Mr. Oldham, Mrs. McReynolds specifically has named you as her benefice and she has left you the ranch, surface and one fourth of the minerals. She has four producing wells and she has left three fourths to the Sunset church of Christ. Since her death, we have received all the oil royalties here and the money has been in escrow until we had probated her will, had made sure she had no creditors and everything was in order before we proceeded."

"Now, Mr. Oldham, your portion of the minerals for the past twelve months is in the sum of this check for one hundred thousand, eight hundred forty five dollars and some twenty six cents. My secretary has the check prepared for you and I have a document here for you to sign plus the deeds for her place, twelve hundred eighty acres. Are you not part of the Sunset church of Christ?" He asked.

When Jake affirmed such, Linger then said, "I have a check for your church too, in the amount of Four Hundred Thousand dollars and some odd cents."

Jake was about to faint, he thought. He was overwhelmed by her kindness.

"I don't really know what to say." Jake said. "I'm extremely grateful but not really deserving of Mrs. McReynolds kindness."

"Mrs. McReynolds held you in special acclaim." Linger said. "She spoke highly of your entire family."

"I guess I'll need to go and record those deeds." Jake said.

"Or I can do it for you." Linger said.

"No, that's ok, I'm sure you've done enough. I'll be glad to take care of it." Jake said.

He left the law office overwhelmed. "Well Lord," Jake begin in prayer, "You sure have blessed me many times over."

He drove straight to Montague and to the County Clerk's office to record the deed changing the name from the James Spence Russell to Jake Oldham Trust. A few years ago, Jake had gone to an attorney and upon his suggestion, put all the land he owned in trust with he and Lois as trustees. It was stated in the trust that upon the death of either he or Lois that the two sons would be added to the trust and now that was what was going to take place.

He drove back from Montague to Forestburg and then to the farm. He had not been in the house long before there was a knock at the door. It was Glen Ray.

"Well, come in old pal," Jake said.

CHAPTER 6

Glen Ray came striding in the house following Jake. "This is your folk's house, isn't it?" Glen said.

"Yup," Jake said. "After mama died, me and Lois had to eventually move up here to look after Daddy. And the house just suited us too, we didn't get in a hurry to go back to our house and then we were going to have to decide what to do with an extra house, then Lois was sick…"

"I got a nice place in Houston, but fixin to sell it. In fact I got a contract on it now. I've bought me a place to build on out on Lake Ray Roberts." Glen Ray said.

"Well, that's is closer to home," Jake said "But what about your law practice."

"Last ten years I have mostly dabbed in oil and real estate." Glen said. "I'm ready to slow down. You know my wife left me and that cost a pretty penny but I'm free and clear."

"No, I didn't know that Glen. Course I hadn't seen you much in the last dozen years." Jake said.

"I don't mind telling you," Glen said, "The years have been real good to me. I don't have to worry over nothing. I sure don't have to feed cows to worry about paying bills."

"I don't either," Jake said. "The Lord has blessed me many times over. Feeding cows is now a pass time, it's not life or death, it's not one day away from the poor house."

"Well of course, I didn't mean it that way about you, Jake, I know you've worked hard, had several successes and are reaping the rewards." Glen Ray said. "Hey you remember how we used to farm watermelons and that usually bought our school clothes?"

"Many times," Jake said, Gladly allowing the conversation to ease in tension. To him there was a little sting in Glen Ray's remark about feeding cows. But, he was willing to let it slide.

"You know I really miss our days growing up." Glen Ray said, "It was a good time in life and we had fun and things were so simple then."

"We think it was now, but back then we were all hustling to survive on the land. We had our cows, we had our hay and peanuts and the melons, we sold eggs, some cream, and raised and sold pigs. My mama and Elzie's mama worked at the dress factory in Bowie and my dad took odd jobs here and there until he went in the dozer business. I think we thought life was pretty complicated, Jake said. And then the dozer work got more and more and the government brought in those contracts for conservation work. Why except for my Army time, we worked a lot and we made good money. Saying all that, I would sure have or I might have done a few things different back in school days."

"Yeah, like what?" Glen Ray asked.

"Oh I think I would have done a few things different with Nell." Jake said in a sort of melancholy way. "I think I would have made really sure she went to the school dance with me instead of you."

"Wouldn't have made any difference," Glen Ray said, "The whole darn night all she could do was watch you and tell me how nice you looked and how good and smooth you danced. Seems like I remember her following you outside. Did you talk to her out side?"

Jake chuckled a bit, "Oh yeah, we talked a second or two, kissed a second or two then she went back in and I stayed out a few more minutes before I went in."

"Kissed her? Why dad gum you, I never got no good night sugar from her when I took her home!" Glen Ray said.

"Sometimes," Jake said, "Women are a complete mystery."

"You can say that," Glen Ray said.

"What happened to her anyway?" Glen Ray asked.

"Oh you know while I was gone to service she was finishing high school and she was trying her best to jump clean out of the chute, she wanted to put Sunset in the rear view mirror and she started dating a guy that promised her they would move to Kansas if she would stick with him." Jake said. "She stuck with him but they never got out of Bowie and he wasn't too good to her and she divorced him. Then she went down to Dallas to nursing school and I think she met a med student and married and they ended up in Mississippi. I guess she is still there like us growing old."

"Don't remind me about growing old." Glen Ray said. "Like members of my family, I have to battle high blood pressure, heart problems and I know I'm fixin to have my knees replaced."

"I guess that is the price we pay for living too long." Jake said.

The men talked another hour and Glen Ray jumped up and said, "Well hey, dog gone it, I hate to go but it's getting late and I need to get on up to Morgan's. I'll be headed back to Houston tomorrow."

"Glen Ray, I'm so glad you came. And by the way thanks for the donation to the cemetery. That was so nice of your family in Lois's memory." Jake said.

"Hey man," Glen Ray said, "You are just like family. I just hated that I was out of the country when you lost her."

Jake didn't answer only shook his head showing that he understood. They shook hands, hugged and patted each other on the back and then Glen Ray was out the door and gone.

Then the room was quiet. Jake would make a bacon sandwich and drink some tea before trying out his new room just off the kitchen.

He chuckled to himself and thought, After all these years, I find out the truth. He wormed his way into getting the most important date of the year with Nell, and he never got a kiss. At least, Jake thought, I got more than one of those from those sweet lips.

CHAPTER 7

J ake slept reasonably well in his new room. He liked it all right. He could get up, get ready for the day, walk into the kitchen and fix whatever he wanted to start the morning and then out to the truck. It was feeding day and he didn't even have a bale on the fork but that wouldn't take long once the cubes were loaded in the feeder hopper. The old cows were ready for him, even watching as Jake undid the bail and put the ring around it. It was a good morning, much warmer than the past days but the weatherman said last night a new cold front would blow in on Thanksgiving.

Once he had fed, he placed a call to his financial advisor Vince Bradford in Decatur. He made an appointment for Monday after Thanksgiving. Next he called the elders at church and requested they get with him for a meeting and they agreed to meet at the church building that afternoon.

It was about time for the carrier to have brought the mail so Jake walked down to check the mail box and found the mail had come. He had a couple of newspapers, the local paper and one from Wichita Falls plus his propane bill and electric bill. He sat down at the kitchen and looked the mail over putting in place for Lois and then it hit him that Lois wasn't there, wasn't going to be looking at the mail. It was painful.

He decided to bake a potato for lunch and make a new batch of sweet tea. Shortly after lunch he drove in his town truck to town to meet with the elders of the church.

Archer was the first to arrive and Grover Meador was the second to arrive but within minutes of Archer. The men went into the church building and sat down in one of the classrooms. The minister Dave Preston was not in his office and Jake was glad he was not. Unless asked, Dave was excluded from the elders meetings.

Archer was the eldest of the men and considered the leader and the one to conduct the business meetings. As usual, once the men sat down and had their greetings, they bowed in prayer and unless Archer asked one of the other's, he would lead the prayer himself and on this day he did.

Archer began the meeting by saying that at Jake's request they meet and turned the floor to Jake to state the nature of the business. He told the men about Mrs. McReynolds gift to the church and how he wanted to set the money in a trust for the church that they could take the interest in the future and use it for the minister's salary and devote their weekly contributions to other efforts. The men had no objection and then decided in addition to what Jake held how much more to add to it to have what they considered a working trust that would pay for their preacher. Jake told them he too had benefited and he was going to donate a portion of his to the trust as well.

Then the next item was the consideration of Jake's position. Jake just flat out told the men that unless there was objection, he saw no reason to resign but he would if any member of the church thought he should. The other two men agreed and with a prayer, they were done with their business. Both Archer and Grover with great affection shook Jake's hand. He was some twenty years younger than the other two but they valued him as someone very wise beyond his years even though he himself was no spring chicken.

Since it was close to five in the evening, Jake drove to the Dairy Queen in Bowie for supper. Once he got home and took care of the chickens, he would be in for the evening. Tuesday night at Dairy Queen is the burger special night and the place was pretty busy with folks after the special. Some were eating there but others were getting take out.

There were no tables empty but Jake knew several there and asked if he could sit with at a table where two couples were sitting. The two couples were all natives of Bowie but knew Jake from church. They attended in Bowie but they knew many of the Sunset members including Jake. The first couple were the Breeze's and the second the Jordan's. Mrs. Breeze said, "We were so sorry to hear of your loss."

"Thank you, sister," Jake said. "It will just take time to get past it. And right now with all the holidays, Thanksgiving and Christmas, it is really a difficult time, but I have good strong kids and good friends, good brethren all looking out for me."

"That's so wonderful." Mrs. Jordan said. "It is all part of a good support base and we all need that."

The five of them ate their burgers and engaged in small talk but as soon as Jake could get away he did because he had to get the eggs gathered before the chickens were trying to roost. So he hurried on home. He put out some feed made sure their water supply was adequate and picked up five eggs. It was enough and would certainly be enough for him.

Inside the house was getting dark as he switched on the light in the kitchen and soon was turning on the TV in the living room. Although the days had warmed the nights got cold and he appreciated his gas log fireplace. It was one thing that gave him a feeling a comfort even though alone. One more day alone and then the kids would be home. He was glad.

He had yet to clean out Lois's closet and things. He hoped his daughter in laws would take a hand in that.

CHAPTER 8

Although he had fed the day before, Jake drove around just checking cows. He was glad he did because he had seven more new baby calves.

It was a cool morning but promising to warm before the next cold front came blowing in. Back at the house, he went out and picked up his mail. Nothing of significance but he was in the habit of wanting to know what was there. Sometimes he got a letter from someone of the past, and sometimes he got a note from a distant relative. But today it was mostly advertisements getting ready for the day after Thanksgiving.

Jake looked and had forgotten to wash the dishes all week. He better remedy that before the kids got there or he would catch it. So, he unloaded the dishwasher which had clean dishes, and loaded it back up and had it cleaning up the past few days of things he had used. Luckily, there wasn't a lot.

At noon he decided to make another bacon sandwich and realized he wasn't doing too well in the cooking department. He had a crock pot and a pressure cooker. He could plan out some meals and put them on while he was out.

Jake's dozer equipment had been sitting idle since last Friday. When his dad was healthy, the two of them had run the equipment and done countless projects. After his dad had given up on running the equipment, Jake found a man who needed work that had experience named Tony

Edwards. Tony had worked in the heavy equipment business for some time but when he met Jake, was out of work and needing a job. Jake put him to work and things went very well. About six months later Tony's cousin Clint Willis had the same dilemma and Jake hired him. He told the two that they would always give an honest day for honest pay. That there would be no short cut's, they would give each job full attention. They were to take care of the equipment as if it were theirs because repairs were expensive. From the time Clint went to work, Jake's job was to secure work for them to do under Jake's company name. He would charge the bills, collect the bills and would pay them. It had gone well and Jake had been busy meeting new clients and securing work for the two to do but when Lois's health got bad, he had cancelled his appointments until he knew what was going to happen. After Lois died, he rescheduled to meet people the week following Thanksgiving. He paid the boys for the week to be off and would see them back on Monday following Thanksgiving.

While the dishes were cleaning, Jake realized he had not swept the house or dusted a thing. He had a feeling of panic that the kids were going to see for the first time since being married dirt in his house. Jake got busy running the vacuum cleaner and dust rag to help the appearance of the house.

He felt like he had just finished and sat down when he heard a car. Susie and Leeza came in.

"Hi ya'll," Jake said.

Susie made a nod to Jake as she was coming in arms full of grocery sacks.

"Hi Grandpa," Leeza said.

Jake looked at his only granddaughter with pride. To others she was her own person but Jake could see a lot of his late mother in this spindly teen. She had long locks of blond hair and very pale blue eyes hidden behind fashionable glasses. She bounded across the room to give Jake a big hug.

To himself he thought Leeza regarding him as some old dinosaur about to fade into oblivion. An old man clad in overalls and antique glasses and a hat pulled down over his head shuffling around mumbling to himself.

But to Leeza, she saw an astounding man who had fixed in his mind his ways about things, a caring man about others and a tower of strength especially in the past few days. She loved him with great admiration.

Jake got up from the kitchen table from where he sat looking at the newspaper and opened his arms to her.

Ely was the last to come in carrying their bags.

"When is Phil coming?" Jake asked.

"Either late tonight or early in the morning." Ely replied.

"Oh shoot, I need to go down and make sure the house is ok." Jake said.

"Don't worry," Susie said, "I'll check the house as soon as we get settled. Who's been down there since we all went home?"

"Really no one," Jake said, "But I don't know that the sheets were changed when you all were here for the funeral. I haven't changed the sheets up stairs. Elzie and I both slept upstairs in our old rooms."

"Don't worry about it, we'll get it later." Susie said. Susie was busy putting up grocery items. Jake had started to process of thawing his turkey the day before.

"Ely, put ya'll's stuff in the master bedroom, it is the guest room now." Jake said.

"When did it become the guest room?" Ely asked.

"Yesterday morning." Jake replied. "I moved into the room by the kitchen. It has everything I'll need and that way you all can have your privacy and Leeza can have the whole upstairs."

"I'm sure Leeza will like that." Ely said.

"I think I'll go gather the eggs." Jake said. "Leeza you want to go and help me?"

Leeza looked up from her phone that she was so intent with and shrugged her shoulders and said, "Guess so."

Out the back door they went as Jake picked up his egg basket, one that had belonged to his grandma, a woven basket a relative of hers had sent her from Alabama.

Next to the chicken house was a small building that the feed was stored in. Jake filled a small gallon bucket with the mash mixture and showed Leeza where to pour it, in the long feed trough made for chickens. It was no more than two inches wide, but six feet long reinforced at the top by a heave triangular shaped wire. The chickens could eat the food out of the trough but the wire prevented them from sticking their foot in the trough to scratch the mash. Chickens love to scratch the soil as they forge. Jake gathered seven eggs that day. He then checked their water and turned on the faucet and filled the container they were getting water from, which was an old tractor tire that had been split in half, which made a good watering trough.

Leeza got some chicken poop on her shoes and was having a gross out- fit but Jake just showed her to wipe her feet and clean them off best she could. She was worried about a nasty smell. Jake only laughed.

"Not funny," she said.

"It's just all part of farm life," Jake replied. "You best get used to this because this is going to be one of your chores."

She only rolled her eyes.

"You got anything specific planned for supper?" Ely asked.

"I should have put some stuff on to cook," Jake said "I'm not running on all my cylinders yet."

"It's ok" Ely said. "We brought up some smoked barbecue and we can make some real nice brisket sandwiches."

"Oh yeah," Jake said, "That will be perfect."

After supper, Jake and Ely were sitting in the living room enjoying the cozy warmth of the fire place, listening to something on TV.

"I'd like for you to go with me in the morning to feed." Jake said.

"Oh sure, I was going to anyhow," Ely answered.

Jake waited for Ely to tell him what he wanted to tell him but Ely never indicated. Jake didn't know at that moment if Ely had changed his mind about coming out or moving out there or if his family had changed their minds or what. Ely was not saying at the moment and Jake decided not to push it. When they were out in the pasture, he could find out then.

CHAPTER 9

Morning came and once Jake was dressed, he had coffee going in the kitchen, biscuits in the oven and sausages cooking on the stove. The bacon was cooking in the microwave when Ely walked in.

"Morning son," Jake said.

"Morning Dad," Ely said. "I smelled the food and knew I better get up.

"I know we are having a big Thanksgiving dinner today but I can't go out and work much without some breakfast in me. You want any eggs?" Jake asked.

"Sure," Ely said.

As soon as Jake took up the sausages and drained off the grease, he broke a couple of eggs in the skillet, salted and peppered them and watched them cook. When the white was done, he flipped the eggs so that the yolk would get cooked.

"I never did understand TV shows showing eggs with the yolks not cooked. Who in their right mind would eat an egg like that?" Jake said.

"I think people up north might," Ely replied.

Jake just made a sour face and shook his head.

He scooped out the eggs in a plate and cooked two more, and got the pan of biscuits out of the oven. They were just right.

"Dad, you make those biscuit?" Ely asked.

"Sure do," Jake said, "My grandma taught me how. I still have her old whiskey bottle for a roll pin to roll out the dough."

"Grandma Bertha taught you how to make biscuits?" Ely asked.

"Grandma taught me a lot of things, as did Grandpa and my dad and my mama." Jake said.

"Each one had their thing." Ely said.

"Well sort of." Jake said. "My grandma was a hard worker, a stringent saver, a real manager. My Grandpa was a fair farmer, a man that never got in a hurry. My dad knew work, was ambitious and pushed to the limits. My mama was just the solidity we needed to hold us all together. She was all love, she was all kindness, but she also insisted on some things and my dad never argued with her on those things."

"Like what?" Ely asked.

"Like going to church." Jake said. "She didn't miss, she wasn't going to miss and she wasn't going to allow you to miss unless you was on your death bed sick."

"So, your saying you got good things from all them?" Ely asked.

"That's right. And I can't say I got more things from anyone of them. I learned all the best things from all of them." Jake said.

Jake's voice almost broke when he said, "And I miss them all. I'd love for them to all be here today and of course including your mama."

Jake plopped his eggs in his plate, got his cup and saucer for coffee and let Ely get whatever he wanted to drink coffee in. They ate their breakfast in silence although Ely noted just before he started he saw Jake bow his head and silently say a prayer.

Dishes in the sink, the two men went out to the truck and headed out to the pasture. Jake had the hay on the fork and the cubes already in the feeder.

Finally Jake couldn't stand much more of the waiting. "What is it you were going to tell me about moving out here?"

"Well dad, you know how I have built up a chain of oil change stores all around Dallas and I've been successful with it and was about to open two more stores when a company approached me to buy me out. And the price is a good profit, and if I wanted to, I could go down in East Texas and buy me a place on a lake and just fish the rest of my life, but that ain't me. Me and Sus's been talking and she's agreeing with me that we are ready to get back to a slower, simpler life and we want to be here close to you and I want to get in the cattle business and whatever else you want to. I want to do it here with you." Ely said.

Jake just sat there as he was driving in the pasture giving all of what Ely said serious thought.

Finally Jake said, "You know when I was still a teen, and Elzie's folks moved and we bought their place, my dad had the place put in my name and started me out sort of directing me in what would be part of my life work. Then when the Jasper's lost their home to the fire and they were ready to give up being in the cattle business, dad pushed the deal and yet it was all for me helping me in getting my start. When I came home from the Army, he had got a good dozer business started and he got another dozer and had me go right in there with him. And you know we worked pretty good together. We built a lot of roads and then the government started a conservation program and we got in on the ground floor of that and just did tons of dozer work through them and then they started building flood dams on all these tributary creeks that feed the main creeks like Brushy and Denton and we got in on a lot of that. And my dad helped me all along. I can't think of a better thing than you coming back and we taking care of this land. You don't know it but I just acquired another twelve hundred and eighty acres, the old Uncle Spence Russell place."

"No kidding!" Ely said, why that's on the other side of Denton creek, all good rich land."

"Are you planning on building a new home out here?" Jake asked.

"Yes sir, if you will help me with planning the site." Ely said.

"Elzie and his wife Angie are going to move out here. I'm going to let them live in our old house where his folks used to live." Jake said.

"Wow, I'll bet you will really like having him back out here." Ely said.

"You don't have a problem with it then?" Jake asked.

"Why no," Ely said. "Old Elzie will be good for you and keep you company."

The feeding was nothing but routine as they put out the hay and distributed, the cubes to the anxious bovines. The wind was getting up and Jake knew it was going to get really cold that day.

Back at the house, he found Phil and his family there. Parking the truck they put on another bale of hay and refilled the cube distributor before going up to the house.

The twins, Jacob Andrew and Elijah Phillip were playing some game on the TV with some kind of box they called an X Box. Julia was working in the kitchen with Susan and Phil was reading the newspaper that had come the day before.

"Did ya'll just get here?" Jake asked.

"No we got here last night, just went on down to the house without bothering anyone." Phillip said. "It was late, and we just went on down there and were pretty quick to turn in."

"Well I never thought to look when we were feeding, or you could have went with us." Jake said.

"It's ok," Phil said, "In the future there will be plenty of turns on that feeding."

"What do you mean?" Jake asked.

"Do you remember last time we was here, I said we all had things to talk to you about?" Phil said. "Well I guess Ely has told you his plans, and mine are almost the same. I've been very successful with my firm, but my partners have offered to buy me out and hire me as a consultant and I can work out of my home. Julie and I came to the same conclusion that Ely and Sus' came to, that we are ready to come back home. We are ready to work with you and partner in the cattle business and I think our children will grow up better if we are here. I want my boys to wake up to the sound of a rooster crowing and to see firsthand where eggs come from, and watch the joy of raising new born calves, to learn to drive a tractor and to learn firsthand how to drive a truck and all the other good things farm life has to offer."

"I suppose you, like your brother, will want to build yourself a home?" Jake said.

"Yes sir, that would be in the plans." Phil answered.

"How would you like to build on the Blane place?" Jake asked.

"The Blane would be fine, if you level a house pad with your dozer." Phil said.

"We can do it." Jake said, "A house pad for you and one for Ely."

About an hour later, the girls called out that dinner was just about ready, for everyone to wash and get ready. The turkey was out of the oven and Phil was carving it. The dressing done, the gravy, the creamed potatoes, the sweet potatoes, the two salads, one green leaf and the other a jell-o, the home made cranberry sauce all done. On the counter were a chocolate pie and a coconut and a sweet potato pie for desert. All things were ready.

As they sat and Jake at the head of the table he bowed and gave thanks to God for all the blessings that could be had and for his children and their families. In spite of the empty seat that Lois would have occupied and had in many thanksgivings from the past, this was going to be one of the best in a long time. Jake couldn't have been happier, he was receiving three great blessings in the form of his two sons building homes and moving back to the farm and his best friend moving back coming home. He was sorry Lois wasn't there to see it as he knew she would have been proud and he knew in his own heart that his parents and grandparents would have been just as proud to see all the family and Elzie coming back to the old place. Thanksgiving couldn't have been better and it was certainly going to be a good Christmas.

CHAPTER 10

Things change quickly. Elzie found out right after Thanksgiving the brick company paid him for all his vacations and sick leave and retired him by the first of December and after agreeing to move out to Jake's old house on the Pariot land, were moved in by the middle of the month. They listed their home with a realtor and had had a contract on it by the time they had moved. Everything moved at a fast pace. Soon Elzie was going out with Jake to feed and spend a lot of his days with Jake. If they had nothing special to do, they went up to Jake's house and played thumps or dominoes. It was just so perfect to Jake and Elzie. It was like old times, it was like their youth except their elders were not there because they had become the elders, and that was tough for them sometimes.

Christmas was about on them, and Angie worried about their kids coming. She wanted them all out there Christmas day but two were coming Christmas Eve and two on Christmas Day, they had other places to be besides Elzie's.

As for Jake, his kids were coming there and they would have supper on Christmas Eve and then be together on Christmas Day as well. The twins and Leeza slept upstairs, Ely and Susie in the master bedroom and Phillip and Julia in Jake's room while Jake slept on the couch in the living room. It was only for one night, Jake believed he could mange one night for his kid's sake.

Christmas day was a big feast and the kids receiving gifts from their parents and surprises. Jake always left all that to Lois so the best he could do was give each grandchild and daughter in law some cash.

The big gift for Jake was Phillip's announcement that he and Julie were planning like Ely, to move back to the farm. Phil had arranged with his company that he could do the work via consulting and computer and wasn't needed in the office every day. He and Julie had grown tired of the rat race in the metro area and the traffic and like Ely, Phil had a longing to be close to the land. He believed he would grow to treasure the times with his father.

The three men along with Susie and Julie sat at the dining table to discuss future plans and Phil and Julie agreed they would build their house on the Blane place while Ely would build his about where Jake's grandparent's home once stood. Everyone was pleased. Jake would get his dozers to build the pads and he would bring up some of his stored sand for the foundation. Back a few years past, when the government started building flood dams on all the tributary creeks that fed Denton Creek, they knew the creek wouldn't always have water. So from the Pariot all through the Blane, Jake had dug a long pit forty feet wide and twenty feet deep running parallel to the creek allowing overflow to fill this channel, would help insure during the wet seasons he would have stored up water that might carry through the dry ones. It would prove beneficial. The silt sand that he dug out of the creek, he stacked up and periodically sold it for house pads, and he still had ample to build theirs.

January proved to be a wet month, delaying house construction. Phillip wasn't on a schedule and Ely and his family were living with Jake, so there wasn't a timetable for them.

When Ely and his family came up, they had to consider the schools for Leeza, and after visiting them decided to send her to Forestburg. Although they were in the Bowie School taxing district, they could send her to either, Bowie, Goldburg, Forestburg or Alvord. Jake banked at Alvord and had since he was a teen even though the First National at Bowie had bought the bank at Alvord, he still banked there and would not have objected had they sent Leeza to Alvord. He knew about as many people in Forestburg as he did Alvord. They chose Forestburg because of the size, the teacher student ratio and they good agriculture program they had believing that Leeza would participate because of her new environment.

For a couple of weeks Jake showed Ely his ropes that is the routine around the farm, the feeding of the stock, the preparing time to work the calves for vaccination and castration of the bull calves, the worming and fly treatments for all the animals. Of course the working the animals was something not done in January but Jake was preparing Ely who in turn could prepare Phillip. Jake was willing to turn the feeding over to Ely and let Ely take a lead. Meanwhile, Jake was dreaming up things for him and Elzie to do.

One afternoon the phone rang and Jake found himself talking to a man who had bought up considerable property between Jake and the farm to market road and even beyond. There was the place that joined the Jasper, called the Harris place that the man was interested in selling. To him it was worthless as it was and going to be too costly to get it in production for his purpose. He had bought some three thousand acres at the courthouse because of back taxes and the Harris was part of that. It was seven hundred acres. Jake agreed to meet the man to discuss the situation but in his own mind he would buy the place if he could. The place was on Denton Creek, but had grown up in heavy river bottom trees, deep rooted and would be expensive to remove. At one time the man who had operated it when Jake was a small boy had made a slew from the overflow from the creek but the owner who had just lost the place had dozed that dam down and drained the water. Jake thought he might could rebuild the slew and set up a hunting business for deer and duck hunting. He knew the slew could be rebuilt even though it might be a year or two before he had the rain to fill it.

A couple of days later he met with the man and they made a deal and Jake bought the property. As soon as his dozers were available he took Tony and Clint and showed them a plan, to build the slew, to make passages or lanes throughout the property and picked three sites for two cabins and a bunkhouse. He and Elzie would use the spring to build the cabins and the bunkhouse. They didn't have to be in a hurry as long as this was all prepared before next hunting season. It would be a pretty good outing for him and Elzie and when they needed some extra muscle, there was always Ely.

It turned out that Ely joined them every day because he could see these two "seniors" needed some extra grunt or they would never have finished the project. They built two cabins that had two separate beds with an open area for a kitchen and den. The bunk house was a large room with eight bunks and a kitchen in the center of the room. Sometimes Ely thought he was dealing with a couple of kids the way Jake and Elzie picked at each other while they worked. Ely sometimes would just yell, "HEY! I need to drive this nail; ya'll shut that up and hold this." The two men would just look at each other and snigger as they obeyed. Ely just shook his head. Jake's idea was during the spring families might want to come up and walk on the nature trails, do photography, and observe the land and wildlife and the bunk was for four hunters who would lease the property during the hunting season for duck, deer, and turkey. They had drilled a water well that would service all three spots and would bring in propane for heat and cooking. Wise Co-op brought in electricity for the three spots as well as the propane. All Jake had to do was put an ad in the Fort Worth and Dallas papers and he was running over with calls. He would not lease to anyone over the phone but insisted they meet in person. The cabins would be completed by the first of April. Tony and Clint were sometimes drawn in to help when a dozer was down for servicing.

He would finally agree to a group of business men who seemed ok. Jake laid down some rules to them too. If you find a gate shut, then you leave it shut, if it is open then do the same. No drinking while hunting. Respect the land but remember they didn't own it and if Jake allowed someone else on the land while they were there, that was his business. He had no trouble with the agreement and these business men who would be up the following September to prepare for their hunting season.

Meanwhile Jake and with Elzie's company were busy drumming up new dozer business for his guys running the dozers. Jake and Elzie would go and meet clients and tell them what to expect from them as the kind of work and services they provided. Elzie was enjoying himself on these business meetings.

One day as they were traveling to meet some new landowner, Elzie said, "Things seem to come pretty easy for you Jake."

"What do you mean by that?" Jake asked.

"Well here when we were kids ya'll was scratching out a living on a hundred sixty acres and now you are sitting here with near three thousand acres and you just keep filling your pockets with money."

"Oh bull," Jake said, "I've worked hard and done without to be where I am today."

"I thought one time the world was mine to have, one special night I thought it was all mine and it was gone in the blink of an eye and I had nothing."

Elzie was confused by what Jake said but didn't pursue the conversation.

"Well you seem to done alright in my view." Elzie said. "You got good land, good cattle and this hunting business will probably be a big success. And you got them boys running dozers and that ain't chicken feed."

"Everybody I guess finds their way to make a mark in life," Jake said. "I try hard, I have worked hard in the past but it is time now in our lives to reap the benefits."

"You just happen to have garnered more BENEFITS than I did cousin," Elzie said.

"I'm turning more and more of it to the boys." Jake said. "I'd rather have more free time with you."

"I guess we'll keep ourselves busy." Elzie said.

"I'm sure we'll find things to keep us busy, they might not all make money but who cares? Let's have some fun, let's raise a little hell," Jake said.

"I'm telling on you," Elzie said.

CHAPTER 11

This time of year Vicksburg can experience cool snaps but it is usually warm and the winters mild. The north fronts that hit the mid west and swing through Texas usually take an eastern swing and just touch the most northern part of Mississippi. Seldom did the bad cold snaps get into Vicksburg, their winters were usually mild. Vicksburg is a fashionable city, full of charm, full of rich history, southern grace, and southern memory.

Nell Hunter Jefferson was very busy with packing her final belongings and loading them into her new SUV Cadillac and about to depart Mississippi for the last time. The last few days had been such a shock and yet subconsciously a relief.

Life had been grand in Vicksburg. When Nell married Mark Jefferson soon to become Dr. Mark Jefferson, she had no idea what their lives would be like. They had met while she was in nursing school at Baylor in Dallas and he was in his third year of school about to graduate and establish his residency as a cardiologist. He was very handsome, had girls on his arms all the time and she felt really privileged when he ask her out. He kept asking, kept wooing, and coaxing her to his bed and she had remained Victorian keeping her ladyship. However, his charm persisted and though he didn't get her in his bed before they married, he did succeed in getting her to marry him. But she found out even though they married within six months he was still wooing nurses and student nurses into side rooms, towel rooms for quickies and leave them wanting more. She thought with her own charms she would win him over and for the next thirty years worked very hard at it.

He had been good to her. When he finally was established as a resident cardiologist, he headed them for his own hometown where his family owned the major shares in the local hospital, a pharmacy, two nursing facilities and two rehab facilities Vicksburg received them with open arms. She started as a nurse and was soon elevated as assistant director of the nursing department in the hospital. Mark's success was well known and soon he was building his bride a modern southern antebellum mansion, fifteen bedrooms, a guest dining room to seat seventy five people, a pool and fifteen manicured acres. His intent for her was to be his grand hostess, his lover when he wanted her and the rest of the time to lead a quite social life belonging to all the right clubs and being part of all the right campaigns when they were fund raising or they were lobbying senators and congressmen for funds. In some ways she felt she was his slave, his prisoner. She knew he kept tabs on her whereabouts all the time. It was the duty of the chauffer to give reports to Mark on where she had been each and every day. When her father died, he took the hospital's private plane and flew her to Bowie and had arranged for a car from Dallas to pick them up to attend the funeral and as soon as the "amen" was said at the cemetery, wisp her back to the airport without much chance to speak to anyone. But he was good to her, lavished her with gifts, jewelry, fine clothes, breath taking vacations, and an elegant lifestyle that most women would envy.

The end for them had come on New Year's Eve night. They were hosting a party for all the hospital doctors and personal staff, some of the city dignitaries and any of the elite society members. She would not know who he was upstairs in bed with but was found alone fully in his pajamas and very dead. A cardiologist had died from a major myocardial infarction apparently. The autopsy confirmed it. You would have thought a president had died the way the town turned out for the funeral and the visitation, and funeral that the family planned was elaborate. They spared no expense. Nell was not even consulted, but just picked up for the event. The next day the family attorney came calling and sat down with her to go over her late husband's will. He had left her his assets and the estate they lived on, but the attorney was there with a proposal from Mark's family, his family consisting of Mark's overbearing and controlling mother, two sons and their wives, all of whom had never extended much hand of fellowship to her. The proposal was to buy the estate and asking her in return to vacate and preferably to leave Vicksburg and even Mississippi. The check was for four and half million dollars. The attorney went over Mark's assets which happen to be stock ownership in the family holdings and his bank accounts, amounting to some ten million dollars. The family was most anxious to buy her shares and would pay above market value. "You'll be comfortably rich and have everything a woman your age could ever need for the rest of your life." he had assured.

Nell asked the attorney if he would come back that afternoon say 3 P.M. for her answer. She told him she needed time to think, time to gather her thoughts and get herself organized. The attorney in his expensive tailored silk suit, stood and with all the charm a southern gentleman could muster, extended his hand and did a slight bow, and said Madame and excused himself.

Nell was in a drawing room, with a coffee tray in front of her feeling more alone than she had ever felt in her life. She needed someone to talk to someone to confide in, but who? The Jefferson's controlled Vicksburg and whomever she was to talk to there, she was sure the conversation would get back to Benetta Jefferson, her mother in law.

She picked up the phone and called Bud. Patty answered the phone and after their exchanges in pleasantries, Patty called Bud to the phone.

"What's going on?" Bud asked.

"A thousand things all at once," Nell said. She proceeded to tell him of Mark's passing and the family offers and them wanting her out of their lives.

"Nell, if you think the offer is half what it is worth, just take it and get out." Bud said, "If you need some help getting home, I'll be down there tomorrow and if I need to, I can bring a couple of old boys that will come down to kick butt."

"Who would that be?" She asked half knowing.

"The baddest in Sunset, Jake and Elzie." Bud said.

"How are they?" she asked.

"I guess they are ok. You know Elzie and Angie have moved out to Jake's farm! Yeah, Jake gave them the house he used to live in after he married. He's living in his dad's house, so he offered Elzie his place. They are retiring and they didn't want to stay in Bridgeport. Jake lost his wife back at Thanksgiving and so Elzie and Angie have moved out there and Jake's youngest is moved out there and Jake told me his oldest is moving out there with all their families."

"Well I hate to hear that Jake's wife died." Nell said. "Had she been sick long?"

"No," Bud said, "it was sudden and it was pretty quick. We went to the funeral and I was a pall bearer. Jake looked so lost that day. But he seems to be doing pretty good. Him and Elzie and I been to lunch and we're planning some big fishing trips in the future. But, hey, what do you need me to do?"

"Bud, when I leave here, I don't have a place to go except come home. I'm not sure I want to come back to Sunset, but for now I guess I have to. You've not rented out Mama's house have you?"

"No, I haven't done a thing, it is half yours but you can have it if you need it but right now it needs work, it needs some remodeling. If you're coming, you come on, we got a nice private spare room on the north end of our house and it's yours baby sister, it's yours for as long as you need it or want it."

"I'll call you the day I get ready to start out for home." Nell said. "I have to sign papers, and transfer money from the banks here to there. I need you to go to the bank and open me a savings account where I can transfer the money."

"Ok sis," I'll call you so you'll have the account number." Bud said.

CHAPTER 12

That afternoon, the family attorney came back calling and Nell was a tad more prepared than that morning. She was sitting at her hand crafted oak desk. The butler brought in the attorney and she motioned him a seat as she sat behind her desk.

"Mr. Bougaurd, she began, "thank you for your patience. In regard to the selling of this estate, I will sign and agree. However in regard to my hospital and all asset shares in all the family business, I'll need 25% above market value or I'll just hold on to them and I believe my husband left me ten thousand shares in the various holdings and the current value is thirteen hundred per share at 25% above would bring them to over sixteen hundred a share. I'll settle for sixteen hundred even plus I'll need a new Cadillac SUV and I'll need a new credit card in my name only. I can't leave or move until all the conditions are met and then I'll gladly comply and leave the state of Mississippi."

Without showing emotion, Lance Bougaurd pursed his lips, inhaled a deep breath and after blinking his eyes, said "And what color of car were you thinking?"

Two weeks later with a new Visa and a new pearl white Cadillac SUV Nell was packing for Texas. Except for a few hundred dollars in cash, her money had all been transferred to a bank in Bowie, into a savings account. She thought she probably just doubled their assets with the twenty seven million dollar transfer. It was on Sunday night and bright and early Monday morning 6:00 A.M. she was ready to leave. The servants lined the front doorway to all bid her adieu. Her personal maid, Adelphia and the cook Miss Dora, had insisted she eat some breakfast and fixed her a thermos of coffee and had packed her some sandwiches. She hugged them goodbye knowing she would likely never see them again.

It was January twenty fifth; it was cool that morning some fifty degrees but the day promised to get up warmer even in Texas. She was not traveling in bad weather. Fifteen minutes and she was crossing the Mississippi River and entering Louisiana and by eleven she would be in Shreveport. The maid had packed her a couple of sandwiches so other than restroom stops she could keep driving and she wanted to do just that. The further west she went, the more she wanted be in Sunset. The closer she came, the more thrilled she was and excited and anxious.

As soon as she could get settled she wanted to go and see Nancy Shelton who had married Brad Pritcher. She had seen her at her dad's funeral and only got to greet her and a brief hug. And where was Deb Crocket? She thought. I'd love to see her again. She couldn't get around it though, even though she was trying not to bring it up she had to admit that of all the people she wanted to see, the most she wanted, the one person that would mean the most for her to see was Jake Oldham.

CHAPTER 13

Arriving early that afternoon in Sunset she was rather shocked at the things that were gone from her youth. No school, no store, no café, it looked like it was a town on its death bed. She shuddered and thought, "Depressing."

Arriving at Bud's changed her mood. It was the first time she had really seen his house. It was lovely and out on their old family farm. He had taken good care of the place, had grass, nice ponds, and fat cows. It looked so warming and inviting. It hit her then right then, she understood probably for the first time in her life, why Jake was so in love with his home. It was home, it was warm it was a welcome mat, it was family. It was a big world in some ways.

Bud and Patty came out of the house and for the first time in their lives they embraced. Although she loved Bud dearly, they had always had this brother sister conflict as kids. He would be going off to do something and half the time wouldn't let her go, and the times he did, he would stick her with Jake. That was how she and Jake started their spark, the spark that she had kept from being a flame.

"So glad you got here safe and sound." Bud said. "Dang what a nice car!"

"It's very reliable transportation." Nell said. "It got me here and the ride was very smooth."

"Well here, let's get your stuff and get you to your room." Bud said

232

as he and Patty started getting bags. She had brought home necessities, nothing of extravagance but day to day wear clothes, casual wear, some nice things for church, but she did bring all her expensive jewelry. She intended to put that to good use, either by sharing it with close friends, her sister in law or sell the stuff and put the money in something beneficial.

In fifteen minutes the car was empty; it was laid on her bed for her to unpack at her own pace. Shortly Patty had a nice supper for them.

Nell looked at Bud and Patty and said, "Ya'll ever see Nancy Shelton?"

Bud thought for a moment and he said "It's been about two years since the last time we saw her. You know her husband has flooring business in Bowie and she works in the office. When we took out our carpet and put down this wood floor, we had them do it and that was the last time we saw her."

"How does she look?" Nell asked

Knowing that Bud couldn't tell the difference between a new hair-do and a woman in curlers, Patty said, "She's still very pretty, no wrinkles in her face, but smooth. She's probably heavier than high school days, and she wears her hair shorter than back then, but she looks good."

"I think I'll try to see her tomorrow." Nell said. "I'd like to see her."

Then Nell said, "You remember Debbie? Wonder where she is?"

"Now that, I don't know." Bud answered. "She went off to some foreign country in missionary works, but I haven't heard of her. Her family here are all gone and their property sold. I don't even know who to ask."

"Seems like she had an older sister." Nell said. "If you knew where she was, she would know."

"If the older sister is still living." Bud said.

"True." Nell answered.

After supper and the dishes cleared, Nell went to her room to unpack. Shortly before bedtime, though, she went back to ask Bud one more question.

"Bud," she said, "I need to talk to someone about my money. I need to either get some CD's or look at some long term investments.

I don't need all my assets in a savings account. And I'll need to set up and open a checking account."

"I'll tell you what," Bud said, "Before I did much, I'd talk to Jake Oldham. I know for a fact he's done right well with investments and the cemetery funds and things. He's pretty money sharp if you ask me."

"Does he still live out on the same place?" She asked.

"Where else would he be?" Bud answered.

CHAPTER 14

Around nine the next morning Nell was out and headed to Bowie to catch up with her oldest friend Nancy Shelton Pritcher. It had been over thirty years and little correspondence and she desperately wanted to see one of the two girls from her past that was back then her very best and dearest friend.

She was astonished at the changes thirty years can bring to a town. Not only was she shocked at Sunset, but she was just as surprised in Bowie. Some of the old haunts she remembered, like the Dairy Hut, were gone. Where car dealers once were, stood empty lots. Where the old pharmacy's once were, now supported antique stores. A big hardware store that had once been the bulwark of Bowie was completely gone. Just north on the highway to Montague, she spotted Pritcher's flooring and carpet store, a large building that sat high off the ground. I guess they didn't want risk flooding on carpet inventory she thought. Nell parked and walked up the stairs and entered the glass door. A bell sounded to let whomever know a customer had walked in.

Coming from a small room that had specific samples Nancy stepped out, saying to Nell not at first recognizing her, "Come in and I'll show you anything we hav..."

She didn't finish her sentence but just gasp, covered her mouth with her hands, then flung them open almost screaming, "Nell, oh my God,

Nell Hunter, Oh good grief, Nell, Nell." Then they were embraced and an intimate hug that would last for full minute.

"I can't believe it is you!" Nancy said. "Oh it has been so long, and I have wondered about you so much and so many times and I'm, I'm going to just swell up and cry."

Nell was happy, was elated to see Nancy. Was teary eyed too and finally was getting a word in.

"I've thought about you a million times too. I've wondered about you wanted to see you, wanted to talk to you. And now we can!" She said.

Nancy put her hand up and then turned around and found a young girl that worked for them. "Cindy!" she called out. "This is my dearest friend from my past. She and I are going down to the sweet shop and I don't know when we will be back, but you take care of things and don't you call me unless it is absolutely necessary. You hear me?"

"Yes ma'am," Cindy replied.

"Come on Nell, we're going for coffee and a talk a long talk." Nancy said.

Nancy took Nell to her car, a very nice and just a year old, Lincoln and put her in the passenger seat and into the driver's seat she sat and started the car. "The Sweet Shop is just down the street, it is quiet and we can have a table and just talk and not worry about a phone call."

Nell was studying Nancy. She looked younger than her years, she was sure she colored her hair because she just couldn't be that blond at her age, and was of course slightly heavier than high school. But for the wear, she looked good.

Nancy too was studying Nell. She was still youthful looking. "I wonder if she's had a face lift?" Nancy pondered. "She's about the same size as high school. She may not have ever had any children, her hips don't say so. And her hair, it is still brown, she probably puts on a rinse, have to at her age."

They pulled up to the Sweet Shop and went in. Although it was bustling with activity, there were a couple of empty tables and they took one in the corner. Nancy ordered coffee for them.

"Well, Nell," Nancy began, "What brought you up to Montague County? You just on a visit?"

"Not exactly," Nell answered, and with that she began her story. She didn't divulge her money but she just told her she had come back and would need some time to decide what she was going to do.

"How about you?" Nell asked, "You been married all this time to one guy, how many kids ya'll have?"

"We just had one boy, Jimmy and he's in partners with his daddy and that girl Cindy, is his wife. It's all a family run business. Brad let's Jimmy do more of the managing and Brad likes to fish and play golf. He's out on the golf course more and more. I'm getting Cindy trained so I can have more time at home. Have you seen anyone else since you got back?" Nancy asked.

"Well no, I just got here yesterday afternoon. You were my first to call on. I just had to see you." Nell said.

"You ought to let Jake Oldham know you are here." Nancy said. "He lost his wife back in November, but I know he'd like to see you, I just know it."

"I'm going to see him, right away, but why do you think he would like to see me." Nell asked.

"I see Jake every now and then. His late wife had a good accounting business here in town and between her and our involvement with the chamber of commerce, we saw them a right smart. And every now and then I'd ask him if he knew anything about you. He always would say no, but there was something in his voice, told me he still cared for you a great deal." Nancy said.

"What happened to you when you got your divorce? Jake was single then and he sure was eligible, very eligible, and you knew how much you meant to him." Nancy said.

"It was complicated," Nell said, "I knew he cared, and in some ways I took advantage of that. I went to him, he helped me get a lawyer, he kept Doug from hurting me but I just couldn't see myself wearing an apron, canning food with his Grandma, and fixing his supper every night and being just stuck out there on that old farm. I had a hunger to see what was out there in the world. Ok, yes, I saw what was out there and Jake told me one time what was out there and I thought he was crazy and I didn't listen but I saw some of the world, and I saw what he told me, the good, the nice, the pretty and the ugly. I saw all of it and I've seen enough. I think I will try to live here, or Bowie or somewhere in the area and make my home. I'm not welcome in Mississippi."

"I hope you find Jake receptive to you and glad to see you." Nancy said.

CHAPTER 15

As usual Glen Ray was racing down the highway doing about 85 when he spotted a Highway Patrol sitting taking radar. He slowed and almost swore under his breath. Swearing made him think of his good buddy Jake Oldham. Once when they were riding down the road he uttered out some curse word and Jake rebuked him saying his mother would not approve of such language. It made him think about that every time thereafter when he was about to cuss a blue streak, that no truer statement was every made, that his dear mother would certainly not approve nor would she have ever uttered such words and it helped him keep that kind of language in check. He improved over the years but sometimes when he was all alone, he would let a few words fly. Today he didn't. He thanked Jake. Jake Oldham, one of his best friends, someone he actually loved like his own brothers. He wished to goodness he had more time to spend with him, had time or should take the time to be together. They could fish, they could make a trip, and since both of them were now single men, they could do just about anything. He figured even Angie wouldn't fuss about Elzie being off with his best pals on some over night or weeklong trip, what kind of trouble could sixty five year old men cause? As he slowed the car to speed limit, the slower speed made him somewhat impatient, he tapped his leg with his fingers, his foot was pounding up and down in nervous twitch.

Glen Ray had driven from Denton to Lake Ray Roberts. He needed to see his new property to check on construction. He had approved his building plans and had them approved by the building committee of the community group home owner's association where he was building. He had decided on a four thousand square foot structure with an enormous back yard deck overlooking the big lake. Down below by some fifteen feet was a stairway to a big floating dock on the lake and boat docking system that he could pull his boat for storage out of the water. It was going to be grand and it would be a lot of fun time in the near future. His goal was to have the house done by spring but that would be pushing it. The weather had not cooperated; a lot of wet weather had marked January. Fortunately the past three days had been dry but cold. He was hoping they had the foundation site ready for pouring. And he was right when he arrived, he found the construction crew on the job and had just about everything tied and ready for the concrete. The contractor told Glen Ray they would check the weather forecast and if they had the right temperatures for the day, they would plan the pouring and work the concrete. Once the concrete had set up which usually they allowed a week, framing would begin, weather permitting.

Glen Ray slapped his hands in approval, shook the contractors hand and was back in his car heading at top speed up the highway to Gainesville and then on over to Bowie to visit and spend the night with Morgan, then to Wichita the next day to golf with Cooper.

Glen Ray arrived around the noon hour and Morgan was on the phone. Of his two brothers, Morgan favored their dad the most. He seemed to have his dad's ways more than he or Cooper. Cooper looked a lot like their dad too but Glen Ray was totally from his mother's side, the Lynch's. His Granddad Lynch was a tall slender man who was a preacher. Everyone said he got his height from his Granddad Lynch. His ways came from his schooling, his arena fights in the courtroom battles and his business sense, a byproduct of his being a good attorney. For his family, his brothers, his late parents, he had made some good oil lease deals where every time a drop of oil was sold, the Shelton's would be receiving royalties. It was sweet icing on the cake as far as Glen Ray was concerned. His days of raising watermelons, cutting hay and feeding livestock were long gone. He was now a promoter, he talked others into investing into the family business, and he leased their minerals that were not in production, promising that if possible, they would drill a well. His brother's car rental, of which he was a silent partner, made him considerable money without him lifting a finger. He liked that kind of business, where someone else was doing the work and he was benefiting from the profits. It had made his family all multimillionaires. They didn't and never would flaunt that, but the fact remained, they were people who were well off.

Cooper's business was also a good payday. He owned numerous car washes and oil changes from Wichita Falls to Childress Texas, which Morgan and Glen Ray shared as partners.

Morgan was hanging up as Glen Ray sat down. "How you doin, brother? He asked.

"Running a tad behind. We still good for golf, it's a tad cool but not miserable." Glen Ray asked.

"I'm in if you are." Morgan said.

"Hey I talked to Nancy yesterday and she had a big surprise visitor." Morgan said.

"Yeah, who?" Glen Ray said.

"Nell Hunter." Morgan replied.

"Nell Hunter! What's she doing back in these woods? She come up to see Bud, nobody in their family died, did they?"

"Well, yeah, somebody died, but not in her family. Her husband died and her husband's family bought her his assets and asked her to leave the state of Mississippi." Morgan said.

"Her husband died?" Glen Ray asked. "My God, do you think she's thinking about moving back to Sunset?"

"Who knows?" Morgan said. "I can't imagine anyone wanting to move back there." Shoot, it is heading to becoming a ghost town, don't you think?"

"Oh, yeah," Glen Ray said, "I don't see anybody but druggies and thugs wanting to live around Sunset. Bunch of losers. Why I bet 90% of the crime in Montague County comes out of Sunset."

"Probably right." Morgan said. "We still going tomorrow to meet Cooper and play golf?"

"Yeah," Glen Ray said, "We're going to knock some balls around."

"I wonder, Glen Ray said, "if old Nell has come back to stay?" He'd have to check that out.

CHAPTER 16

A couple days later, another Norther was pushing through. The wind was strong, raw and cold. The temperature was dropping by the hour. It was just going to be a cold day. Ely had gone alone to feed, Elzie and Angie had gone to Wichita Falls to do some shopping and eating out, and Susie was in the kitchen making homemade pot of hamburger and vegetable soup. She told Jake she had thawed out some frozen peeled tomatoes, had cut up an onion, salt, pepper, had cut up some potatoes and carrots and would add some corn cut off the cob and some English peas. She asked Jake about adding some macaroni.

"I never put over a cup once the mixture is boiling. Once it starts to cook, he said, it swells up and that one cup will feel like three cups is in the pot." Jake replied.

As the wind howled, Jake told Susie he was going up to the cemetery a minute and be back soon. He was thinking about ordering his and Lois's tombstone but he wanted to do some measuring. She wondered why he didn't just wait until the weather was different but knew how determined he could be and if he was determined, and then you better stand back because he was going to do it come hell or high water.

"You better bundle up, it sounds very cold outside." She warned.

"I got my heaviest coat and my hat. I'll be fine." Jake answered.

Jake jumped into his "going to town" as Ely was in his one ton. In just three minutes, he was pulled up at the cemetery. No one there

and no danger on a day like this, he thought. He had no more than
walked through the gate into the burial area when he heard a car pull
up. It was pretty white Cadillac SUV. Wonder who that is? He thought.

Shortly a very youthful looking woman of middle age got out of
the car and slammed the door shut and started toward him. Jake was
standing there in his heavy jacket, head covered in his work felt hat. He
thought he might recognize who that was and as she passed through
the walk in gate he about fainted. It was Nell Hunter!

"Jake, is that you?" she said.

"Oh my God," Jake said, "Nell, it's been a ton of years but you look
like you did the last time I saw you, a beautiful woman."

They hugged and Jake had to all but restrain himself to keep from
kissing her and Nell half expected that he was going to kiss her and
she would have welcomed it.

"What are you doing up here in this country?" Jake asked.

"It's a long story but I don't think I can stand here and tell you in
this cold wind." Nell said.

"Yeah," Jake said, "It is too cold for conversation. How about
following me back to the house?"

"Ok," she said, "Let's go."

And he took her arm and helped her to her car, then got in his
truck. He was almost shaking he was so taken by seeing her again.
He was excited yet he was remembering how she had just up and gone
and left him hanging those thirty five plus years ago. He had wanted
to cry at times over that, he had wanted to ram his fist through the
dash at times and at other times he thought it was for the best. All
his emotions were stirred to the brink. He was anxious to get back to
the house where they could relive their past, but was on the brink of
wanting to just scoop her up in his arms and make mad love to her.
He wondered what she was feeling. Good grief she looked so good,
so elegant and beautiful and youthful! She hadn't aged all that much,
still looked young. Mississippi must have been very good for her and
to her. Jake put the truck in reverse and back away from the fence and
then headed toward his house. "Oh shoot, he thought, I'll have to make
some sort of excuse to Susie."

Nell was thinking as she was driving what her first impression was when she saw Jake at the cemetery. She saw a man who didn't really look in his sixties but still had some of his youth. She saw a man that reminded her of Jake's grandfather a bit, she supposed because of the glasses and hat, but his frame was more of his Grandmother. She was truly excited to see him. She couldn't help feel a sense of rush as they embraced. She fought the hope that she wished he had kissed her.

In short order they had driven up to Jake's parent's house. She could clearly see the Pariot house only it wasn't the Pariot house. She could see that his Grandparent's house was gone but construction had started on a new house she supposed. She remembered Bud telling her he was living in his dad's house.

Jake opened her door and helped her out and they sprinted to the door and in out of the cold harsh wind.

Inside Susie was cooking the soup she had told Jake about that morning and was testing its flavor as they came in. She had a sort of surprised look on her face as Jake greeted her.

"Nell, this is my daughter in law Susie Oldham, my youngest son Ely's wife.

Susie, this is a fine lady from my past Nell Jefferson, Bud's baby sister." Jake said.

Nell in all her gracious ways said how pleased she was to meet her. She had never seen Jake's sons let alone the wives of the sons.

Susie in turn returned the gracious introduction with a remark, "I am pleased to finally put a face with a name I have heard a time or two."

"Susie, Nell and I are going into my living room to talk. We have so much to catch up on and I don't want to bother you." Jake said.

"You won't but go ahead. As soon as the cornbread's done, I'll fix ya'll a bowl of soup, cornbread and ice tea." Susie said. "Ya'll just have the best visit you could ever have and don't worry about me."

"I love that girl," Jake thought, "what a perfect daughter in law, in fact he thought, they both are."

Jake led Nell past the kitchen and into the ROOM.

"I don't remember this room on your parent's house. This is your folk's home isn't it? But I don't remember this room." She said.

"My dad added this room when my grandma started needing special attention." Jake said. "Then when he needed special attention, after my mother died, well he moved in here and now I'm in here to give privacy to Ely and his family. I can shut this door off the kitchen and they wouldn't know I was even here." Jake said as he pulled the door to. "My son Ely and his wife and daughter have retired from their business in Dallas and have moved back home and are building themselves a new house. Then my older son, Phillip and his family are moving here and are building a new house on the Blane place." As Jake was telling Nell this he lit his fireplace.

He took Nell's coat, took off his own coat and hat and laid them in his favorite chair. Motioned Nell to the couch and he sat beside her. In his mind, he didn't know why he did that but he didn't want to sit anywhere else but beside her. It made him think of their youth, when she and he would ride from school to the café for lunch or riding back to school and even in the café how he just dreamed of having her to sit beside him, what thrills that gave him, and today was no different. He was almost mad at himself for the way he felt, he was struggling to keep control. Yet on the surface of things he seemed a man most calm and collected.

With his hat and coat off, Nell could study him further. What beautiful blue eyes he has, she thought. And those big blocky shoulders, he's still strong as an ox. That shock of white hair gives him distinction she thought. She liked everything she was seeing.

"In a minute, Sues' will bring us some tea, I betcha." Jake said. "So tell me what brings you to Texas?"

"Well," she began and she told him her story. How her late husband's family wanted her out and totally out of their lives. They believed she was below their social standing and they wanted nothing to do with her.

Then she said, "You may not remember, but you told me no matter where I went I would find my world no bigger than the one I was in and Jake Oldham, I hate to admit it but you were exactly right."

Jake wanted to lie at that moment and tell her he didn't remember telling her such a thing but he remembered, he remembered every second their lives were together.

"I don't know that I knew what I was talking about." Jake said. "You know I saw some of the world, I was Korea, Germany, and even England and France for a little while. It wasn't as good as home either."

"You are hopeless aren't you?" Nell said. "You just couldn't get past Sunset in your life, could you?"

"Is that so bad?" Jake answered.

"I don't guess it is, it just sort of looks like you have limited yourself." She said.

"Limited?" Jake asked.

"Yeah, you know, you limited your potential in life by staying here. You couldn't break the apron strings. Now those that held you are gone and what do you have?"

Jake chuckled. "Well to tell you the truth, I've been successful in all my ventures. I've got a good dozer business, got a good bunch of cows that are mine in the clear, don't have no notes on them at a bank, have more than doubled the amount of land we had when I came into this world, got a good family, had a good marriage, good boys and good grandkids but most of all, Nellie Hunter, I got good, wonderful and lasting memories of my youth. I had the best grandparents, I had good parents, I had good friends and I had a love one time that I thought would make my life so complete and she left me."

Nell was struck with the last statement. It stung a little. For she knew what Jake was speaking of, the time she came to his house and spent three nights escaping her abusive husband soon to become an ex-husband. The last night she had been at Jake's, she came to his room, and she gave herself willingly to him and she now imagined that he thought that was the beginning of them to be together forever and it was not. She had realized just how much that had hurt him.

"Jake, you have to understand something," she said. "I was under so much stress, I didn't' know what to do. The lawyer you took me to and paid my fees, without so much as a glance and I still was wanting to rid myself of this small place, it just caved in on me Jake. For what it is worth, I never dreamed that I had hurt you, and I wouldn't hurt you on purpose. And really no one has ever come close to you in my books. I just never gave you all of me."

"I suppose we could say it is water under the bridge, now." Jake said. "It is part of our past, it is how fate played out. BUT my dear, what of our future, what are we to become?"

"Right now Jake I need some advice," she said. "Bud said you would be good at helping me with my money. I need some advice."

"I've got just the man down at Decatur, Vince Bradford. I'll get you an appointment. I'll even call him directly. Right now, his office is closed for lunch." Jake said.

Just then Susie entered the room with a tray, carrying two bowls of steaming vegetable soup and small saucer plates with hot cornbread.

"I'll bring ya'll some tea but I couldn't carry it all in one trip." Susie said.

"That's all right," Jake said, "I'll just dash in the kitchen and get the glasses"

And Jake bounded up off the couch and went and prepared two glasses of sweet ice tea. Susie had set the tray on the small table for two in Jake's room. Nell was seated at one side and Jake pulled up across from her.

"Oh, this looks so good," Nell was saying as Susie was leaving the room.

"Shall we pray?" Jake asked.

"Of course," Nell said. And Jake bowed his head and uttered thanks to God for the meal but he also thanked his heavenly father for the chance meeting with Nell. He even said it was the "fulfillment of a lifelong dream."

They ate quietly and for awhile didn't resume their conversation. When they were finished, Jake took the tray back to the kitchen and when he came back closed the door.

"Nell, listen to me." Jake began. "The last night you were with me, and you came to me and we spent the night together, was the most special night of my life. And right then, I just knew that once you were divorced, that you and I would marry and we would begin life here and we would build our lives right here. I just knew it. And the next day you left this note and I still have it, still carry it in my wallet. You left me with that note and my world about came to an end. I was hurt, I was devastated and never in my life felt so rejected and alone. But I had to get right on and go right on as if nothing were wrong. I could not show it, I couldn't tell it, I couldn't let anyone know how I had been played."

"Jake, for what it's worth, I never intended you to be hurt. I don't know how to even begin to explain that night. I wanted to be with you but I had so wanted to get away and the pull to get away was just too much. Is it too late for me to say I'm sorry. Will you or can you forgive me?" Nell said.

At that moment they were just looking at each other as they had moved from the table back to the couch. Their eyes met, they just drew close and Nell instinctively kissed Jake. When she started to kiss him she took her hand and wrapped it around the back of Jake's head and just pulled him to her. The kiss lasted a long time, and then there was another and another followed that. Jake wanted to resist but he could not and would not. As she kissed him, he returned each kiss with another, they were embraced and holding each other tightly. Their emotions were at a high. Neither Jake nor Nell knew whether to laugh or cry, they were both so happy and their emotions were so strong at moment, they could not stop embracing or kissing. It was something long overdue.

Finally they drew apart only to keep their embrace with each one on the neck of the other. And Jake uttered, "Oh God, Nell, I love you, I have loved you since I was at least fifteen and I have never ever stopped. I think this is the second time though you have let me tell that I love you."

Nell replied, "I love you too and I know I have always loved you."

They were drawing apart when they heard the door of Jake's room open and Susie came in. Acting like nothing was wrong, she said, "Uh Jake, I'm going to Forestburg and pick Leeza up. I'll be back in about an hour."

Jake stood up from the couch and said slightly breathless, "That's fine. I'll be here when you get back. By the way, where is Ely?"

"Well he came in to eat lunch, then he was off to the McReynolds place to check a fence and make sure it wasn't down. He said you wanted to plan a pasture over there for weaned calves and he thought he better be checking the boundary fences."

"Good idea," Jake said.

Susie was turning to leave but she glanced at Jake and with a grin whispered, "You devil you."

Susie was gone and the house was then empty except for Nell and Jake.

Jake sat back down and sort of ran his hand through his hair. He was thinking very seriously. "Nell, listen, you and I have been honest with each other today and I can't be more happy. I hope you want what I want and that is that you will marry me? BUT, we need to wait and give time for what everyone says a proper grieving time. You just lost your husband a few weeks ago and I lost my wife back at Thanksgiving. I really don't care what people think but I sure want my boys to accept what you and I want. Do you want what I want?"

"Yes, I do, I will marry you and I will marry you when you feel it is proper, whether that is next week or next year. I feel like a thirty year load has been suddenly lifted from me and I feel so refreshed. I just want you to hold me and I want to kiss you and I want you to make you the happiest man on this earth."

Jake kissed her again and then drew his breath. "I want to make you the happiest woman in the world. Just being beside you makes me happy."

"Oh, Jake said, let me call Vince and get an appointment." Jake took out a cell phone and punched it and waited for the answer and then asking for Vince. Vince would see Nell day after tomorrow at one thirty.

"Nell, he will see us Friday at one thirty. I'll pick you up at eleven thirty and we'll have lunch down there and see him. Now when we get to his office and I introduce you, I'll wait outside while you discuss your business. I don't need to know your financial affairs." Jake said.

"Jake, I don't mind you sitting in. I rather would want you to know my affairs in and out and I would value your advice over your advisor." Nell said.

"I'll do whatever you want." Jake said.

"Let's have another glass of tea. I want you to meet my granddaughter

Leeza and if Ely comes in, him too. For now, we won't tell them our plans, let's just get you acquainted with my bunch." Jake said.

It wasn't long before Susie and Leeza came back and shortly Ely. Jake was most anxious to introduce Nell to them. Leeza was polite, grinned like she suspected something and of course Nell was most gracious.

Jake and Nell went back into the Room and behind closed doors spent the afternoon talking. Jake wanted to take her to supper after he made sure Leeza had gathered eggs and fed the chickens. But Nell said she would go on back to Bud's and they could talk tomorrow. Jake told Nell that he and Elzie would be working on this cabin that they were building as part of his new business venture. He wanted to see her that evening and she agreed.

Jake said, "I'm going to call my oldest son Phil and see if they are coming up and if they are I want us to have a big supper out here where we can tell everyone what we are planning and then maybe we set a date. I don't mind telling you Nell, I'm excited, I feel like I'm 20 again."

Nell chuckled and said it would be fine. She was anxious to meet the other son and his family. Ely seemed very nice and his wife was a doll. Their daughter was just a typical teenager that she hoped in the future would get to know.

CHAPTER 17

Elzie and Jake were up at one of the cabins. They were about to start the outside covering of the house in eight inch hardy planks. Jake was glad he and Elzie had nail guns else nailing by hand would just take forever. Setting the first plank on the bottom and then having to mark and measure the second plank and hold it while shooting took awhile but after the first two were set the others were set with a block of wood and quickly nailed. Once the ends were nailed then they nailed the middles working toward each other. The hard part was cutting around objects that were on the outside and trimming for windows, otherwise the work went at a good pace and a lot was accomplished.

"Well," Elzie finally said having waiting for Jake to say something, "how was your meeting with Nell?"

"I'd say it was very nice, very cozy, very friendly, but we didn't make out on the couch like you and Angie." Jake laughed.

"Dad gummed you Jake, you silly ass," Elzie said, "You bringing up sompin from fifty year past. Don't you let up?"

Jake was laughing so hard he couldn't nail.

"It was a reunion, cousin, it was like we just picked up where we let off thirty year ago." Jake said. "Now tomorrow night you and Angie come over for supper if you want to know anymore. Now you get that plank over here and let's get it marked and sawed and nailed up here!"

"You don't pay me enough to order me around COUSIN!" Elzie said.

And thus it went all the day as they two men picked and poked at each other in jest and fun which made the day for them more pleasant, and passed quicker as they progressed.

Ely drove up and got out of the feed truck. "Hey you two, Susie said come on in for dinner, she's got chicken fried steak, mashed taters, fried apples and gravy for you."

"Wooo, that sounds mighty tasty," Elzie was saying as he clapped his hands. "You ready straw boss?"

"Naw, I think you ain't earned your way this morning, and should have to work your way through the noon hour. You're too lazy, you're too slow, and you talk way too much!" Jake said.

"My foot!" Ely said, "Just get in my truck and I'll take ye, and bring ye back.""

In the house, on the table was a plate of tender fried veil cutlets and a big bowl of flower gravy and beside that a bowl of creamed potatoes and on the stove was the apples.

"Mm, those apples sure smell good." Elzie said.

The men had washed and were seated when Ely and Susie sat down with them. Jake asked Elzie to say a prayer which he did, then they began to pass food and fill their plates.

"Is all you want to have tomorrow night for supper, steaks, baked potatoes, a salad and some rolls?"

"Yeah, don't you think that will be enough?" Jake said.

"I suppose along with a desert." Susie said.

"I guess Ely will cook the steaks." Jake said. "Phil and his family are coming aren't they?"

"Oh yeah, said they wouldn't miss it."

"Good" Jake said.

CHAPTER 18

Dressed up like he was going to Wednesday night church, Jake picked up Nell at Bud's and headed to Decatur. They went to a restaurant called the Whistle Stop and had a lunch of roast beef, creamed potatoes, green beans, a salad, rolls and iced tea. Both Jake and Nell felt almost like school kids, they were totally excited to be together and wanted the moment to last forever.

"Tonight we are having a family supper. We need to invite Bud and Patty out. Both my kids will be there and of course Elzie and Angie. I think we can tell them all our intentions and then we can just decide later when we want to set a date." Jake said, "That is if that is all right with you?"

"Of course it is all right with me," Nell said, "I'm nervous about your kids, how they will react, if they will feel like you have betrayed their mother or something."

"I really don't know but I don't think they will feel that way. For one thing, they know that Lois and I had a good and happy marriage. We made a point to be devoted to one another and to the boys. I really think they will see this as a good thing and a good thing for their old daddy." Jake said. "They better anyway."

Finishing their meal, they drove over to Vince's office and as soon as he called them in, Jake introduced Nell and went ahead and told Vince their history and their future plans. Vince was very congratulatory.

Although Jake would have stepped outside while Nell discussed her private affairs, she would not have it and insisted Jake sit and listen and offer any advice. Jake's bottom jaw about dropped out of socket when Nell disclosed her net worth. It was astounding.

After listening to the possible investments, Jake made a few suggestions, like setting up a trust for Bud and Patty, and for Bud's children. Then he suggested she set up a trust for the Sunset Cemetery where her parents and grandparents were buried and finally suggested she benefit her home church and perhaps the local fire department. She did both, feeling she was making a gift that she would be pleased to make. She kept herself a nice trust that she would benefit from every year for the rest of her life and she felt she had nothing else to worry her.

However, Jake had Vince bring out his own portfolio so that Nell would know that although not near as wealthy as she, he had a good trust income for himself and had things set up for his sons and three grandchildren. It made perfect sense to her why he made the suggestions he had made since he suggested she do almost the same thing he had done for his own estate.

Several years back when Jake and his dad were running dozers, they had the opportunity to purchase some three sections of land. After they had fixed up the land, clearing just the right amount of timber to have good grass pastures, built ponds on all the draws in order to have plenty of water, they had divided the properties in 80 acre tracts. For a couple of years after they had established their grass, they had run a couple of hundred head of first calf heifers and about the time of selling the stock, there was an influx of people coming to the area looking for land to build on. They had made a very tidy profit selling tracts but they also been fortunate enough to obtain the minerals when they bought the surface and about the time they had sold all the land, there was a huge oil boom. It seemed to Jake these companies and lease hounds hitting the county were seeing just how much they could pay and out bid one another. When they were offered fifteen hundred dollars an acre for a lease, Jake, with his dad's approval signed off. The lease alone was considerable. The six wells drilled then were icing on the cake and

Jake's net worth increased into the millions. He had wisely put it all in safe but good interest bearing investments with Vince.

It would take Vince a few days to set everything up before Nell transferred the money which would mean another trip but she didn't mind as long as Jake came with her.

Driving back to Sunset there was a certain calm about her. Nell thanked Jake for taking her to his man. For the first time in over thirty years, she felt a contentment and calm that she had never had although she knew that a long time ago she could have had.

"What time are we to come out tonight?" Nell asked.

"I think they will plan our supper around 7, but you all can come when you want to. It is to me, just that much more time to be with you." Jake said.

"And I with you, Jake." Nell said. "I with you."

CHAPTER 19

Jake was a tad nervous about the evening but things were going smoothly. Susie had the salad tossed the potatoes were wrapped in foil and baking in the oven, the table had been set, she made a nice chocolate cake for desert and she wasn't even trying to rush. Ely was going to cook the steaks around 6:30 so things were going as planned. Phil and Julia came in before four thirty and the twins were simply running all over the place excited to be there.

Shortly before the company had arrived, Phil told his dad he was planning on moving a mobile home out to the place and they were going to move out as soon as possible. The kids were prepared to change schools, they had a viable contract on their house, it was all falling in place and they didn't mind the temporary quarters while their new house was being built, besides Phil would be there on hand to make sure all things were being done to his requirements.

Close to six Elzie and Angie arrived followed by Bud, Patty and Nell. Nell was dressed in slacks and lose hanging blouse but Jake was stunned by her beauty. He was almost speechless just admiring her.

Jake formally introduced Nell to his family, one by one. Before Jake or Nell could tell them anything about their intentions, it was very obvious to the boys and their wives. They just waited to hear it from their dad. And they were very aware of his nervousness. They had actually never seen him act this way. To his family, Jake had always seemed like a rock, a solid anchor, but he was clearly out of his element in some way.

Phil remembered a time when his dad had been providing dozer service to a man who wanted to complain about some of the work done. They had shaped some gullies and they had built a nice dam but the man was insistent that the work was sloppy, and was threatening not to pay. Phil was with his dad, a boy about twelve, and was sitting in the truck as he heard the man speak so critically to his daddy. Jake patiently listened to the man but when the man cussed Jake, Jake stuck his finger up in the man's face and very calmly said, "Oh my friend, you will pay every penny for this work. And not only that, when I leave here you will shake my hand. Now right now you and I are going to have a little prayer with almighty Jesus Lord, to give me patience that I don't stomp you into the ground and to give you wisdom to shut your mouth. Otherwise I'll make you eat every word and make you regret every word you have spoken to me."

Phil remembered the man was visibly shaken by what Jake said. As Jake was calm and collected and yet deliberate. The man was shaking all over but Jake was cool as a cucumber.

But today to Phil's amusement, his dad was like a schoolboy caught in a prank and about to be punished.

Phil helped Ely cook the steaks and when they brought them in, everyone sat down and with Jake leading a prayer, had a fine meal. Jake sat where a long time ago, his grandpa had sat, and later his father and now he, at the head of the table. To Jake's right was Nell and Phil noticed how they looked at one another and the soft speaking they were saying to each other. There was no doubt to Phil, his father and this woman of his past were in love. "It didn't take long." Phil thought. But he didn't really know their past.

After the dessert was served, Jake asked for the attention of all. All heads were turned to him.

"Many years ago, there are several in this room that grew up with me. Elzie, Bud, Angie, Patty to some extent, and Nell. We grew up together, we went to school and community events and we have known one another all this time, it is like we are family. When I was a teen,

Nell was my sweetheart and we spent time together and I wanted to plan our life together but she had other notions and she went one way and I another. We have both experienced love, marriage and our own happiness. Recent chain of events has brought Nell back here and because of my circumstances and hers we are both single people. When we met just recently we found that the spark we had years ago still was still there and we discovered we were um, we were in love again and we want to put our lives together, we want to get married. But we also are here tonight to seek your blessings and best wishes. I would never hurt my children, but I am in high hopes they will respect my feelings."

Jake reached his hand out to Nell and she stood up beside Jake and she said, "I can only echo what Jake is trying to say. He was very sweet on me in our youth but I kept him at some distance because I had a notion that the world was waiting for me and I needed to get far from Sunset and I knew Jake couldn't, this was his world and right then it wasn't mine. And now fate has brought us back together and his world has become my world. And he was right about something he told me almost forty years ago, that the world right here is just as big as the world I thought I had to find. He loved me and I really was in love with him but I wasn't ready for this life, but I am ready now and with your blessing, I want to make Jake a happy man as he is making me a very happy woman."

For a moment there was total silence and then Ely and Phil were looking at each other half grinning. Finally Phil spoke first.

"I think I can speak for all of us, that we couldn't be any happier. There is nothing I want more than my dad to be happy and content and I don't know what you all had before Ely and I were ever even thought of, but I can sure see it and I would never stand in your way."

"Amen to that," Ely said. "I guess I should tell you dad that just before mom died, she told me and Phil not to let you mope and grieve too long. She hoped you would find someone to share your life with. Lord I don't think in the short time I've seen ya'll together, that two people could be more matched."

Elzie clapped his hands and said, "Oh I couldn't agree more. When we was in school, poor old Jake was almost miserable he was so much in love with Nell Hunter. Half the time he couldn't even get the chores done for being so sick on her."

The room erupted in laughter and Jake was turning red. Bud then spoke up. "I've known how crazy Jake's been over Nell since we was in our teen's. I used to pair them up when we went a hunting trying to push them to a match. I'm glad it's finally shaping up."

Julie then ask, "Have ya'll set a date?"

"Uh, no, not yet, we wanted you all to know our intentions, we wanted to know how you felt and then we wanted to know what you all thought about when would be a proper time for a date." Jake said.

Elzie and Angie almost spoke at the same time saying, "I think you should marry right away."

Ely beat his brother to the punch saying, "If you all want to get married tomorrow, just tell me what time, so I can clean up and be there!"

Jake then said, "I tell you what, Nell and I will sit down right away and make plans and then we'll have another supper."

"Whoopee" Elzie said.

The women were hugging Nell, and the men were either shaking Jake's hand or patting him on the back of his shoulder and everyone was all smiles.

CHAPTER 20

G len Ray and his brothers had a good session of golf but as usual for Glen, he was sometimes preoccupied not concentrating on his game, thinking about other things not excluding Nell Hunter.

After they had played their full eighteen holes, dropping off Cooper and then a quick trip to Bowie to leave Morgan, he was flying down the highway headed for Denton. Since he had sold his place he had movers store his furniture and had rented an apartment until his house on the lake was finished.

Tomorrow was Saturday and he usually didn't do much business. He thought he would make a run back up to Sunset, see Jake and then go see Nell. He was thinking he would take her down and show her his house under construction. He might convince her to buy the lot next door or just plan to move right in with him once his house was finished. He was ready to make plans with her.

Saturday morning, Glen Ray was up and slurping coffee and trying to get off and head back to Sunset. He was anxious to take Nell to his new place, take her to lunch, maybe take in a movie and then coax her right over to his apartment for the night. He had it all planned.

His Lexus SUV roared to life and he was out the drive and headed north. He would be in Sunset in forty minutes or less.

Jake leisurely walked into the kitchen where Susie had coffee ready and was scrambling eggs. A plate of bacon and sausage was on the table.

"You are energetic this morning young lady." Jake said.

"I figured you'd be up, and Ely is down at the barn and will be back in a minute and I know he needs his breakfast before going out checking stock." Susie replied. "You and Nell doing something today?"

"No, she said her and Patty and Nancy might do a little visiting and shopping. Me an Elzie are going over on the hunting cabins and do some work. We are about ready to move inside and then it won't matter what the weather is doing. Like right now with it fair, we need to finish outside, then if it's cold again, or even raining or worse, we can work inside. She's going to church with us Sunday and then after lunch, she and I will sit down and make some plans and set a date. I'll tell you if she'll go along with it, I'd sure like to marry in the old Pleasant Hill church. I've spent enough of my own money rebuilding it and keeping it from falling down. We've got siding on the outside, we've added an inner wall and insulated it, we got heat and air, and we got water. We can have a nice antique type wedding. We don't plan a big thing, just our family and our very closest friends."

"You know that would be great!" Susie said. "Julie, Leeza and I can fix things for the reception and we can do a little decorating and it would just be perfect. I'll bet she'll go for it. I can tell she is really fond of you, Jake and that is what sold all of us on her. You worry when a man decides to remarry if he's rushing into something and the woman is looking for a meal ticket and bank account, but I just don't get that from her."

Jake laughed a bit and then said, "Susie, she's got a lot more money than I do. She don't need someone's bank account. But I feel it too, I feel that love, I feel that devotion and I sure hope she feels mine."

"I don't doubt it one bit. I see the happiness in her eyes." Susie said.

Shortly Ely and Elzie came in.

"Ah, you would know that any time there is food, old Elzie's got a nose." Jake said laughing.

"Maybe so, but I done et about twenty minutes ago." Elzie said.

"Well have some coffee Cuz," Jake said.

The men sat and Ely told that Phil and the twins were going with him to feed and check the stock.

Jake told Ely that he and Elzie were going to the cabins and when they got done to come up there and they could finish up today where next week they could start inside.

After Ely had eaten, Phil and his rambunctious boys came bouncing in. They both wanted to get on Jake's lap for a minute and he let them, hugging them with great affection.

Soon they were out the door with Elzie and Jake still sitting. "Did ya'll all sleep ok last night?" Jake asked.

"Oh yeah, we have plenty of room, the boys are sleeping in your boys old room and Phil and Julie are in our guest room, so it is all fine." Elzie said.

"Well I appreciate you letting them stay there for the weekend." Jake said. "They are going to move a mobile home up here and go ahead and move next week. You won't have to board them again."

"Well we didn't mind." Elzie said. "That will be good though, they can be right there while their house is going up, they can get them rowdy boys in school and established this year and not next."

"Yup," Jake said.

There was a knock at the door.

Susie went and let Glen Ray in and brought him to the kitchen.

"Well I'll be dang!" Jake said.

"How you doing Glen Ray?" Elzie chimed.

"Oh I've been busy, been here and there, yesterday was with my brother's playing some golf, then back to Denton and I come up here and I wanted to ask you sumthin and then I got to go."

"No need to be in a hurry," Jake said, "it's Saturday, this is sort of a slowdown day, have some fun stuff. Have some coffee."

Elzie chuckled knowing that if they went up to the cabin, that wasn't exactly fun.

"Have ya'll seen Nell Hunter yet?" Glen Ray asked.

Elzie was about to explode, but Jake sort of shook his head and winked at him for silence.

"Yeah, we have, fact, Bud n'em was out here last night for supper." Jake said.

"How's she look?" Glen Ray asked. "She get fat or does she look good?" And then he leaned in to them not wanting Susie to hear as she was in the utility room, you know is she ripe for the picking?"

Jake wanted to about slap is friend for that, but he kept his calm, slapped his big hand on the table lightly. Jake smiled and said, "She's right purtty, Glen Ray, she looks real fine, a real lady."

"Well I'm going over to see her right now. I'm going to take her out and see what happens." Glen said.

Jake looked over at Elzie who looked like he was going to pop, his mouth gaping open, then back at Glen Ray.

"You know she's a staying with her brother Bud?" Jake said flatly.

"Yeah, that's out on Sunset School Road isn't it?" Glen said.

"Sure is." Jake said.

Then Glen jumped up and said he had to go.

"You can hang around with us, we're getting ready to have a little party," Jake said.

Glen hardly heard as he was bounding across the kitchen toward the living room and out the front door.

"Are you sure that is the same Glen Ray Shelton we grew up with?" Elzie asked.

"I right think it is, Elz", Jake said. "He's changed some, sort of gotten himself self centered a little but I spect he'll be in for a little surprise when he gets out to Bud's."

"I hope so." Elzie said, "He was acting like a horse's ass."

"Let's go knock out them cabins." Jake said.

CHAPTER 21

Before they left, Jake called Bud's and talked to Nell. She happened to be there alone. Her shopping trip had to be cancelled because Nancy was under the weather. So, Patty and Bud had gone to Bowie to get some groceries.

"Just wanted to give you a head's up," Jake said. "Me an old Elz here are working on the cabins but you got company coming. Glen Ray Shelton is on his way out there. I didn't get a chance to tell him our plans, he was in too big a rush to tell us he was going to take you out tonight and see what took place. I just let him fly out of here but wanted to call ye."

"Thanks for the warning, but you have nothing to worry about." Nell said.

"I'm not worried a bit," Jake said, but wanted you to know that I just didn't tell him what you and I are planning. You can break it to him."

"I'll handle him with gloves." She said in a chuckle.

Jake and Elzie were then out the door and in the truck headed to the hunting cabins. Soon they were fast at work knocking out the siding on the outside. Jake wanted that job done by the end of this day.

There was a knock at the door and Nell opened it and tried to look surprised to see Glen Ray Shelton.

"Why Glen Ray, is that you?" She sort of shouted. "My oh my, it has been a long time."

He expected a hug and a generous one, then he was all smiles and charm. "My goodness, I thought I was looking at some 16 year old, not Nell Hunter!" He said. "How nice to see you, Nell. Nancy told me you had come up and said you had left Mississippi."Glen Ray said.

"Come in Glen and have a sit. Yes, I have left Mississippi. My husband died and I decided to come back here to see what I wanted to do with my life." Nell said.

"Mississippi was certainly kind to you, Nell." Glen Ray said. "You just look marvelous."

"Oh you are too kind." Nell said.

"Say, Nell, I have just sold my place in Houston and I've got me a nice, and I do mean a nice, apartment in Denton and am building me a real spacious place out on Lake Ray Roberts. It has the greatest view overlooking the lake and I've got a nice floating dock and a boat and I can have some really nice parties out there and we can plan some nice fishing fun. I'd love to show it to you and we could go in to Denton for dinner and a quiet evening, what do you say?"

"Sounds nice Glen but I don't think I should. You don't know and few do know but since I've been back I went out to see Jake and we found out that the old spark we had back in high school was like a full blown forest fire. We are making plans to marry fairly soon."

Glen's jaw just about dropped to the floor.

"Well I'll be d..." He didn't finish. "Why didn't Jake tell me!?" He rather shouted. "I was out there this morning asking about you and the turd never said a thing not a dad gum thing!"

"Glen maybe you were in some sort of a rush and he didn't get the time to tell you. It's ok, no harm done. I think I've been in love with him all these years and now both of us have a chance to live in that love."

"Yeah Yeah, and ain't that nice." Glen said in a sarcastic manner. "I'm going back out to Jake's. I need to clear the air with him."

"All right Glen but remember, he has always been your friend, he thinks of you like a brother."

Glen didn't answer just got up and headed toward the door, feeling like a big fool. "God durn why didn't Jake say something to him when he was asking about Nell? Glen thought Jake had made him look small, look foolish and he was going back out there and give him a little piece of Shelton philosophy and maybe a butt kicking. Elzie better not interfere either."

Glen hardly said goodbye as he jumped in his car and was roaring down the county road too fast, kicking up a stream of dust that looked like one of them jets in the air leaving a trail.

Twice he met cars that were hugging the side of the road and he seemed not to even notice them. When he came to the stop sign in Sunset he slid to a stop and then gunned it out toward Forestburg to Jake's.

At the Oldham house, Glen found Susie and she told him where to find Jake and Elzie on the old Harris land. He knew the land and all he had to do was drive in and follow the roads. It would be easy to find where they were.

In short order he found the Jake's truck and saw them nailing up the siding.

Jake saw Glen and gave his traditional grin and wave as Elzie smiled showing they were in a welcoming mood. They had no idea Glen was mad.

"Hey Glen, nice to see you again. How was your visit with Nell?" Jake asked.

"It sure didn't turn out like I wanted, you big ass!" Glen said. "Why didn't you tell me you had her all wrapped up in a nice little package for yourself?"

"Glen, that's not how it is. We found out after we met how much we meant to one another and we are planning on getting married. You was in such a stir and half in heat that you didn't give me a chance to tell you. Besides you wanted to see her!"

"You made me look like a darn fool!" Glen said.

"No Glen," Jake said, "you did that to yourself."

Glen sat down on a work horse they had for laying out siding to cut and then to Jake and Elzie's surprise, he broke down. Tears came down his face and he was almost shaking.

"You know I had a wife and she left me. She left me for a man that didn't have much above his weekly paycheck and she left me for him.

I'm scared to death I'm going to be all alone." Glen said. "I got no kids, I got no family, I'm all alone and I'm scared to death."

"Oh come on," Elzie said, "You got two brothers that adore ye, you got me and ole Jake here that loves ye. You ain't alone."

"Glen," Jake said, "You are not too old to find someone. I just know in your social circles, there are women out there who would love to spend time with you and get to know you and probably marry you. And be a good companion. It isn't the end of the world old buddy."

Glen Ray looked at his two best friends in the whole world. He had chummed with some big name people down in Houston, in Austin, and even with Washington socialites making and wheeling deals, but right now he realized that these two old boys had always been his friends and would always be no matter what happened in life, whether he was a peacock or a feather duster. He stood up and just hugged Jake and then Elzie.

"I've been such an ass," He said. "You guys forgive me huh?"

Jake said one of his famous lines to people that sometimes rubbed him the wrong way, "It is water under the bridge."

"As soon as I know when we are tying that knot, I'll let you know, cause we couldn't have that without you being there." Jake said.

"And I wouldn't want to miss it either." Glen Ray said. "I've been out and missed so much already."

"Can I help ya'll with this?" Glen Ray said.

"Well shoot yeah," Elzie said. "You hold this plank while we nail er up and it will speed things up."

The three of them worked on for awhile before Phil and Ely showed up.

"How ya'll comin along?" Phil said.

"We're making good time," Jake said. "I just want to get the outside covered so that we can move inside and work in there regardless of the weather."

"Well, looks like thanks to Glen Ray here, you'll sure make it." Ely said.

In two hours the three buildings were now complete as to the siding on the outside. They could now move inside, and do the finish work regardless of the weather.

Although they invited Glen to stay for supper, he insisted he had to get back to Denton, although truth be told, he had no real reason other than his on antsy ways.

Jake put in a call to Nell. She and Bud and Patty were getting supper ready. She told Jake about Glen's visit and getting upset but Jake assured her he and Elzie had calmed everything down and everything was fine.

"I'll pick you up in the morning at 9:45 for church." Jake said, "Bible class is at 10 and church is at 11. This will be my first time to go back to bible class since Lois died."

"I'll be ready." Nell said.

Jake told Elzie to come with him down at the shed where they kept the chicken feed. He had something to show Elzie.

The two walked together and Elzie said, "You know you sure defused old Glen Ray this afternoon. He was hotter than a Saturday night pistol."

"Yeah he was," Jake said. "I'm part to blame. I could have told him about Nell and me but I thought better of it and let Nell tell him. It sure did make him mad for awhile but then he told us what the real problem was, his own fear of being alone."

"Well Cousin, were you afraid of being alone, is that why you going to marry Nell?" Elzie asked.

"I was not really afraid to be alone. After you went home that Sunday, I was alone until Wednesday. It was a tad uncomfortable and I'm glad my sons are moving out here. It will be a good thing. No, Elz, I'm not marrying Nell to avoid loneliness. It wasn't like that at all. It was something magic, I tell you. We were sitting there on my couch and all at once we were just drawn together and we couldn't stop kissing one another."

"I knew it!" Elzie said, "You did make out on the couch, only it was your couch not the pastors!"

"Oh shut up!" Jake said laughing.

At the shed Jake pulled a tarp off of a truck that had been stored there for several years.

"This is your grandparent's old truck!" Elzie was saying in almost a whisper. "I didn't know you still had that old bucket of bolts."

"I never got rid of it and now I have a use for it." Jake said. "There are people in Wichita Falls who restore old antique cars and trucks. I called them the other day and I'm making a deal, I'm going to completely restore this truck, including a modern V8 engine, air conditioning, power windows and an automatic transmission. I'm going to have this thing completely ready to drive Nell from the church where ever that church is, when we get married."

"My God," Elzie said, "that will cost thousands of dollars."

"So what?" Jake said. "We don't take it with us, besides it will be like it was when we was kids."

"Oh sure with that big V8 and automatic, this thing never ran that fast in its life, sure it will be like it was when we was kids." Elzie said.

"Well it will look like the same old truck when we was kids, smarty." Jake said.

"I'll tell you something else I'm going to do." Jake said. "I had Leeza look up where I can get a tailored suit made and I'm taking Nell down there to get it and we can sort of spend the day together. Going to do that next week."

"That's another big expense." Elzie said.

"Would you quit worrying about my expenses!" Jake said.

CHAPTER 22

Sunday morning Jake was running around like a chicken with his head cut off. He wanted to be sure he was ready, that all the family was ready even though they were not riding with him. He was annoying everyone. Ely finally told Jake to calm down and settle down everything was under control.

A little early, yet he got into his go to town truck and headed for Bud's. What he was really nervous about was that Nell had not been raised in the church of Christ and she wasn't now a member and for Jake wanting to marry her was to some a violation of Scripture when Paul had instructed widows to marry "In the Lord." Because some would not view Nell as being "in the Lord," since she wasn't a member of the church of Christ. Of all the things that might worry Jake, this was a big thing. It was so big that he considered it an issue that if need be, nothing would prevent him from marrying her, no preacher, no elders and no matter what the members of the church might think or say. But he sure didn't wish nor want her to be hurt by something someone might say. It boiled down to one issue, and that was; was she or was she not In THE LORD?

Arriving at Bud's, Bud and Patty were about to leave for their own church service, the Sunset Baptist where Bud as well as Nell had been raised and where now Bud served as one of their deacons. As Jake parked in the drive way, he saw Bud and Patty about to get in Bud's truck.

"Good morning Jake," they both said.

"I guess you're going to take my little sister to your church and make her into a Cambellite?" Bud said as he laughed.

Jake laughed too and was almost at a loss for words but said, "No she only needs to be a Christian and I know what she is."

"Well go on in, we've got to get there, I got to bump up the heat, get the sound system up and running." Bud said.

"We'll see ya'll later." Jake said.

Inside, Nell was sitting in the living room. She was dressed in a very nice blue trimmed in white dress. Her hair was combed out and she looked absolutely beautiful.

Jake walked over and gave her a light kiss and she in return.

"Good morning," she said.

"Good morning to you. You look so beautiful." Jake said.

"It is chilly this morning, you should take a coat," Jake said.

"I am." She said. "Jake you are early, you want to have a little cup of coffee before we go, we have time."

"That would be fine." Jake said.

They sat down at the kitchen table, she pouring the cups, him adding the cream and sugar.

She reached over and touched his arm. "You look troubled, are you?"

"I am, I don't even know where or how to begin." Jake said.

"I hate to even bring this up, but you know my church is in many ways like yours very conservative and they have a view that if you don't follow the bible as they follow, well then you are not right. And there is in the Scripture the instruction that widows that marry should only marry in the Lord. There are some people that would say because you are not a member of the church of Christ, you are not in the Lord. But Nell I've known you a long time and I believe that as a person you have always been a better person than I ever was. I believe your heart has been and was always more pure than mine. I don't want you hurt by how some people at the church may act." Jake said.

"Jake, don't worry a minute about this. I have decided that since we are going to marry that I would become a member of your church and whatever that takes is fine. I expect they will want me to be baptized again and that is fine. I was baptized when I was about seven and truthfully I didn't understand why, only that it pleased my mother and father. I have been reading in Acts lately and I think now I have a much clearer understanding of baptism and I don't object to being baptized again. It would be better for me because I now understand it so much better."

Jake was so relieved to hear her say those things, he almost cried, tears came down his cheeks. He couldn't help but hold her in an embrace.

At church Jake told Brother Preston he needed to see him, perhaps that afternoon around four or so. Brother Dave agreed to come out at that time.

Jake and Nell and Jake's family were all there but Jake was not prepared for the surprise of Elzie and Angie coming and sitting beside them.

"Are you all mixed up?" Jake whispered to Elzie after he sat down next to Nell. "You are at the church of Christ."

"Don't you think I don't know where I am?" Elzie asked. "Me an Angie enjoyed the service that Sunday we wuz here, we wanted to come back, that is if'n it's alright with you?"

Jake straightened up in the seat. He cleared his throat. "Of course it's alright with me as long as you don't snore while our preacher preaches."

"I'll bet I can stay awake as long as you can cousin." Elzie replied.

The service went well and many people came over to welcome Jake's guest. Many were there that knew Nell, Elzie and Angie.

Jake was glad to get home and out of his suit but felt like overalls was a bit under dressed for the day and to spend with Nell. So, he put on a pair of khaki pants and a dress shirt.

Julia, whom sometimes the family called Julie and sometimes Jul, and Susie got the noon meal ready to serve. They had put a pan of chicken in the oven to bake while they were gone to church. They made creamed potatoes, and they had cooked a bag of cream peas and had made yeast rolls. A peach cobbler was also in the lower oven baking.

The family all sat down and after prayer were enjoying the feast. Everyone bragged on the delicious cobbler. The boys were going into the living room to watch football and the girls, after cleaning up the kitchen, were going for naps.

Finally Jake had Nell to himself in his private quarters and they could sit down and start planning.

"You know Jake, I was thinking," Nell said, "And I want to do what you want to do but I wanted to make a suggestion about where to have our wedding." She paused a minute waiting for him to say something and Jake just nodded meaning he was waiting to hear what she had to say. "I noticed the first time I came out that you or someone had done a lot of restoration work to the old Pleasant Hill church building and I was wondering since we were having a small family close friend gathering, why not use that old building, can we?"

"I was going to suggest the same thing!" Jake said. "Yes, I think it would be wonderful to have it there. The building has electricity, has indoor bathrooms, running water, has a fellowship room and a chapel and I think it would be perfect. I mentioned it to my daughters in law and they thought it would be great, and they are willing to serve at the reception."

"Perfect." She replied.

"I've got something cooking for us but I will not tell you about it and I can't set a date until this project is done and they told me three to six weeks." Jake said.

"What in the world are you up to, Jake Oldham?" Nell said.

"Something I hope will be special for you, and that's all I'll tell you." Jake said.

"But there's something else. Leeza looked up for me a tailor in Dallas that makes suits. I want to have one made for our wedding and I want you to go down there with me to see that there tailor." Jake said. "In fact, I'ze hoping you'd do the driving. I don't like driving in Dallas."

"You could get married in your overalls as far as I'm concerned." Nell said. "When will we be going?"

"Tuesday, if that's ok with you. I've got a noon board meeting Monday at the Farm Bureau office. I'm on the board, a county director." Jake said.

"Wasn't your dad a county director?" Ness asked.

"Yeah, he was and it was through those connections he got in the dozer business." Jake said.

"Ok, Tuesday will be fine." Nell said.

"I'll come over and then, I'll buy your gas but I'd sure like to have you drive us to Dallas." Jake said.

"You better know where we are going." She replied.

"We'll get Leeza to show us and get all the directions." Jake said. "She knows how to do that stuff on a computer. I kinda think it will be fun to spend the day together and away from everyone else."

"Why Jake, don't you think for one moment you're going to get me down there and do something immoral!" she teased.

Jake blushed, "Oh no, no, I was just meaning just being together no phones, no kids, nobody to interrupt or worry about someone busting in but I, uh I, oh I sure have stepped in it, haven't I?"

"You sure have, you naughty boy." Nell said.

"Why do you want to have a suit made?." Nell asked.

"Cause I can afford it, cause I want to, cause I think you deserve the very best and I want to present myself as best as I can and I thought a handmade suit would just fit that bill." Jake said.

"You know I'm sort of getting excited about this trip to Dallas," Nell said.

Jake could hear voices coming from the living room and then Susie was knocking at his door.

She came in and said, "Jake the preacher's here and so are Elzie and Angie."

Jake knew why the Brother Preston was there but he had no idea what Elzie and Angie were up to.

Nell and Jake walked into the living room with Nell on Jake's arm.

"Thanks for coming out, David," Jake said. "Elzie what's up?"

"The two times Angie and I have visited your church we found we liked it. And things have changed so much at ours, we just don't feel welcome, but we do at your church so we wanted to talk to Brother Dave here about joining." Elzie said.

David spoke before Jake could, saying, "Well Elzie, no one joins the church of Christ, when we are baptized, Christ adds us to His church. Now what we need to do is come to an understanding about your status. I want to just read some Scriptures to you and then you decide if you have done these things then you just make the request to be a member and you will be without question." Preston made his point reading Acts 2 and Acts 8 to them seeing if they understood what took place with those people in finding their salvation and to ask themselves if they had done the same. When he started reading Leeza had come into the room. When he finished he asked them if they understood what this passages meant.

Leeza said, "I understand and tonight this very night I want to be baptized, because I sure believe that Jesus is my Savior and I want to be baptized into Him that I might receive the gift of the Holy Spirit and my sins be forgiven.

"Bless you Leeza," Preston said.

Jake hugged his granddaughter.

Then Nell said she would like to request to be baptized, as when she was baptized as a young girl she didn't understand it then and she would rather do it again to be clear about why now. Then Elzie and Angie said that although they had been baptized in their churches, they were not told the reason and now that they understood, they too would ask that they might be baptized again.

Brother Preston told them to bring some clothes for the baptism and come to church tonight and they would be baptized then. He said a prayer and then he bade them goodbye until that night. It was almost five in the afternoon then and church was at six.

After he left Jake was elated and very surprised and very pleased at all of them. He couldn't wait until they all went to church. He could not contain himself and had to hug his old friend Elzie. Both men had tears, tears of joy.

That night at church there was enthusiasm everywhere. The air was electric. Everyone seemed to know beforehand that four new people were about to be baptized.

Brother Preston started the service that night before any singing took place and announced what had taken place out at Jake's house. He asked the four to come forward immediately and then asked each one if they believed in Jesus as the Savior and then he had prayer and was sending them, the women on one side of the building and Elzie on the other side to prepare for their baptism. But then he told the church that normally we had an invitation song after the preaching but because he knew these were ready, he wanted them to receive their salvation then. But he asked were there others who were considering obeying the gospel that they could and they should come forward then and now. Amazingly, four more, all teens who attended the church came forward. Again Brother Preston asked each one their belief in Jesus and had prayer for them and sent them to change. Jake knew they didn't have enough baptismal robes for eight and he was glad Dave had suggested they bring extra clothes. Because they were not going to go out to Bud's, Jake was sure Nell could use one of the robes.

Then each one was baptized and upon the last one coming from the water, the church stood and sang the Hymn "O Happy Day." It would take some ten minutes for all to change into dry clothes and come back to the auditorium and while they waited, the church sang songs. One by one they came out and just sat on the front row. When Nell came, Jake got up and went and sat with her, holding her hand and she squeezing his. After they came out, the men served communion to them and to any who were not there that morning. Then the preacher gave a very short lesson on "let us not forget these," referring to those who had been baptized that night and the service was closed. The congregation surrounded the eight and for a long time there was rejoicing, hugging and even crying for joy for these.

Jake was very choked up because half of the people who were baptized that night had direct association with him: his granddaughter, his best friend and his wife, and then the woman who was to become his wife. It was very emotional.

Jake, Elzie, Angie and Nell were all riding together and they drove out to Bud's to take Nell home. Jake walked Nell to the door and was saying to her, "I wish I could spend this very night with you. I don't mean from a sensual way but I just want to be with you and I can't hardly stand not to be with you."

Nell was almost giddy and probably was happier tonight than she had been in many years and said, "I know exactly what you mean, but it will come soon enough. You have to wait until your tailor made suit is ready and that three to six week surprise. So just suffer!"

They had a laugh and then as if they were teens, he kissed her good night on the porch and she went in.

Jake felt nine feet tall as he strode back to Elzie's car.

"Dang if you don't act like a teenager." Elzie chimed as Jake got in the back seat.

"Well I'll tell you cousin," Jake said, "If you'd kiss ole Angie more, you might feel like one too."

With that Angie said, "He might be right," and she turned Elzie to her and kissed his lips. Then she pulled away and said, "It sure does, I feel sixteen again, hurry up Elzie Tatum and get me home, I've got plans for you."

They all had a big laugh as Elzie sped home.

CHAPTER 23

Tuesday came soon enough and Jake was loaded with the information he needed to get them to the tailor's shop off Harry Hines in Dallas. He arrived at Bud's and there was Bud in the front yard, picking up more pecans.

"That last Norther really blew off some nuts," Bud said. "This will be the third five gallon bucket. You know Jake you should have called us if my sister was going to be baptized. We would have come. Why didn't you call?"

"I should have Bud, don't be mad. I was excited and happy and just forgot my senses for awhile. My Granddaughter was baptized too and so was Elzie and Angie and four more!" Jake said. "I was sort of overcome with emotion. And I wasn't sure how you'd feel, like maybe she was doing something she didn't need to do or whatever, I just didn't know what to do."

"I understand. I guess for awhile I was annoyed about it, but Nell explained that when she and I was baptized, it was under some pressure from our parents and she was small and I'm sure wasn't really understanding why it was done. I'm not mad, really I wished we had been there for her and for you." Bud said as he sort of slapped a gentle hit on Jake's shoulder.

"Nell says ya'll going to Dallas to look for you a suit." Bud said.

"Yeah, going to have one hand made." Jake said.

"I'm going to see about having her dress made too," Jake said "but she don't know that yet. She'll learn that after we get there."

"Well lets go in there and fetch her out," Bud said.

As they entered the kitchen Nell was coming through the living room. She was casually dressed yet looked sharp as a tack.

Jake drew a deep breath and smiled.

"Are you ready to head East?" Nell said.

"I'm ready," Jake said.

They said their goodbyes and walked out to Nell's car. In a way Jake felt funny not driving but would get comfortable with the idea.

"I like your car," Jake said, but not sure it will hold up to these dirt roads."

"I might sell it and get a nice four door pickup," Nell said.

"I bet this car would cover the cost of new pickup." Jake said.

"It should, it has less than two thousand miles on it." Nell said.

In a few minutes they were in Sunset and then on the highway headed south. When that got to Rhome they would take 114 to Dallas. It was a pleasant trip and the traffic was light.

At Harry Hines, they got off as Jake would read the instructions to Nell. Exit Harry Hines, go five blocks and exit Springer, go right on Springer and then ten blocks turn left on Logan, and on Logan the shop would be five blocks once they had turned on Logan.

They were in a small business district, what to some were known as a garment area. There were some stores that carried material and others that carried leather items. Nestled between a dress store and a cleaners was the tailor's shop, called "Golden's."

A little bell went off as they came in the crowded shop. There were some four clerks working around the store with tape measures around their necks. A man about seventy years old came up to them and with a strong accent asked how he might be of service.

Jake cleared his throat and said he was looking to have a custom suit made.

"Umm," the man said, "And vot style, color and all do you have in mind?"

"I was thinking gray or a blue or something in the darker gray that was more blue than black," Jake said.

"Umm" the man said, "I tink I got just the ting."

He took Jake and Nell to a boat of material that was a darker gray but blue as well.

"Yes," Jake said, "I like that, what do you think Nell?"

She ran her finger and then her hand across the material and said, "It is a nice color and it will certainly highlight your eyes and hair."

"Well," Jake said, "What is next, do you measure me?"

The conversation went back and forth as the man meticulously took the measurements needed to make the suit. Jake asked about a vest wanting it to be of a slightly different color. The man brought out a lighter gray that was a compliment to the suit and it was agreed. Jake was insistent on one thing, he wanted the coat to be longer than normal. He wanted it to come down to about his knees. It would give the suit an antique look, and that was what Jake wanted.

The tailor asked the occasion why they were buying a new suit, a birthday perhaps or an anniversary? Jake explained that they had been childhood sweethearts and were now getting married. The tailor clapped his hands, smiled and congratulated them both.

Jake asked the man if he knew a seamstress as he wanted to have a wedding dress made for Nell.

"I know just the person, a cousin of mine, too." The tailor said. He then went to a phone and called someone and speaking to her in Yiddish. Coming back to them, he said his cousins would come over to his shop.

Nell was looking at Jake. Jake you don't have to have me a dress made, I was going to pick out something.." she said.

"No you're not," Jake said. "If I'm getting a new suit, you shall get a new and a special dress. I want you to have it."

About the time the tailor finished his measurements, a small elderly lady came in and walked up to them. She was smiling and looking Nell over. "What do you have in mind?" she inquired.

The tailor introduced his cousin to Jake and Nell, her name was Ester.

"Miss Ester, Jake began, I would like to have a dress made for my bride here, that would compliment my vest, something close to it and then the collar's and cuff's trimmed in the same color as my suit. That is if that would please you Nell?"

"Well the idea sounds cute, we would sort of match and be the opposites of each other." She said.

Ester examined the vest and the suit fabric and looked at the tailor and made an expression and then back to Jake and Nell. "I have just the thing. Let me measure you ma'am and all shall be done."

Nell obeyed and while they were measuring, Jake asked the tailor to show him a couple more fabric's for future suits. "I'd like something light in color, near white, and a tan for spring and summer," Jake said. "You've got my measurements, all you got to do is make them. But this here suit, it needs to be made first cause when you get these clothes made, and I get my special gift for her in, well then we can get married."

"It is no problem, I can have them all made at once." The tailor said. "But I need to give you the price, you may not want even one. I charge fifteen hundred dollars for a suit, but I will make you a price for three, say four thousand."

Without blinking an eye, Jake just said, "Done. I'll give you cash money, no credit card, just cash." Then Jake pulled out his wallet and began counting hundred dollar bills. "What's the dress going to cost, a thousand?" Jake said.

"I think that will be fine," the tailor said as Jake gave him the money. "You'll pay Miss Ester?"

"Of course I will." The tailor said.

"Good, we are in business. Now, how long do you suppose it will take to get our clothes?" Jake asked.

"Two weeks," the man said.

"Fine I'll give you my phone number and you can call us, and we'll come a' running." Jake said.

The tailor wasn't sure what that meant but accepted what was said to mean they would hurry back. He agreed and they shook hands.

"That was a nice place to do business." Jake said. "I hope you are pleased and don't think I'm running the show, I just had this idea for you a dress and for me a suit."

"I love the idea and I love you for thinking of it." Nell said."I'm starving, where have you planned to feed me?" Nell asked.

CHAPTER 24

I t seemed to Jake the next two weeks just crept by. He and Elzie and Ely after feeding, worked daily on the hunting bunkhouse and the two cabins. They wired the buildings, but hired the plumbing and insulating but they did the sheet rock work and then Jake had them cover the walls with some kind of board or bead board paneling as he was not for painting the walls or ceiling. The work progressed and other than when Jake or Elzie went to meet clients and schedule dozer work, they were at the cabins and bunk house most of the time.

Evenings, Jake would journey over to Nell's and they would either have supper at Bud's or go out, and sometimes Nell would come out to Jake's for a family supper and then spend the evening in Jake's quarters with him. They might watch TV, or sit and talk, as they still had many years of the past to catch up on. They held hands, they embraced and they could not depart without kissing each other with passion. Neither Jake nor Nell knew that they could have had such emotion for any person like they had for each other.

When the tailor called for the suits and dress to be picked up, Jake insisted that Angie and Elzie go with them. Angie had been working at the hardware store and had to schedule the time off, but otherwise they were all able to make the trip.

Nell drove in her car with Angie in the front and the guys in the back seat. Elzie and Jake couldn't keep from teasing each other which to someone outside the family might even confuse with a real argument. But for them it was just the way they showed affection for each other.

Arriving at the tailor shop, the man who had originally measured Jake brought out the three suits and let Jake and Nell examine them for their approval. He called his cousin Ester to bring the dress but Nell told Jake he could not see it only Angie could. So, Jake had to look away while they examined the dress and while they were he took Elzie over to the supply of material and had Elzie to pick out a three colors he liked. He picked a dark blue, a light blue and a tan. Jake told the tailor to measure Elzie and if he would make the same deal, well they would buy three more suits.

"Wait a minute," Elzie said, "I don't know that I can afford three new suits."

"You wait a minute," Jake said, "This is an early Christmas and birthday present to you from me and Nell."

"You are not spending a bunch of money on me." Elzie said.

"I'll spend whatever I want, and you can just hush up." Jake said.

"Go ahead and measure this fat boy." Jake said motioning to the tailor.

At that same time Nell was doing about the same thing for Angie. She was asking Miss Ester to show them her garments and have Angie pick out pieces for dresses.

It was something Jake and Nell had decided that they wanted to do for Elzie and Angie, gesture of their long friendship.

The four ended up at a Mexican restaurant before heading back home.

"Well in another two weeks, I guess we'll be coming back for ya'lls new stuff." Jake said. "Or I suppose ya'll could come yer selves, if ya wanted to." Jake said.

"You know," Elzie said, "Me 'n old Angie might just slip off and come ourselves, and spend the night in some high dollar place, who knows?"

"You'd probably get your butt lost down here." Jake said. "Or worse than that, get Angie pregnant." There was a howl of laughter as Angie said, "Oh God no!"

One week later, Jake got a call and he and Elzie headed up to Wichita Falls to pick up a 1950 flat bed half ton pickup with new paint, new tires, new suspension, new engine and new upholstery.

When they arrived at the business and saw the truck, Elzie was ready to faint.

"Wow, oh wow, Jake," Elzie was saying, "Can I drive that back to Sunset?"

"Sure, but don't you let anybody see ya." Jake said. "We gotta hide that thing in the shed."

Jake wouldn't let Elzie see what the truck cost but he was sure it was near ten thousand dollars.

The two headed out and headed back to Sunset as quick as they could. Coming to Sunset, Elzie exited off 287 and headed up through the main part of town and only stopped at the stop signs, then was out headed to the farm. At the farm, they didn't see Ely or Phil or anyone and parked the pickup in the open part of the shed and covered it back up with the tarp.

There were carpenters working on Ely's house and they all saw the new/old truck. They were all eyes and after parking it, and Jake went to talk to the contractors. "If ya'll want to look at my Grandpa's old truck, when you get ready to go home for the day, I'll take you down and show it to you. It is a surprise for my wedding and my boys nor their wives don't know a thing, so don't say a word."

Jake and Elzie went in for lunch and Susie was just about to call them not knowing where they had been all morning.

"What ya'll been up to?" she asked.

"Um, well," uh, Jake stammered, "we went over to Sunset to look at some property I heard about and I had to go to the post office and warn the post master about my chickens."

"What do you mean?" Susie said.

"Oh well, I decided to get Leeza in a project that will serve as a future project for her in her FFA class. And later we will rope in the twins. Leeza and I are going into egg production." Jake said. "So I ordered three hundred mixed chicks, which means at least 80% will be pullets and she and I will start selling eggs next year. Since me 'n

Elzie's going to start selling produce at the Fort Worth farmer's market, we are going to start taking eggs with our melons and Leeza too. She will learn how to deal with the public and learn how to sell. It will be good for her. And when the twins get older we will make them partners. Right now they are going to just work for us although right now they don't even know that."

"And Leeza is all for this?" Susie said.

"As a matter of fact she is." Jake said.

"So, I was letting the post office know of the shipment of live chicks and how they need to call me when they arrive so I can get them out here quickly and out of the boxes." Jake said. "It will be about six weeks and we will have our laying shed built by then."

"Next year, we will expand our pecan orchard, increase the acreage and it will be part of Leeza and the twin's own projects. They can earn the money, they can use part of it for whatever they want, and the rest for their future educational needs." Jake said. "I need to see Nell, my surprise for her is here and all we need to do is set our date, buy our rings, get our license and tie the knot." Jake said. "I'm going to do that tonight."

"Oh shoot," Elzie said, "I thought we would play thumps."

Jake knew Elzie was just kidding him, razing him some.

CHAPTER 25

Jake drove over to Bud's so he could sit down and make final plans with Nell.

Nell was sitting at the dining table talking to Patty when Bud showed Jake in.

"Well well, Mr. Jake," Patty said, "have you been slaying dragon's today?"

"Perhaps," Jake said. "My surprise has arrived, and I needed to talk to Nell about setting a date and it just hit me today that we haven't even looked at a ring."

"Jake Oldham," Nell said, "you've got me on pins and needles wondering about your surprise! As far as rings are concerned, Jake we don't need a ring or rings, I notice you don't wear one, and I don't think you wore one from your past marriage, because there's no lighter skin on your ring finger."

"Well you are right. I had a wedding band but never wore it much. I couldn't wear it around machinery, you risk getting your finger torn off, if you was to hang your ring on something and so I never had the habit. But, I thought whatever you wanted, I was sure willing to get it, don't care what you want, maybe not the Hope diamond but I'll get you what you want."

"Jake I've got all kinds of jewelry and I don't wear much of it. The ring is not that important if isn't to you. I'd be just as pleased with a simple band and nothing else," Nell said.

"Why don't we do that then, let's go tomorrow to Wichita Falls and get what you want and then let's get down to the nut cutting," Jake said.

Everyone knew what Jake meant but the girls had to giggle a little at the plain way Jake had put it.

"Can't we get our license and then set the wedding for the next Friday?" Jake asked. "Is that too soon?"

"Not for me Jake Oldham," Nell said. "Since we are having a little small wedding and asking a handful of people, two weeks should be just right."

"Ok, I'll pick you up at ten and then we can go and get there around eleven. The mall will be open and then we can have lunch before we come back and go right over to the courthouse. We can get all that done and then we can call, invite and be ready." Jake said matter of fact.

"Where would you like to go tonight?" Jake asked

"Nowhere, we are staying here. Patty and I are cooking supper and we will all eat here." Nell said. "Now you and Bud trot off to the living room and sit and rest and visit and Patty and I will work on the meal." Nell said.

Jake didn't argue or say a word but he and Bud obeyed except instead of going to the living room, they went outside. Out to Bud's shop and then Bud took Jake in his truck to give his cows some cubes while they talked.

"What is your surprise for Nell?" Bud asked.

Jake had to grin a little, but finally he told Bud about the old truck.

"That is neat, good gosh!" Bud said. "As many times as we rode that thing to Hulet's, sure ought to bring back some memories."

"I hope it does and I hope she will be pleasantly surprised and not disappointed."

"When you going to show it to her?" Bud asked.

"I'm going to drive to the church and drive her away in it." Jake said.

"Well I'll be dang." Bud said. "I like that. I know she will."

"Don't you dare tell her a thing." Jake said.

"Don't worry, my lips are sealed." Bud said.

CHAPTER 26

Jake had put in a call to Wichita Falls and had found Debbie Crocket's sister. She told Jake where Debbie and her husband Dr. Ralph Harper were now living, which was Raleigh North Carolina since they had retired from missionary work.

Jake immediately called Debbie. She was the one who answered the phone.

"Hello." She said.

"Debbie, is this Debbie Crocket Harper?"

"Yes it is," she replied.

"This is Jake Oldham." Jake said.

"Oh my, Jake Oldham, how in the world are you?"

With that Jake launched into his story and his wedding plans and wanted them to come as a surprise to Nell.

"I know it is sort of short notice, but if you all will come, I'll buy your plane tickets and everything, and have you picked up and take you back." Jake said.

"Let me talk to Ralph, and I'll call you back now that I have a number." Deb said. "I'm so glad you called, and so excited for you two, you two deserve one another and should have been together all these years!"

"Well it didn't happen that way but by George we are going to put it together now and live whatever time the good Lord has for us." Jake said.

"Listen Deb," Jake said, "I'm going to go and pick up Nell and she and I are going to get her a ring. I found out we have five days once we get the license, so we'll get that first thing next Monday of the week we are marrying. I'd like ya'll to come out here a couple days before we marry so we all can visit and catch up. We've decided, and I mean Nell decided this, we aren't going off on a honeymoon. When we get married we're just coming right here to the farm and start life. She said we can plan us a family trip next summer, so I'm doing whatever she says. So if ya'll can come, we can visit and even stay after we get married we can take you back to the airport together. I'm planning on getting Glen Ray Shelton to pick you up, because I know how glad he will be to see you. But, don't call me back until tonight cause I don't want Nell knowing I found you."

"I guess if we can come, it will be a big surprise for her." Debbie said. "What about Nancy, is she around?"

"She is, she married a local guy, they have a good business a new daughter in law and life seems good for them." Jake said.

"I'll call you tonight, say nine or so?" Deb said.

"That will be perfect." Jake replied.

Jake got in his truck and drove to Bud's finding Nell ready and waiting.

Bud and Patty were sitting in the living room with their TV on.

"Ya'll ought to just go with us," Jake said.

Bud and Patty looked at one another and said why not. So Bud got his truck for them to ride in since it was made for four. Jake and Bud rode in the front seat with the women in back.

"I'll tell you one thing," Bud said. "We'll not go in any jewelry store with ye, we'll leave that to you two."

"That's fine," Jake said. "But now when we eat dinner, we can sit together then can't we?"

"I'll think about it." Bud replied.

They arrived at the Sikes Mall and parked at the Penny's parking lot. Bud said he liked to walk through the men's clothing to see if they had anything on sale.

"Let me tell you Bud," Jake said, "Before Christmas, we'll take you down to Dallas to this tailor we met, and he'll fit you fine for a suit and I'll get you one for Christmas, since you're about to be my brother in law. You're going to increase my Christmas list some."

"Did you get a suit from that tailor?" Bud asked.

"Sure did, got one special for the wedding and got two more just cause they had some material I liked." Jake answered.

Walking through Penny's, they headed out into the mall and mid way in the mall were two jewelry stores. The first one they went in, the people seemed not to anxious to wait on them but finally made an effort but they did not have a simple band in stock.

The second store seemed more friendly, and they had two bands, a yellow gold and a white gold. Nell chose the white gold. They actually had one to fit her small finger. When she tried it on, there was something to Jake that just seemed so woman, so feminine seeing the ring on her hand. He was very moved by the sight of the ring.

"Is that what you want Nell?" Jake asked. "If you want one with a diamond, or a whole bunch of them or..."

Nell cut Jake off, "Jake I told you, a simple band is all I really would want and this one is exactly what I want."

Without asking the price, Jake told them to put that in a box and sack and ring it up. He paid them in cash.

Bud and Patty were in Dillard's but came out just about the time Jake and Nell came out of the jewelry store. Nell had her arm locked on Jake.

Bud rather beamed looking at them thinking they are a good looking couple.

They headed downtown to McBride's Steak House for lunch. Everyone was excited, Bud and Patty at the upcoming marriage, Jake and Nell at the prospect of getting one more thing done so they could marry.

"Have ya'll decided what time you're going to have the service?" Bud asked.

"Well," Jake said, "if I could get everyone together, I'd have it before breakfast. But I 'spect, Nell will want to have it before supper. Maybe six or so, in the evening?"

"Yeah," Nell replied, "Six will be fine. Bud you will walk me down the aisle and give away won't you?"

"Of course baby sister, there's no one else to do it and I am ready to give you away." Bud said with laughter.

CHAPTER 27

Jake depended on his daughter's in law to get all the things necessary for the wedding. They had simply called the people they were inviting which was their immediate families, Bud and Patty, their children. Elzie and Angie and it was an option if their children wanted to come, since Nell didn't know them and Jake hardly knew them.

There were Jake's boys, and his grandkids. And then there were the Shelton's, all of them were invited, Glen Ray and his brother's and their wives, Nancy and her husband and son and daughter in law. Nancy's older sister was at the time out of state with her husband on a trip to California and would not be there. Then there was the preacher and his wife, the two elders of his church and then Jake told Nell to invite whomever she wanted from Bud's church since she had grown up there, surely there were still a few families she knew. Of course Jake's two employees Clint and Tony and their families. All in all there would be no more than fifty people. Of course Nell did not know that Debbie and her husband would be there. Debbie had confirmed with Jake they were coming and would arrive on Wednesday afternoon. Jake had asked Glen Ray to get them since he was in Denton and it would take him about forty five minutes to arrive at the airport. He was glad to do it. After his spat with Jake, he had really found a renewal in his life. He was still busy but he took more time to smell the roses. He was even thinking about asking a woman out that he had met while still living in Houston. He didn't mind driving down there for a visit. After all, he knew Houston.

Jake was as happy a man as he could be. He had tried to stay busy but it was hard to concentrate. Elzie gave him a hard time about it too.

They had finished the hunting cabins, and they had constructed a large laying barn for the chickens Jake had ordered.

Jake had shown Leeza and the twins how to care for them and the chicks were doing well. Although they had lost a few as expected, the chicks were thriving and growing fast.

Since Ely and Phil were doing all the feeding, and the extra projects were complete, Jake and Elzie had some time on their hands.

One day Elzie suggested they take the truck and just go for a ride and do some catching up.

What he meant by that was, they would drive around the county roads and they would talk about their days past, they would be reminded of an event at certain places. They had no destination in mind, but Elzie wanted them to just drive and talk and wherever they wound up, well they could duck into some eatery.

They first looped Pleasant Hill then headed up toward Forestburg but detoured to New Harp. From New Harp they drove out east of New Harp on roads they had actually never been on. But, it was an interesting drive. They relived the days of plowing their bottom's with the old Ferguson's tractors of their dad's and how that after breaking the land they had to chisel it, then disc it and re-disc it. If they wanted to hunt or fish, it was as far as Jake's dad was concerned, unnecessary, but Jake's Grandma would prevail and get P.D. to let the boys go fishing.

They talked about their love life and of course Jake thought about all the times with Nell. He had got to spend some time with her but she had really resisted him and his advances. There was the one time they drove to Lover's Lane and he got some sugar from her, plenty and it was nice and it was sweet, but she would not commit to saying nor would she let him tell her he loved her. But, to think about it, Jake was seventeen at the time and she was hardly fifteen. You don't expect a fifteen year old girl to think she's in love with the "man of her life," at that young age. Then again, Jake didn't think they were at that young of age, they were just about to dive off a cliff called adulthood and they were expected to grow up and to be adults and marry and have a family and work and slave and wonder if they did the right thing or if there had been a better life waiting for them if they hadn't jumped the gun and married the first whim of their life.

There was Elzie, as he had been sweet on Angie when they were but fifteen and then off and on, Elzie had dated different girls but he came back to the one he started with and they ended up husband and wife and they still were. Shoot they knew a bunch of people that had got married and later got divorced, twice as many as their parents generation and four times the number as their grandparents generation. Jake wondered why. How come each generation more and more was getting divorced? Who knows, he thought. Must be something to do with how we are schooled, how more and more women were working full time, or social changes that Jake and Elzie had no idea what they were.

One thing Jake knew and that when he married Lois, they had been happy but sometimes, he had to suppress thoughts about Nell. There were times in his life he had to fight the idea of getting in his truck and just driving to Vicksburg and ask the woman he had been in love with, did you find a bigger and better world? And now he knew that when the first time they met after thirty five years, the buried love he had came to the surface and he made a move to let her know and she met that move. She had kissed him first and it was a deep and emotionally charged kiss. Jake could tell when she started kissing him, she was letting go all the suppressed emotions she'd had and couldn't contain them a second longer. Yes, he was a lucky man, to have had two great loves in his life. Lois had filled the void that Nell had left and then she was gone. Somehow fate had brought them back. Nell was going to refill that void she made from long ago. He had no fear they would be happy. He may have to leave the farm some, you know, go on some darn trip, but go so that she would be happy. It just didn't hurt to do what you could to make someone happy.

The guys wound up back in Forestburg and pulled up at the old country store where they had a grill.

"Come on old lover boy," Jake said to Elzie, "Let's go eat a big burger and plate of French fries!"

"Elzie clapped his hands, and said, "I'm all for that cousin. Yep, all for that."

CHAPTER 28

G len Ray was overjoyed that Jake had asked such a favor of him, that he would gladly drive to the Dallas Fort Worth Airport and find Debbie Crocket and her husband Ralph Harper. He believed he would know old Debbie right on spot but Jake told him, just for to be sure, he should make a sign that said Dr. Ralph Harper and that way for sure they would find one another.

She and her husband were arriving that Wednesday at noon on an American flight arriving in Dallas at gate 34 Terminal A. So Glen Ray was parked in the parking lot, and with his sign he had placed himself where they should come out. He felt like someone's driver, but he knew Jake was being cautious. But, Glen Ray thought over cautious, shoot, he should be able to pick out Debbie in a crowd, thirty five years or not.

As he stood there two small, petite, almost elderly people walked up to Glen Ray. "I'm Dr. Ralph Harper." He said.

Glen Ray stood there for a moment and then he said, "Debbie."

The small olive skinned woman with very white hair smiled and said, "Glen Ray Shelton, yes it's me."

Glen was almost knocked over. He knew it was her, but she was now a senior citizen. She was old, yet she retained her fine line beauty. She had been extremely pretty as a girl and she still was. She had just aged yet gracefully.

Her husband was somewhat a surprise; he was white headed, very small man not much over a hundred and twenty pounds, wore a new style of frameless glasses, with a heavy prescription. He also had Native American blood, at least partially as it showed in his face and skin color.

"Um, forgive me, I'm Glen Ray Shelton." Glen said shaking Dr. Harper's hand. "I grew up with your wife but thirty five years does change us a bit."

"We are pleased to see you, Mr. Shelton," Dr. Harper said. "I understand, but to me she looks just like she did when I first met her."

"Of course she does." Glen Ray said.

"How was the trip?" Glen Ray said, as he began walking them to the car. They were carrying a bag each and Dr. Harper was pulling a large suit case on rollers behind him.

"It is less than three hours from North Carolina to Texas," Dr. Harper said. "We usually take us some reading material and it shortens the time."

Glen Ray popped the trunk, put their bags in and then opened the back door for them. Debbie motioned for her husband to get in and said she would ride in the front so she could visit with Glen. That was fine with Dr. Harper.

"By the way Dr. Harper, Glen said, just call me Glen, no one calls me Mr. Shelton."

"The same here," Dr. Harper said, "just call me Ralph."

As they left the airport, Glen asked them if they had been fed on the plane. They had not. So, Glen's first project was to take them to some place nice and get them fed. Glen knew Dallas pretty well and knew where some of the better restaurants were.

Once they had eaten, Glen figured they would feel much better and would probably rest as he drove the hour and a half back to Sunset. However Debbie was anxious to visit with him catching up on Nancy, Glen's own marital status, his family, and she was especially curious how Nell and Jake had come back together.

"I think when Nell came up to see Bud, he told her to go and see Jake. A couple of months back, Jake lost his wife and of course Nell had lost her husband New Year's Eve night. Bud had her to go and see Jake for some financial advice and as I have heard Jake say, they found that the old spark from the past just about caught ablaze when they were together. So, now they are going to get married and she's going to ride around with Jake in an old rattling truck and feed cows and try to be happy."

"If she is with Jake, then I'll bet she will be just that, happy." Debbie said. I'm really excited for them and can't wait to see them."

"What about Elzie? Where is he? Debbie asked.

"Well, you know, for years he and his wife, and you know his wife Angie Freeman, they lived down in Bridgeport for a long time but he was retiring in December. After Jake's wife died, well old Elzie goes out to see Jake and Jake just offers them his old house. He's got two houses on the place. He built one on the Pariot place and then his dad's house and he and his late wife were living there taking care of P.D. and after he died, they stayed and so the other house is empty, at least it was empty until Jake's kids came up for visits. But, now his boys are both building new houses out there and are living out there."

"Jake has two boys?" Debbie asked.

"Yeah, Phillip and Ely." Glen said.

"And grandchildren?" she asked.

"Three," Glen Ray said.

"How about you Deb, do ya'll have any children?"

"Well yes we do, we have an even dozen." She replied.

"Good God, you don't say, twelve!" Glen exclaimed.

"You know we spent the last thirty five years in missionary work and we were in India a long time, and while there we adopted ten children; and we had two of our own, two boys and both of them are ministers." Debbie said.

"Reckon all them kids helped to turn your hair so white?" Glen Ray asked.

"Probably so," Deb said, "Probably so."

"Let's see, what of Billy John?" Deb asked.

"Sorry to say Billy John died last year. He had some heart trouble and one day they just found him dead at his desk." Glen said.

"So sorry to hear that." Debbie said. "Did he have a family?"

"No, he never married and his folks have been gone awhile." Glen said.

"Deb when we get to Sunset, you may not recognize it. It never grew after the depression. It just declined and after the school consolidating with Bowie, the bank, the store, then the highway went around us and all the stations closed. I guess people would call it a bedroom community, but I think it a deplorable community." Glen Ray said.

"It can't be that bad," Debbie said. "You have no idea what a deplorable town is until you have been to places where Ralph and I have been."

Glen didn't answer. He was fast approaching the Sunset exit. They eased into town and Debbie was looking things over.

"Oh, Glen, please drive by my old house, if it is still here, I want Ralph to see where I grew up." Debbie asked.

"Why sure," Glen Ray said as he turned left at the intersection and headed toward Chico. And there it was, her home, the house she knew as a girl growing up there with her parents and her Grandmother Crocket.

"Someone has added a room, but it doesn't appear anyone is there or using the house." Debbie said.

"After your folks past and you and your sister sold the place, it has had a few people living there I think. The last person that bought the house never rented it out or used it. I'm not sure who owns it now but you are right about one thing, I don't think anyone is using the house these days." Glen Ray said.

Debbie made an expression with her face but didn't reply. She was aware that Sunset was not likely the same town it was when she was here. All the old people she knew were likely all gone and she didn't know or would know the people living in the homes that were there. Some she recognized from her days, but there were many that were gone, just empty spaces on the street. There were a few new homes too, and she wondered about the people that lived in them, if things were as bad as Glen Ray said.

"I see there are several churches here and of course my old church is still here and the same building." Deb said.

"Ah yes, that would be right," Glen said, "But you know my old church is gone, that is the old building, and they have a new building but I understand not a very large group attends."

Glen was speaking of the Methodist church where he had grown up. As a kid the church was always full and was very active as a church back then. According to what he had heard, there were less than two dozen now attending. At least they had a nice new building, he thought.

Glen had now headed out of town and on toward the Oldham's place. Debbie was getting anxious. It was a tad slow on the bumpy road and that brought back considerable memories to her remembering that was one thing that had never changed, the bumpy country roads.

She thought, as they were driving out, how the farms had changed so little. Of course she saw a few new homes that were not there in her past but she expected that. But the land the use of it was the same.

Soon they were pulling up to Elzie's house. They had hardly gotten out of the car when Elzie, Angie and Jake were all over them hugging and greeting them.

Debbie was looking at Jake and Elzie and it amused her to see those two together as they were from their youth only they were some heavier, very gray and white headed and yes they were older. Angie was of course Debbie's age and she thought Angie looked younger than her years with a surprisingly nice figure.

Jake looked like Jake, only with his glasses suddenly reminded her of his Grandfather Oldham. He sure favored him but not in size. He was more his grandmother Oldham's size, or at least her build, thick boned, no neck and blocky.

As she looked around, Debbie asked, "Where is Nell?"

"I'm going to fetch her for supper and you all being here is going to be a surprise." Jake said. "I'm going after her right now."

CHAPTER 29

Jake quickly drove over to Bud's. Nell and Patty were trying to decide about supper as Jake arrived.

"I've got an extra surprise for you Nell and it is out at the farm. I think it would be a good idea that you pack an overnight bag and you'll spend the night at Elzie's. Trust me and just go pack yourself an overnight bag." Jake said.

"What is up?" Bud said.

As Nell was off packing, Jake said, "We've got Debbie Crocket and her husband Ralph Harper out at Elzie's. I thought Nell would like to have tonight and tomorrow to catch up with her. We're having supper out there so, ya'll follow us out but stay back that she don't know your coming."

Patty said, "Jake you are so mean! You are sure going to shock Nell!"

"A pleasant shock, I hope." Jake said.

Nell soon came back with a small overnight case and was carrying a change of clothes. She took his arm as they headed out the door and Jake let her pass first and he turned back to Bud and Patty and said, "See you in a minute."

As they were driving out and heading to Sunset, Nell said, "Are you getting nervous about getting married?"

"Not really, Nell," Jake said, "I feel confident that I know what I am doing and to tell you the truth, I wished we already were."

Nell had to smile because in some ways she had wished the same thing. As far as she knew they had everything ready, they had the license, it was a matter of Brother Dave signing the papers and sending them back to the county clerk for recording, and he would do that on Saturday morning after their Friday night wedding. All was ready.

"What are you up to tonight?" Nell asked.

"You will have to wait and see but it won't be long. I hope you are pleased." Jake said.

She could only wonder when they pulled up to Elzie's drive and got out and went inside. She had never seen this house and was curious.

Coming in the front door they were immediately in the large spacious living room. To the left lay the dining and kitchen and to the right was the master bedroom, she could only presume the arrangement of the bedrooms. Inside in the living room seated on the couch side by side were Debbie and her husband Ralph, beside them in an easy chair was Glen Ray all smiles when they walked in.

At first Nell was unsure who the couple were and then she knew, it was Debbie.

"Oh my Lord!" Nell said, "Debbie, oh Debbie." Debbie was then standing as the two met in the center of the room embracing. Nell was almost in tears.

"Nell, I want you to meet my husband, Ralph Harper." Debbie said.

"Oh, I'm so pleased to meet you and so grateful you are here, but how did you even know?" Nell asked.

"Why, Jake of course," Debbie said.

Nell looked for a moment at the man she was about to marry. She couldn't believe all the kindness and good things he had done, would do and was doing on her behalf.

"You certainly know how to surprise a girl!" Nell said.

About that time Bud and Patty came in and there were more greetings and introductions. Every one sat down and starting visiting and talking and at times all at once. Jake slipped out the door to check on supper since his daughter in laws was preparing it. They were cooking enchiladas with fried rice a tossed Mexican salad and a carrot cake. It was just going to be great, he thought.

When Jake went in Susie and Julia were busy but they said to give them about half hour and bring them all up and Jake did.

Everyone was sitting and enjoying the wonderful meal. Afterward the men retired to the living room while the women visited in the kitchen. As it was getting late, Bud and Patty went home, Elzie and Angie headed to their house, Deb and Ralph to follow. Glen Ray was making his way to leave and Jake asked him to just stay over and go home in the morning. Glen Ray decided to do so. Jake asked Nell to wait for a moment and then he would take her down to Elzie's. He walked Nell to his own living room and looked into her eyes.

"I hope tonight has been special." Jake said. "Tomorrow you and Deb and Nancy can all get together and just visit all you want. I'll take Ralph with me 'n Elzie." Then he kissed her and she pulled herself closer to him, and with her arms wrapped them around Jake and held on for a good while. When they pulled back, Nell was feeling so dreamy.

"Oh how I love you Jake." She said.

"I love you, Nell," Jake said. "Oh how I wish I could just sweep you into my bed tonight."

Nell smiled as she wanted the same thing but knew in two days he could sweep all he wanted.

"Come on, I'll run you down to Elzie's. You and Deb can talk all you want or just go to bed." Jake said.

It was a chilly night, but no wind. They got in Jake's truck and drove idly down to Elzie's. He walked her to the door but didn't go in but kissed her one more time for the night. He quickly went back to his house as he had left Glen Ray sitting in the big living room.

Glen Ray was watching TV as the news was about to come on.

"Come in my room," Jake said. "This couch is really comfortable and I'm going to sleep on it and you can have my new king size bed."

Glen Ray looked at the bed and said, "As big as that is, we could sleep on each side and never touch and who would care?"

"Suit's me," Jake said, "Back when we was kids and even teen's me and old Elzie shared the same bed over at Grandma's several times. And it weren't no king size bed."

"I wasn't expecting to stay but I am tired." Glen Ray said. "I do keep a spare tooth brush but I don't have a change of clothes. Won't matter, when I get up in the morning, I'll be out of here pretty quick."

"Just get some rest Glen, just rest and be refreshed tomorrow." Jake said.

They were laying in the bed both on their backs both thinking about the day.

"I'm sure glad you had me pick up Ralph and Debbie," Glen Ray said. "Lord, she's so small, and he is too."

"Yeah," Jake said, "I'm just so glad I found them and they are here for Nell."

"I know you too will be happy." Glen Ray said. "I don't know why I suddenly had the hots for her, thinking she would just fall into my arms."

"I'm sorry that didn't work out," Jake said, "but you know I've had a thing for her for a long time. And when she came out here to see me it was like a slow burn, it just got hotter and hotter and before I knew it, I was kissing her and she was kissing me."

"I want you two to be very happy." Glen Ray said. "One of these days, I'll find a nice lady."

"No doubt about it," Jake said. "You have always been such a good friend, you, Elzie, Bud, Billy John… I had other friends but none like you boys. Well my friend, I hope you are as tired as I am. I am drifting off…." And in less than a minute Jake had turned to his side and was sound asleep.

With Jake on one side of the bed, Glen Ray on the other and three feet between, neither knew the other was there for the night. Except for a few times Jake heard Glen snore and occasionally Glen heard Jake; they never knew the other was there.

That morning Glen Ray was up before Jake, he took a quick shower and was getting dressed when Jake got up.

"As soon as I'm dressed, we can have some breakfast." Jake said.

"I might drink some coffee, and then I'm going to head to Denton." Glen Ray said. "I'll be back tomorrow evening and so will my brother's."

"Good," Jake said. "By the way did you sleep all right? This is a brand new bed, new mattress and everything."

"I slept as good as I usually do." Glen said. I've gotten to where I wake all hours of the night. Sure is annoying."

"I know what you mean," Jake said, "Must be old man's syndrome."

They went into the kitchen and Jake rustled up coffee as Susie was not yet up. It was probably an hour before her normal getting up time.

"Why do you have to go?" Jake asked. "I'm going to get Elzie and Ralph and show Ralph our place."

"I've got a meeting with my housing contractor and I've got to meet with a potential client this afternoon who may invest in some leases I have," Glen Ray said.

"Well sometime come out here and spend the day. We need to visit more and you need to slow down. You can't take a dime with you," Jake warned.

Glen didn't answer but nodded slightly.

The coffee brewed, they had a cup and then Glen Ray was quietly out the door and off in a flash.

Jake decided to treat Susie, Ely and Leeza by making his Grandma's famous biscuits, and cooked a plate of bacon, sausages and eggs. It was done shortly after they were getting up stumbling into the kitchen.

"Wow," Ely said, "somebody got real industrious this morning. What's up with you?"

"Oh Glen Ray spent the night and he wanted to drink a cup of coffee and head out and so we got up and did that. And then I decided to do something nice for Susie," Jake said.

"How'd you get old Glen Ray to sit still that long?" Ely asked.

"I guess he visited so much last night that he got plum tired and couldn't go another step," Jake said. "He didn't put up any argument."

"I don't have to feed this morning, but I'm going to help Leeza and the twins move them noisy chicks from the shed into their laying home. They are getting so big, they fly out of those boxes and we just need to move them," Ely said.

"I'd help but I need to entertain Debbie's husband," Jake said.

"Me an the kids can handle it, Dad," Ely said.

"Elzie's supposed to call me when they are up and I'll go down there and take the good doctor around. Besides I'd like to hear about some of their adventures in their missionary work," Jake said.

Toward nine that morning, Elzie called to say that everyone was up and stirring around and that he could come down anytime.

Jake cranked up his go to town pickup and drove down to Elzie's. Everyone was dressed and sitting at the breakfast table when Jake went in.

"Have you ate yet?" Angie asked. "Yeah, I had breakfast earlier and saw Glen Ray off. He spent the night and he said he had some things he just had to do so he went to Denton."

Jake sat down and poured himself a cup of coffee. Since he usually only drank one cup he was breaking tradition. He asked and got a saucer and after cream and sugar was looking around to see that only he and Elzie were fixing the coffee in a saucer. It seemed like for a minute all eyes were on him though. Jake looked about and especially at Nell and sort of indicated "What?"

Jake then said, "You see it was the way my grandparents drank their coffee and it's how I drink it." And then he took a sup from his saucer.

"Pass the biscuits," Elzie said, as he broke the silence and then everyone seemed to talk at once.

"Did you all have a good visit last night?" Jake asked.

"Well we did," Nell said, "But Debbie and Ralph was pretty tired out from their trip and we didn't really stay up too late. We are going to really catch up today." "Angie, Debbie and I are going to Bowie and pick up Nancy and we are going on a shopping trip to Wichita Falls and lunch and just have grand time."

"That will be fine," Jake said, "cause Elzie, Ralph and I have our day planned out, no need to worry 'bout us. No sir, we will be fine."

Ralph looked at Jake and said, "Now Jake you and Elzie don't have to try to entertain me, I can stay right here and do some reading and just relax."

"No sir," Jake said, "Me an old Elze' got the day planned, we'll take care of you."

"I think," Jake said, "I'll have one of them hot biscuits and pass the butter."

"You know that makes me think of you dear old Grandma." Elzie said. She kept us in butter. She milked her cows, she took that good sweet cream and she churned it and made the best butter!"

Jake said, "What I wouldn't give to have some of her butter right now."

CHAPTER 30

As soon as breakfast was over Jake, Elzie and Ralph loaded up in his truck and started out over the pastures.

"Oh wow," Elzie said, "Ralph feel special, we are touring around in the go to town, go to church and stepping out truck of Jake Oldham's."

Ralph didn't really catch the joke, but Jake told Elzie to just shut up and ride.

They drove out, as was Jake's custom, on the old Pariot place first, and as it was, they found the herd in the northern corner of the place. This herd also ran on Jake's family place but he had a separate bunch grazing on the Blane.

"You have a good looking bunch of cows," Ralph said. "Different breed to what we saw in India."

"All I ever saw pictures of was Brahma's," Jake said.

"Yes a dominant species for that country," Ralph said.

"Tell us about your work there," Jake said.

"Well we went under the support of the church, the church of Christ, which Debbie and I are members. I think you are a member, right?"

"Yes I am, Elzie and Angie are, my wife to be is, my children and one of my grandchildren," Jake said. "In fact I was right there the night Debbie obeyed the gospel and was baptized."

"By the way, how did ya'll meet, you and Debbie?" Elzie asked.

"I was a student at North Texas and met Deborah in a class," Ralph said. "I had decided to go into the ministry but I was also studying pre-med and later I went to med school and at the same time worked as the associate minister at the church in Waco while attending Baylor. We married after I finished at North Texas and we were in Waco until I graduated and finished up my residency down at Scott and White and we both made the decision to go into the missionary and at the time we were going for five years but we ended up being there some thirty years. We adopted ten native children and had two sons of our own and they are both ministers in the Carolina area within an hour of us. When we decided to semi retire, Deborah had liked the area of North Carolina as we had a sponsoring church from there and we would every five years visit our sponsors and she just fell in love with that area and I wanted her to be totally happy when we made the decision to come back to the states."

"Are you still in practice?" Jake asked.

"I do a limited practice," Ralph relied. "I work in a clinic that sees the poorer section of the community and I work three days a week."

"Did you do any preaching while in India or just practice as a physician?" Elzie asked.

"Good question," Ralph said, "I did both but spent more time in the hospitals treating the very poorest of society there."

"And you Jake," Ralph asked, "You have spent your whole life being a farmer?"

"Sort of," Jake said, "I practice some veterinary science, I'm a soil scientist, I'm an agronomist, I'm a horticulturist, a welder part time mechanic, plumber electrician, you name it."

Ralph had to laugh because he did understand what Jake was talking about. Being on the farm, a man has to do a little bit of everything.

They were crossing the dam onto the Blane and seeing a new heard of cattle. Jake pointed out Phillips home under construction.

"Your family has owned a lot of land." Ralph said rather matter of fact.

"No, not really," Jake said, "Over the years I have accumulated most of it. Back when I came into the world we had a hundred sixty acres, and Elzie's folks had the same. Then by stroke of events, Elzie's parents decided to move to town we bought their place and my dad put that in my name. Then the Jasper's lost their home to a fire and they decided to build a home in town and my dad leased their land and again it was in my name. Ten years later, I would buy that place and we will see it in minute when we drive over there. Then the Blane came up and I leased it and later bought it and most recently I bought a place that joins the Jasper place and I inherited twelve hundred and eighty acres from the McReynolds family. It has four good oil wells and it produces income. I've got some other oil interest that in the past has made considerable money. We have a hundred and sixty cows and that many calves. We have twenty acres of pecans and I'm starting an egg production operation for my grandchildren to get them started. The place that joins the Jasper is heavy in timber and we are making it a wildlife operation leasing it out seasonally for hunting deer, turkey, and ducks. We are also going to sell wildlife tours during the non hunting seasons. Joining the Blane there is another four hundred acres that is about to be for sale and I may buy it if I can and across the road from that place is another two hundred that I already own one fourth of. I have been a silent partner to a young man that wanted to be in the dairy business. But he has taken a buy out from the government and his wife wants them to move to town and for him to have a day job that pays a regular pay check, so I'll have first option since I already own one fourth of the property. When I get it, I'm going to convert the house to two homes for the guys that work for me running dozers. We're going to build a big welding shop and they are going to build cattle guards and fence corners when they aren't running dozers. I'm a business man and I work at keeping our operations operating at a profit."

Jake pulled out to the county road from the Blane and showed Elzie and Ralph the land next to the Blane and the property across the road from it. It was all good working land.

They drove to the Jasper and made their tour and counted their cattle and then to the Harris and showed Ralph the hunting lodge and the nature cabins. Lastly they toured the McReynolds property. Jake was just starting to make use of this property having only obtained it a few months before. The whole morning they had taken their time observing and talking as they showed Ralph the property. Leaving the McReynolds it was noon and Jake wanted to take the guys to Lindsey to the Smokehouse.

On the way back both Elzie and Ralph dozed while Jake ambled back at a slow but deliberate pace. He aimed to drive the doctor out toward Cap's Corner to show how drastically different the landscape was but since the more he drove the heavier they slept and did so until he pulled into Elzie's driveway. The women were not back but Elzie woke as they were coming to a stop and Ralph soon woke as well.

"What a delightful lunch," Ralph said, "I don't think we have barbecue that good in North Carolina, although almost, but that was just delicious."

"It must have been," Jake said, "Both you and Elzie slept all the way back. I couldn't believe how sound you two slept!"

Elzie was standing outside the truck stretching saying, "Well I'm not so sure I got my nap out."

"Well you'll have to stay up because otherwise you wouldn't sleep tonight." Jake said in a sarcastic tone yet Elzie knowing he was kidding.

"You needn't be worrin about my sleepin," Elzie said.

Inside the men took to the easy chairs in the living room but Jake told them he'd be back later. He needed to check in with his daughter in laws.

Up at Ely's the girls were visiting and cutting up tomatoes, onions, and had some shredded lettuce. They were cooking hamburgers for their supper tonight. They had already made two cakes, and Italian cream and a chocolate.

"Looks like ya'll got everything under control." Jake said.

"Are you getting nervous?" Julie asked.

"I'm not nervous about getting married, I'm not nervous about a church ceremony, but I am nervous, and I can't explain that. I guess I am nervous for everything to go without a hitch, I suppose," Jake said. "I probably won't sleep a wink tonight and I don't want be tired and sleepy tomorrow night."

"Why Jake, your embarrassing us!" Susie said with a laugh.

Then Jake realized what he said and was blushing himself. "I didn't mean... um, boy have I stepped in it or what?"

They were all laughing.

A couple of hours later Jake saw the women arrive and he hurried down to Elzie's.

Nancy, Debbie and Nell were all aglow almost like school girls with a secret. Jake drove up as they had come back out and were getting a few things they had bought out of the car.

"Nell could I talk to you for a minute?" Jake said.

She came over and he motioned for her to get into his truck. "I just wondered" Jake said, "If you wanted to move your belongs tonight into my or should I say OUR room. I thought maybe you would want your stuff there and I thought since we are not supposed to see one another until tomorrow evening at the church, I just thought..."

Nell answered before Jake could finish his statement or his question as he was about to start stammering.

"I'll send Bud out in the morning with my things," Nell said. "That will be ok, won't it?"

"Of course it will, my sweet," Jake said. "I was just trying to be helpful."

"Well you are," Nell said as she leaned over and kissed his cheek. "You are more than thoughtful and I am so grateful to you that my oldest girlfriends have gotten together. You made that possible. Are you getting nervous?"

"My daughter in laws asked me the same question." Jake said and I told them, I wasn't nervous about marrying you, wasn't nervous about a church service, but I was nervous about the event coming together without a hitch and I was nervous about that. I told them I probably wouldn't sleep a wink tonight."

"Well Jacob Oldham," Nell said, "You don't want to be sleepy on your wedding night."

CHAPTER 31

It was Friday, March 5, and the day of the wedding. The boys had taken care of all the farm chores, Clint and Tony were busy on a job and there were no appointments to see a potential client, and worst of all, until that night, there was nothing all day for Jake to do.

Bud had come out with all of Nell's things and all Jake could do was to put the baggage in his and, what would soon be, their room. Fortunately when Jake's dad had built the room, he made a large walk in closet and there was ample room for Nell's hanging clothes. She had sent her dresses and he and Bud hung them but did not and would not touch the suit cases.

Jake didn't quite know what to say to Bud on this occasion. Finally he said, "I guess I'll be glad when we get this wedding past us. Getting ready for it is been a little worrisome."

"It will be alright soon, Bud said. "I think you and Nell are going to be real happy."

"I will see you tonight, old friend," Bud said, and with that he got in his truck and headed back to his farm.

Nell was back at Bud's and so were Angie, Nancy and Debbie. Elzie was to entertain Ralph and Jake was unsure if he could even go down to Elzie's. Finally he called Elzie.

"Ah, hello," Elzie said in a drawn out tone. "This is Elzie's mule barn and I'm the head mule."

Jake had to laugh. "What ya'll going to do today?" Jake asked.

"Shoot if I know," Elzie said, "Tain't nobody here but me and the Doc."

"Hey bring him and yourself up here and we'll play thumps and dominoes." Jake said.

"Now that's capital, cousin, that's right capital," Elzie said.

The three men played thumps. It was new to Dr. Harper but he quickly understood the theme of the game. He watched Elzie and Jake go at it and then he had to play the winner while the loser watched and then the one watching would play the winner. They played for a couple of hours then got the dominoes and started playing dominoes and that went on for another hour before Susie came in and said that she had run to town and bought some chicken cause there wasn't time to cook since she and Julia had been decorating the church and they were not finished. The photographer would be out about an hour before the ceremony and the reception room was not yet decorated.

"I don't care," Jake said, "I'm not real hungry."

Then Elzie was poking Ralph and teasing saying, "Oh he's hungry alright, but not for chicken." They were laughing softly with Jake looking over at Elzie with somewhat a stern look.

"Oh shut up cousin," Jake said. But Jake was blushing, turning beet red which caused the two men to laugh even more.

"I know it is kinda cold, but let's go down to the creek." Jake said.

"Sure," Elzie said, "But not before we sample this here chicken, mmm mighty good."

"You know Jake, the secret to a good marriage is sex and supper." Elzie said, "Aint that right Ralph?"

"Well, come to think of it, yes, a man likes a woman to fix good meals, and then he loves to share his love for her and with her in the most intimate way." Ralph said.

"Like I said," Elzie mused, "Sex and supper."

Jake looked at both men as if in a panic. "Do ya'll think I might be rushing into things, maybe Nell and I need to spend some time talking and really having a good understanding about what we are getting ourselves into?"

"Oh, good gosh!" Elzie said. "Here you been knowing that girl all and I mean all her life and when she started looking good to you, that's all you ever wanted was to live with her, to spend your time with her, well now by gum it's time to pay the fiddler! No, you don't need to do no more talking, you need put your words to action! Rushing my foot!"

Jake was almost not hearing, and was beginning to ponder and to worry. Both men could see he was nervous.

"My friend," Ralph begun, "I have seen many people who thought they were in love and I have seen people who were in love. I have watched the two of you. You are both sincerely in love. No you don't need to worry about a thing. Just relax and in a few hours, you two will be bound together forever."

Jake wiped his face with his hand and pushed it through his shock of white hair as he sometimes did when he was pondering and thinking heavily. He took a deep breath and he said, "You know I think you both are right. I'm just having some flutters and for no reason whatsoever."

"Now come on, let's take a walk to the creek and maybe by the time we get back it will be time for me and ya'll to get dressed," Jake said.

So they took a walk from the house to the creek. It was in the mid forties but the wind was light. At old Denton creek, nothing looked as Elzie remembered.

"You've re-shaped this bank to where I don't know where the old creek was and where we swam." Elzie said.

"I dug a channel beside the old creek to catch any water coming down since the government has dammed up all the tributaries that feed Denton Creek. It isn't a live creek anymore. This channel runs from your old place to the end of the Blane and enables us to have water during the dry spells," Jake explained.

"I know it's not the same, I miss that old swimming hole too. We had some great times back then," Jake said.

"We sure did, we did for a fact and fishing too. We'd come down here to fish or swim but your Grandma expected you to bring back your catch cause, she'd sure cook up a mess of fish." Elzie said.

As the three stood there looking at the old creek, Ralph of course knew not the things of Jake and Elzie's past, knew not what the creek had looked like before a dozer changed things, but he respected their memory.

Jake turned to walk back to the house. It was now getting close but yet still at least an hour to kill before changing into his wedding clothes.

"Elzie, I'll park my old truck behind the church and maybe Nell won't see it, and after the wedding, you sneak out there and park in the front where we come out and where she can then see it," Jake said.

"Don't worry about a thing, cuz, cause I'll cover that for sure," Elzie said. "There's sure some surprises for people tonight."

"I sure hope she will be pleased with the restored truck," Jake said, "I'm sure it really means more to me than her. But I did get my first kiss from her in that thing."

"Let's go have some ice tea, play one more best of five games of thumps, then maybe it will be time to get dressed." Elzie said.

"I think, I'll let you two have the thumps," Ralph said, "My fingernail is already going to be sore."

CHAPTER 32

Finally it was time to get dressed. Elzie and Ralph had gone down to Elzie's house and Jake was there alone. He was unsure where his two kids were and everyone. Perhaps they were at Phil's but why, they could get into their clothes here. "What is up?" He thought.

Jake got out the tailored suit and vest, his best pair of boots, his new hat and laid it out on the bed. He was looking at the bed. He and Nell had bought a new king size bed for them as Jake had been sleeping in his old bed from his grandmother's house, an iron stead bed of regular size. He felt they should give themselves more room and so they bought the new bed which had adjustable sections on each side. You could elevate the pillow part just like in the hospital. They had bought new sheets, two new machine sewn quilts, the works. He was thinking about the time some forty years back when Nell came to his room that night and just dropped her gown to the floor and lay next to him and he had taken her, gently and he thought it was the best night of his life, at least it was up until then. And now, they were in their sixties and he knew tonight would not be like it was when they were in their twenties. But he hoped it would be a night they would both appreciate. God how he loved this woman and how he wanted her to share this place, this home, this bed; but it was not wild running passion, it was a deep set intimate commitment, something life long, not as in passing. He wanted every moment to be joyous and good and happy. He hoped he could do that.

He took a shower, even though he wasn't sure he needed to he did. He shaved again for the second time that day, splashed on his favorite Old Spice and then dressed.

The house was still empty. Where is everyone? He wondered. Nonetheless, it was time to go to the church building. He had removed the tarp and brought the truck out of the shed but left it at the shed entrance which faced opposite the road. No chance of anyone seeing it. He laid his hat on the seat, not sure why he was bringing it. Then he changed his mind took the hat back to the house and came back and got into the old truck and cranked it up. It roared to life, and he was slowly coasting out the drive and down the road turning back to the old cemetery. There were a number of cars there and some pulling up behind him.

"Oh my," he thought, "this is really it." I feel a little sick. It is only your nerves, he told himself. He pulled the truck around the back and fortunately someone had flagged a spot and put reserved on it. It had to be his spot, he thought, because the rest of the back of the church parking was taken.

He got out and made sure his clothes were straight and walked to the front of the church. The front of the church was an area that had been created when Jake started working on the building. He had downsized the chapel part and made the fellowship area larger because of the annual meetings and the lunch served. The chapel would easily seat fifty people but the fellowship part would accommodate almost twice that many. Although the fellowship room would be full of people during the annual meetings, when they went into the chapel part, a lot of the younger ones just stayed out and the older ones sat in the chapel room for the meeting.

Jake opened the door to find a large audience inside the fellowship but he didn't see his own family. The preacher was there, the elders, the two dozer hands with their families, the Shelton brothers and their families and the closer family friends who had been invited, but his family was not there! The preacher came over and shook Jake's hand, then the elders, then Glen Ray and his brothers were all seeking his attention. He wanted to ask but they were dominating the conversation and he was not able to get much in. Finally he asked Brother Dave about his family.

"Jake they are inside the chapel and they have a surprise and wanted us to come in just before the ceremony and right before your bride comes in," Brother Dave said.

"Hmm," Jake mused, "I thought I was the one giving a surprise."

It was only ten minutes to wait and then the preacher took Jake's arm and led him into the chapel. The entry was covered with a curtain and removed to allow Jake in. There to his surprise, Jake understood and understood then what Elzie had said a few hours before regarding surprises. Elzie and Jake's sons were standing there in suits that matched Nell's colors. Their suits were the color of Jake's vest and their vest was the color of Jake's suit. At the pulpit behind where the preacher would stand was a stringed band, three violins, a bass and guitar. Elzie, Phil and Ely all lined up at the pulpit awaiting Jake and the preacher to take their place. The audience of friends and family came filing in and taking seats in the folding chairs. The band started the wedding march and in came Nancy, Angie, Patty and Debbie, then Bud wearing the same suit as Elzie and Jake's sons, bringing his sister on his arm to the front of the church. All were standing and Jake was utterly amazed and totally surprised.

Nell was smiling as she strode toward him on Bud's arm. Jake was unsure if she was smiling because she had somehow behind his back, dressed the wedding party and he did not know it until now, or if she was smiling because they were about to join hands or both. He certainly couldn't ask right then.

The music stopped and Brother Preston begin with the traditional announcement of why they were all there gathered in the sight of God and men but finally he asked who gave this woman and Bud spoke up, he did and she left his arm, and stood beside Jake. Bud then moved to the side and stood with Elzie and Jake's boys. On the other side were Deb, Nancy, Angie and Patty and were dressed in dresses that were the opposite of Nell's but the same color as Jake's suit. Jake was so amazed how Nell had coordinated the event in such short time.

They said their vows, he put the ring on her finger and they were pronounced husband and wife and Jake softly and briefly kissed his bride, then they were introduced and everyone stood and applauded. Brother Preston said a prayer, the band struck and they marched to the back of the fellowship part of the building. The preacher invited all to enjoy and dismissed them. The band was to continue playing as the chairs in the chapel were moved to the sides.

They cut the cake and Jake and Nell hand fed each other while the photographer continued to shoot. He had been taking his photos all through the wedding. Except for a few poses, they were not delayed by shooting. Jake and Nell wanted a picture of them together and then all the family and one with the wedding party and the preacher.

Once they had had their cake, Nell led Jake, who all this time had been speechless, to the chapel and said, "The band is going to play a waltz, and I want you to dance with me."

"Of course, Mrs. Oldham," Jake said. "Your wish is my command."

Nell then motioned to the band that had just finished a number. In unison they struck the chords and began a ball room waltz. Jake whisk his bride around the room and all were smiles. Phillip, Ely and their wives looked at one another in amazement watching Jake as he perfectly performed as a dancer.

Phillip looked at his brother and their wives and said, "Wow, the old boy's pretty light on his feet. Where did he learn that?"

"I don't know how you done this, but when, how, did you get all those clothes done?" Jake asked.

"I had Elzie keep you busy where we could do that. Bud and I went down to Dallas and your boys went one day for measurements. I took the girls and I just thought the clothes would be a nice touch. I thought I'd surprise you. Are you pleased?"

"I love it all," Jake said. "Your surprise will be outside when we get ready to leave. I'm scared you will be disappointed."

"Jake I will not be disappointed even if you bought me a milk cow, only you better not have bought me a milk cow." Nell said laughing.

"It won't be long and you will see," Jake said.

The crowd joined in the dance including the elders with their wives, for everyone loved a good waltz. Even Brother Dave and Alberta had to waltz.

Jake told Nell he wanted one dance with Deb and Nancy before they just quit. Nell said she would give Glen Ray a dance too.

And so Nell went over and asked Glen to dance who was more than happy to oblige.

"I don't know that I've ever seen a better wedding," Glen Ray said. "It was nice to the core and two people who are so in love!"

"So nice of you to say," Nell said. "I know that someday you are going to find that special one."

"Well I hope so, Nell," Glen Ray said, "I hope I find someone like you."

Jake had asked Ralph if he could dance a dance with his wife and he bowed as to give consent, not that he needed it and Deb was willing to dance.

"Does this remind you of our prom night?" Jake asked.

"Not really, I was so young then and I had a crush on a guy I went to church with and he was kind to me and he let me down very easy and he never broke my heart." Deb said.

"Deb, I was so in love with Nell, I never saw anything else." Jake said. "Tonight is fulfilling a long dream and I buried that dream for a long time, but tonight it is so alive. I would never have hurt you. I sure tired to give you a special night at the prom."

"And you did." Deb said. "I was really mad at you when I found you outside with Nell. Oh yes, I was standing there watching and I saw you kiss her and then you stayed back when she came back inside and I moved back in like I was inside when she came back in. I was so mad and was going to make you take me home but you talked me out of it and I'm grateful you did. But that was a long time ago and this is a new time, a new day and you and Nell get to start life together."

"I'm going to do my best." Jake said. "Do my best."

Jake had a dance with Nancy then Patty and Angie before he and Nell were to leave.

They announced they were going to leave and Elzie whispered the key was in the truck and it was right out the door.

They joined hands and walked through the crowd of well wishers and when they opened the door there was the old flat bed truck only it looked brand new.

"OH Jake," I can't believe it. Is this your Grandparents actual truck?"

"Sure is, only rebuilt, new suspension, new engine, automatic with power and air." Jake said.

Everyone was clapping and being overjoyed at the sight, the two getting in the old truck. Jake opened the passenger door and let Nell in and went around and entered the driver's side. He turned the key and the engine roared to life. He put it in gear and they slowly drove out of the churchyard. At the road he turned right instead of left and headed out.

"Where are we going?" Nell asked.

"Oh just for a minute a trip down memory lane." Jake said.

He drove toward Alvord and just before getting into town turned off on a dirt road that went north. In ten minutes they were driving down Lover's Lane. He pulled over, not killing the engine but just parked for a moment.

"Over forty years ago, we came out here and we talked and I was about to pledge my love even ask for your hand and you stopped me.," Jake said. "But tonight I pledge my love, I have your hand but I want you to know just how much I love you."

Jake kissed with passion and then pulled away grinning.

Nell looked with admiration on her husband and said, "I love you with all my heart and I will until I die."

"Now you better take us home before we do something indecent in this truck," Nell said.

Jake obeyed and headed back to his farm. In fifteen minutes they were back at the house. Hopefully by this time Ely and his family were on the road to Fort Worth to visit Susie's folks. That had been the announced plan.

In his haste, Jake had forgotten to leave even the porch light on and it was now very dark.

"Let me get the porch light and then a light inside and then I'll come back and get you," Jake said.

In short order the porch light came on and then the living room light. Jake came back and opened the door for his wife.

She took his hand and the two strode to the front door.

Jake opened the door and then proceeded to pick Nell up.

"What do you think you are doing?" Nell asked.

"Ize going to carry you over the threshold." Jake said.

"Oh come on, that's for the young, I don't need you to do that." Nell said.

"Why Nell Oldham, I've carried lots of feed sacks that weigh more than you." Jake said.

And with that he whisked her off her feet and into his arms, lovingly carrying her into the living room and then holding her a moment just looking at her admiring her before setting her down. She had not realized that even at his age of almost sixty six, he was still stout. It was a comforting feeling to her.

Jake locked the front door and as they left the living room and entered the kitchen he turned out the living room light and turned on the kitchen.

Nell sat down at the kitchen table and said she was thirsty.

"Ice tea, or coke?" Jake asked.

"You keep cold Dr. Pepper?" she asked.

"Yeah, always have." Jake said. He got two glasses and poured from a liter bottle. The clicked their glasses as they drank the beverage.

Jake chuckled and said, "You know we have this entire house to ourselves."

"Do you mean to say, Jake, if we wanted to run naked in here we could?" Nell asked teasingly.

Jake had to laugh, "Well I suppose if we wanted to. I have never done that in my whole life, but I'm willing."

Nell was laughing too. "Neither have I come to think of it. It would be my luck if I did, someone would knock on the door."

"Yeah, Hello, I'm Jehovah's Witness!" Jake said laughing.

Nell leaned over and took Jake's hand, a gesture that she had never done when they were young. "Can you believe it, we are really married." She said.

"It does seem like a dream." Jake said. "But I love a good dream, and I don't want this one to end."

"Me either." Nell said. "You know what? It is only eight o'clock. We never ate any supper. What say we go somewhere and dine?"

"Are you asking me out?" Jake said. "It is the first time, you ever ask me out."

"I am, I am asking you out." Nell said.

Jake stood up from the table and extended his arm. "Shall we go? I know the Dairy Queen is open, don't know what else."

"Perfect lets go and we will wear our wedding clothes, cause I'm proud of what happened tonight, let's go show off." Nell said.

And thus they did. They went to the Dairy Queen in Bowie and to their surprise, half of their wedding party was there. Elzie, Angie, the Shelton's including Glen Ray, Phillip and his family, Nancy and her husband, Debbie and Dr. Harper and Bud and Patty. They had pushed some tables together to fit them and when Jake and Nell came in Elzie got up and pulled another table to their group. They were all laughing.

"What are you all doing here?" someone from the group asked.

"Surely, ya'll got more to do than come to the Dairy Queen." Elzie said.

"Well we get hungry too and realized we hadn't ate since lunch and Jake said he hadn't eat since breakfast."

"He had a good shot at some fried chicken at lunch and passed it up, he was too nervous to eat." Elzie shot.

Again everyone had a good laugh. Jake and Nell went to the counter to order. The manager came out to ask what they had been to as they were so dressed up. Everyone else had changed to more casual look.

Jake told the lady they had gotten married so she wanted them to have whatever they wanted on the house, including ice cream for dessert.

They all had a good visit and all left at the same time.

As Jake and Nell were about to leave, Glen Ray came over and admired the old truck. "Man what memories we have of that old truck. A few times we filled it with melons and many times with peanut hay."

"Don't I know it!" Jake said. "She's all new now and got a nice 350 with auto, power and air. Runs like a scalded assed ape too."

"Jake Oldham." Nell said, "You better watch your mouth, I'll be washing your mouth out with soap."

Jake looked at his bride and said, "Yes ma'am."

"One time my mama did that to me, not for cussing but for sassing but it don't matter, either crime, the punishment is not pleasant. NO sir."

"Jake you are already started, getting hen pecked." Glen said.

"It's alright, Glen, I think I'm going to like it." Jake said.

Back home both were feeling the day and ready for bed. Jake was nervous about it but Nell put him to ease.

"Jake, I don't know about you, but it has been awhile since I slept with another person and longer than that to have been intimate with anyone. So, we are not in a hurry, we are not trying to perform here. You just relax and I will too. We will just get comfortable and let nature take its course." Nell said.

"Well," Jake said, "Whatever happens, I know you are the most beautiful bride a man can have and I love you to the core. We might be so darn tired, we might hug and fall asleep."

The undressed for bed, they got in bed, and Jake tuned out the light. His mind was back to the first time he was with her in this way. He was elated that she was surrendering herself to him and him to her. That night, he had fallen in love for life only to have that dream shattered. But tonight she was his forever and he was going to do whatever it took to make her happy.

They kissed tenderly and their passion rose and soon all inhibitions were gone and they were absorbed in each other. They were both satisfied and both felt a great revival in their lives. Soon they were both asleep in one another's arms.

Jake woke first that morning. It was early and no reason to get up and so he lay there for awhile just thinking. Glad the ceremony was over and they could start a regular life together, they could plan together, they could work together and they could enjoy each other. It was almost like a second chance in life.

After half an hour, Jake did get up quietly, showered and shaved, then dressed. He slipped into the kitchen and was brewing coffee when Nell came in.

"I smelled the coffee," She said.

"I sure didn't try to wake you, I had laid there about as long as I could and just had to get up," Jake said.

"You didn't wake me, I smelled the coffee." She said. "But I am ready to get up. What's on our agenda?"

"Well I have something to show you and an idea. But let me pitch something at you that we ought to go see Vince about. I was thinking we ought to put a trust up for Deb and Ralph. They gave their lives to the Lord, spent their good years in missionary and they had no opportunity to save any money. I want to put a trust up for them so they can live a little better. But I want to do that for Elzie too. I know I'm furnishing him a house and he's got retirement but I want his life to be a little more cushy and comfortable. He's like my own kin, a brother by different parents, a brother I never had. We've been together for a long time and him and Angie coming back out here has been a real blessing to me," Jake said.

"I can't believe it," Nell said. "I was thinking almost the same thing! I thought about Debbie and her husband's devotion deserved something more than what they have now and I thought the same thing. And I don't blame you one bit for doing something for Elzie. He's your sanity. If it weren't for him, you might just work yourself to death. He sort of gets you to let up."

"Here's what I propose." Nell said. "I'll set up Debbie's trust and you set up Elzie's"

"Ok," Jake said. "I'll call Vince first thing Monday."

"You want some breakfast?" Nell said.

"Yeah but I don't want a big breakfast. Oats and coffee is enough for me." Jake said.

"Oatmeal and coffee coming up," Nell said.

Jake told her how he made oatmeal and she said that was about the same way she did as her mama did and her grandma did.

She served the hot oatmeal and Jake added the butter and brown sugar. Nell did the same.

"Nell, last night was as special as I ever experienced in my life." Jake said. "It was just wonderful."

"Better than when we were so young?" she asked.

"Yes, ten times because the next day you are still here and the day after and the day after that." Jake said.

Nell could only smile to herself because she knew how true that was. She was overjoyed with her new life.

After breakfast, they took the flat bed and drove down to the Jasper place.

Jake parked the truck overlooking the bottomland.

"Nell, I was thinking about building us a new home right here." He said.

"You don't have to build a new home for us, we can live really well in your dad and mother's old house," Nell said.

"No, I think we are starting a new life and let's build us a new house to start it in. We can sit down with Phillip and he can draw us up anything we want. The one thing I want is an enclosed but with windows, back porch, and I want a porch outside that, one that wraps around the house. I want to be able to sit on that back porch and look out over the little kingdom. I've always loved this place. When I was kid Grandma and I would come down to visit Mrs. Jasper while Mr. Jasper was plowing his fields and Grandpa was plowing ours. They had a nice old white Victorian house here. It was really I think originally three rooms like a "T" just like my Grandparents house, then they added rooms on each side of the kitchen, and they had a screened in back porch. This is a good place, good land, a good bottom and it will afford us a little bit of privacy."

"I'll look at house plans and then we will come to a decision together," Nell said.

"That's fine. Let's drive around and look at the stock, I know Ely and the twins fed them yesterday."

CHAPTER 33

Thirty years had passed since Jake and Nell married. As Jake would have said, since then there had been a lot of water under the bridge.

They built their dream house on the Jasper land and lived there comfortably and happily. It was a two story home; the upstairs was for the grandkids and as often as their parents would let them; all three were fond of staying with them. In time Jake's sons felt comfortable calling Nell, "Mother Nell." The grandkids called her "Nanny Nell," but when great grandkids started arriving, the Nell got dropped off and they only knew her as Nanny.

Jake and Elzie had a genuine ball during the golden years of their lives. They fished and would often take the drive to Glen Ray's and spend a day on Lake Ray Roberts. On several occasions Jake and Nell had extended cruse trips. Sometimes they took Bud and Patty, or Elzie and Angie and sometimes both. They tended to lend to romantic adventures revitalizing their youth. For Jake, the trips were enjoyable, but he preferred to be at his farm, counting cows and calves, helping Leeza and the twins with their chickens, harvesting pecans and teasing Elzie. He treasured every moment with Nell, thanking his God daily for her.

At the age of ninety five, Jake was somewhat feeble, but of strong mind. Nell was so thankful that she and Jake had strong minds.

The twins had married and between them had five children. Leeza had married a man that like Jake, had a great love for the farm, agriculture and cattle. He fit right in with them all. His name was Leeander Sells, but the family called him Lee. Lee and Leeza had one child a son they named Jacob Elijah and Jake insisted they call him Lige.

When Jake turned ninety, Leeza felt she and Lee should move in with her grandparents. Lee was always an agreeable sort, which was what made him so likeable. He greatly respected Jake as a good man, and a good church leader and a suburb farmer. Through his leadership they had increased their holdings to six thousand acres. They managed three hundred cows, and the hunting and photo nature business. Leeza had grown her egg business to twenty thousand hens. They still had their dozer business, along with grass planting, welding and fence building operations. All three grandkids were part of it and their own families. Ely and Phillip were slowing down and letting their children take the lead. All of them were faithful in being involved with their local church in Sunset.

The last few years there had been sadness. Both Nell and Jake had witnessed time and time the loss of their friends and family; Bud, his wife, Glen and his brothers, Nancy and her husband, Angie, Debbie and Ralph. The most recent and most painful, Jake's loss of Elzie. He had grieved his passing more than all his friends.

He had been so proud that Elzie and Angie went to church with Jake's family. Within a couple of years, Elzie was made a deacon along with Jake's own two sons and later would be a co elder with Jake. That never stopped them from picking at one another.

When Elzie had become frail and ill and after Angie's death, his children had insisted he move in with them but he ended up in the nursing home for a short while. Jake was there every day with him and they sparred one another continually. Shortly before Elzie died, he was laying in bed with Jake by his side. With his typical mischievous grin, he said, "Well Jake, all our lives I've bested you in racing, in hunting, shooting, in fishing and even in loving women and now I'm going to beat you again, and go to heaven before you do."

Jake jerked back in his chair, and snorted, "You never out shot me, never could run as fast as I could, and of all that other stuff, you sure ain't gonna beat me going up there, they don't allow liars up there."

Then with all he could muster Jake put his hand on Elzie's chest and said, "I can't stand the thought of you not being here with me."

Elzie looked at his lifelong friend tears streaming down his thin cheeks, "Not to worry, I won't be far, and Nell will look after you. You can't look after yourself you old man."

Before Jake got back to the home next day, they called to say that Elzie had died in his sleep.

Jake took great comfort in knowing what a good man Elzie was, but his grief for a few days was almost inconsolable. Nell was his anchor and brought him through.

Part of Jake's habit was in the evenings after supper to sit in his porch rocker facing the bottomland. He would gaze out the windows on the enclosed back porch. Nell would join him after she had helped Leeza in the kitchen and the two of them had had their special talks. Sometimes Leeza and Lee would sit out with them until they headed for bed.

After Jake's ninety fifth birth day, he was moving slower and more cautious. The kids would not let him drive but on occasions one of them would take him around the land for a look. The fifth of March was his and Nell's thirtieth anniversary. All the family had come for a special supper and afterward Jake had said he was going to sit on the back porch. He told them he had felt awfully tired that day. The kids attributed it to him being driven all over the place and he had insisted they go by the cemetery. About a year after he and Nell married he had with her approval a triple tombstone installed. Lois was buried on his left, with Jake in the center and Nell would be on his right. Everyone thought it was fine. Jake wanted that day to go by the cemetery.

He first took a tour of the old church building, thinking about the funerals he had been to. He remembered his great grandfather Oldham, then Elzie's grandpa Pariot, then his great grandmother Oldham's, Uncle Spence Russell's, his grandparents. He had made a request that his own funeral be here in this building. Even though he had served faithfully as an elder at the Sunset church of Christ, he'd rather his funeral to be at Pleasant Hill. He walked leaning on his cane to his family's plots. He looked at Lois's grave, and visited his parents, and all his grandparents stones. He spent some time with Lige and Bertha.

Back home he settled down for an hour nap.

That evening had been one of the best to him with all the family there. There had been joy and laughter.

But he was tired and he went to his chair. As he gazed out in the "little kingdom" he saw some boys in the bottom land. They were running and jumping having fun. It couldn't be the twin's kids, they were in the living room, he could hear them. Who is this?

They were almost identifiable as they reached the fence that separated the yard from the bottomland.

It looked like Glen Ray, Billy John, Bud and, and Elzie? They were waiving at him, motioning him to come, to come on, he could almost hear their voices calling, beckoning him.

Next he knew, he was standing in their midst. It was them, his old friends. "Hey Jake, they said, we're going to the creek and swim, come on, last one in, is a rotten egg!"

Jake turned and looked at the house and the old man sitting in the chair looking out the window. Jake waved and the old man waved back.

And then they were all running, they were screaming with delight. At the far side of the bottomland was a boundary fence that they simply sifted through and kept on running. As they neared the creek, the creek that Jake had known as child, was there as it had been in the past. They were all stripping clothes and screaming as they were jumping in the water splashing and enjoying every moment. It was good to be home.

Nell had with the help of her walker gone out to check and to sit with Jake. The rest of the family save Leeza and Lee were preparing to leave.

She thought something was odd about Jake. He was motionless, he was staring out but it seemed to her not seeing. She touched him and his face was chilled.

She gasped, "Leeza!" she yelled. "Oh no, oh no, my Jake, my Jake has gone. He's gone!" Nell was softly crying.

Leeza, Ely, Phillip and all came running back to the back porch.

They gathered around their patriarch and all knew by looking, Jake had passed away.

They held the funeral at the old Pleasant Hill church as Jake had requested but it was the second funeral. The response of the public who had been touched by his life and his family was so outreaching, they held the first funeral at the Sunset church although it could not contain the mass. It was a large funeral and the family had a second memorial at the Pleasant Hill building for the family but many people came and stood outside in respect. They surrounded the family at the grave. The outpouring was a demonstration of a final tribute to a good man.

Two years later Nell would join her Jake. On her final day, Leeza was by her side and she told Leeza that Jake had been to see her and that right then he was waiting for her on the porch. Shortly she breathed her last.

Jake's family paid as much tribute to her as they knew how. She had mothered them, she had loved them all as much if not more had they been her own flesh and blood. She was laid beside Jake in the little cemetery where their happiness had been rekindled thirty two years before.